The Art of Brevity

The Art of Brevity

Excursions in Short Fiction Theory and Analysis

Edited by Per Winther,
Jakob Lothe, *and* Hans H. Skei

University of South Carolina Press

Published in Columbia, South Carolina,
by the University of South Carolina Press

Manufactured in the United States of America

08 07 06 05 04   5 4 3 2 1

Library of Congress Cataloging-in-Publication Data

The art of brevity : excursions in short fiction theory and analysis / Edited by Per Winther, Jakob
Lothe, and Hans H. Skei.
    p. cm.
  Includes bibliographical references and index.
  ISBN 1-57003-557-1 (cloth : alk. paper)
  1. Short story. I. Winther, Per, 1947– II. Lothe, Jakob. III. Skei, Hans H., 1945–
  PN3373.A67 2004
  808.3'1—dc22

2004012286

We gratefully acknowledge financial assistance from the Norwegian Research Council, the Norwegian Academy of Science and Letters, and the following divisions of the University of Oslo: the Section for International Services, the Faculty of Arts, the Department of British and American Studies,
and the Department of Scandinavian Studies and Comparative Literature.

Contents

Introduction

An anecdote about Somerset Maugham goes something like this: The celebrated writer once visited a girls' school where he lectured on the art of writing short fiction. In the lecture he pronounced that the essential ingredients of a short story are religion, sex, mystery, high rank, nonliterary language, and brevity. The next day the schoolmistress set her charges to write an essay according to this recipe. After a minute one said she had finished. The incredulous mistress told her to read her work aloud, and she did: "'My God!' said the duchess, 'I'm pregnant! I wonder who done it!'"

Prefacing an academic book on short fiction theory in such anecdotal fashion is perhaps not entirely frivolous if one considers that except for the bit about sex and nobility, the "definition" of the genre proffered in the Somerset Maugham anecdote reflects key concerns on the part of practitioners in the field. The short story's origin in myth and its aptness for capturing the mysteries of existence continue to command the interest of genre theorists like Rohrberger and May (in pages here following and elsewhere); the genre's similar origin in oral storytelling and its frequent penchant for vernacular stylistic registers keep informing discourse on the genre, including essays printed here (New, Nissen, Skei); and the matter of length—a point of crucial interest in commentaries on the short story back to Poe, Goethe, and others—remains a mainstay in theorizings about the genre, be it in the form of reader response experiments (Lohafer, here and elsewhere), analyses of the contemporary attraction to "short shorts" (Mose), concerns with fragments and fragmentation (Lothe), examinations of the role of closure (Winther), or discussions surrounding the generic exchanges between short story and novel (Skei, Lee Kleppe, Nissen, Löfgren).

When short fiction theory is referred to above as a "field," this is a matter of fact as well as policy. Let us start with some of the facts: though it has perhaps been overshadowed somewhat by other branches of "theory," theoretically oriented work in the area dates back some four decades, to the pioneering publications of Mary Rohrberger (*Hawthorne and the Modern Short Story*) and Charles May (*Short Story Theories*) in the 1960s and 1970s. May's book collected essays approaching short fiction from various angles, thereby drawing up an agenda for the future study of the genre; it may well be this book to which the field owes its name. Another leading voice of long standing is that of Susan Lohafer. Her conceptually ambitious study from 1983, *Coming to Terms with the Short Story*, as well as the aptly titled 1989 collection of essays, *Short Story Theory at a Crossroads*, brought further theoretical rigor to the field. In her introductions to the various sections of the latter work, Lohafer documents the versatility of the approaches to the study of the short story that have emerged since May's book and reflects on their possibilities and limitations; the comprehensive bibliography at the end, compiled by Jo Ellyn Clarey, testifies to a broad-ranging and multifaceted attention to the short story genre through the 1980s. Important monographs devoted to the study of short story form during the decade were Helmut Bonheim's *The Narrative Modes: Techniques of the Short Story* (1982), Valerie Shaw's *The Short Story: A Critical Introduction* (1983), and John Gerlach's *Toward the End: Closure and Structure in the American Short Story* (1985). Moreover, interest in short story theory during the 1980s was by no means confined only to American short fiction. W. H. New's 1987 study, *Dreams of Speech and Violence: The Art of the Short Story in Canada and New Zealand*, provided a welcome postcolonial perspective on genre developments. Clare Hanson's *Short Stories and Short Fictions, 1880–1980* from 1985, as well as her edition of articles titled *Re-Reading the Short Story* (1989), added new British voices to the debate. Since his influential 1977 monograph *The Short Story* in the Critical Idiom series, the Australian scholar Ian Reid has been an important contributor to the discussion, not least through interdisciplinary work on the short story and discourse analysis.

Interest in short story theory continued into the 1990s. During the decade Charles May published several more books devoted to the study of the genre, including *The New Short Story Theories* from 1994. Since the First International Conference on the Study of the Short Story was held in Paris in 1989, there have been altogether seven such conferences, alternating between Iowa and New Orleans; offspring of this activity were the formation in 1994 of the Society for the Study of the Short Story, and the foundation of the journal *Short Story*. In 1998 yet another collection of articles on short story theory was published, with Susan Lohafer as one of the editors, titled *The Tales We Tell: Perspectives on the Short Story*. In her introduction, Lohafer seems quite justified in making the following claims: "We are seeing the end of the romance of the short story critic and theorist as 'outsider,' fitting as that label may [once] have been. . . . Students of the form are looking askance at the very boundaries that brought the field into existence (tale versus sketch, novel versus story, oral versus . . .). We're losing our defensiveness about genre; we're bored by taxonomies. Indeed, discussions of the short story tend now to be genre-bending and interdisciplinary, as many chapters in this volume suggest" (x–xi).

As for the "policy" part of referring to short fiction theory as an autonomous field of academic study, a few notes are in order. As the list of authors and titles above reveals, a major part of the theory building in this area has been carried out by Anglo-American scholars. The present collection of essays springs from a desire on the part of short fiction scholars at the University of Oslo to combine the forces of established Anglo-American scholars with those of Nordic researchers in an effort to build academic bridges and expand the field, geographically as well as conceptually. A long-term Short Fiction project was launched to this effect in 2001, and *The Art of Brevity: Excursions in Short Fiction Theory and Analysis* is the first publication to come out of this effort. Further publications are planned, and efforts will be made in the future to bring in voices from other European countries while maintaining, as well as increasing, the number of contacts with Anglo-American scholars.

The dissemination of new knowledge, not least across language barriers, is one of the main objectives of the Oslo Short Fiction project. A case in point: Gitte Mose's article on the centrality of the brief format (so-called short shorts) in Danish short fiction and its links to German Romanticism opens a window on a textual practice that, for reasons of language, might otherwise have remained closed to non-Nordic readers. Similarly, though language is not an issue with regard to W. H. New's thorough discussion of the longstanding tradition of the Australian tall tale, issues of geography and cultural difference may well come into the picture, and we sense that many readers will receive many of the findings as new knowledge as well. New's essay also documents a welcome interest in an area of short fiction theory that has been somewhat neglected until now and that our project will want to encourage further in the future: the situating of genre in relation to social and cultural conditions. Furthermore, in cases where the texts of study fall more readily within the established confines of Anglo-American theoretical discourse, the aim is to enter into dialogue with existing research in efforts to broaden the scope of inquiry, as well as to sharpen analytical tools already in use.

One last "political" note: the title of the present volume, as well as the name given to the Oslo project, privileges the term "short fiction" over "short story." This distinction reflects the fact that genre theory in recent decades has moved away from essentialist notions of what text types may be said to be, speaking instead of genres as sets of textual tendencies and practices that are present in varying degrees in different texts. As pointed out by Susan Lohafer, discussions of the short story now tend to be "genre-bending and interdisciplinary," and the editors felt that a slight shift in nomenclature might help to signal an allegiance to this wider view of genre. This certainly does not represent a disavowal of or break with former short story theory, but rather a willingness to align our analytical efforts with recent developments in the theory of genre.

Commencing the collection with Mary Rohrberger's retrospective essay is a natural choice for several reasons. She has been a prominent contributor to contemporary Anglo-American short story theory since its inception in the 1960s; she was one of the cofounders of the Society for the Study of the Short Story and has been its executive director since the beginning. In her contribution to the present volume she takes the reader on a tour of the field over the last forty years. Her experience in establishing short story theory as a bona fide area of systematic study has been an uphill struggle. Although short stories were widely taught as part of "Introduction to Literature" courses when she started her academic studies in the 1950s, scant attention was paid to the formal and/or artistic features specific to the genre. In the second half of her essay, Rohrberger reviews key issues in her own thinking about the form of the short story during the forty years since she completed her doctoral dissertation on Hawthorne and the modern short story in 1961. She anchors her understanding of the form in Romanticism, with its celebration of transcendence, its ambition to capture "the beyond" in art. Aligning herself with Frank O'Connor, Charles May, and Nadine Gordimer, among others, she posits an opposition between, on the one hand, the novel, generally privileging causal and social modes of experience, and, on the other, the short story, which borrows much more heavily from the conventions of what Joseph Frank has identified as spatial form. She further links her analysis of short story structure to Henri Bergson's distinction between diachronic and synchronic perception of time, arguing that the novel typically presupposes a linearly diachronic reading, whereas the short story must be read synchronically: "Embedded with images forming patterns, metaphoric designs, allusions that resonate, linking small actions or objects in the extensional world with cosmic wholes, short story surfaces occasionally parallel but usually diverge from their substructures, creating tensions, contradictions, ironies, ambiguities, paradox, flux."

As indicated already, Charles May has made major contributions to short story theory and analysis. In his essay in the present volume, "Why Short Stories Are Essential and Why They Are Seldom Read," May examines five generic issues that, for him, are closely associated with the short story as it has developed historically. First, May asks how the short story deals with the relationship between sequence and significance. Referring to Claude Lévi-Strauss's essay "The Science and the Concrete," May concurs with Lévi-Strauss's point that "the reduction of scale or number of properties in an art work creates a reversal in the process of understanding," creating the illusion of perceiving the totality before perceiving the parts. The second significant generic issue is how the short story mediates mystery and control. May finds that its "focus on mystery and the unfamiliar is partially attributable to the fact that, as Boris Éjxenbaum has pointed out, it is a fundamental, elementary form." The title story of Alice Munro's collection, *The Love of a Good Woman*, provides an illustrative "example of the difference between novelistic elaboration and short story mystery and intensity." May then proceeds to discuss the third generic issue: how the short story constructs character. The problem of character looms large in short fiction theory, and May shows how closely it is related to, for instance, the way in which human beings act (or fail to act) in a given situation, for example in several of Hawthorne's best known short stories. The fourth generic issue is metaphoric resolution. Why is the short story's resolution often metaphoric? Since the short story cannot reconcile "the tension between the necessity of the everyday metonymic world and the sacred metaphoric world," May finds that "the only resolution possible is an aesthetic one." Turning to the fifth generic issue associated with the short story, he asks why this genre refuses to explain. One possible reason why it does not or cannot do so is related to May's concluding point that the short story's brevity "force[s] it to focus not on the whole of experience . . . but rather on a single experience lifted out of the everyday flow of human actuality."

In an essay at once academic and personal, Andrew K. Kennedy writes about "occasion, tonality, and direction" in his "double story," referring not only to his work with the short story genre as a teacher and scholar but also to experience gained by writing stories himself. As far as his own creative writing is concerned, Kennedy notes that he "nearly always start[s] thinking toward a short story . . . from a situation fairly clear in outline." Even though this situation (or "occasion," as the philosopher White-head defines the word) can incorporate a significant aspect of memory, Kennedy stresses that, for him, even the more personal stories are not directly autobiographical. He goes on to emphasize the important role played by the narrator in a short story. The choice of the narrator is fundamental, and so is narrative perspective or "point of view." Under this heading Kennedy subsumes the narrator's language and tonality: "what I call *tonality* involves controlling the voices—of narrator and characters—in something like a verbal score." The different styles are supposed to be held together by the score, not by absolute "unity" but by what he refers to as "a sense of *direction.*"

Susan Lohafer's essay reflects her continued interest in areas of short story theory that have concerned her for some time (closure/preclosure, reader reception, and interdisciplinary approaches to short fiction), but it also signals a more recent research interest: the relationship between "creative nonfiction" and the genre of the short story. In "Real-World Characters in Fictional Story Worlds: Robert Olen Butler's 'JFK Secretly Attends Jackie Auction,'" Lohafer reports on and analyzes some of her findings in a reading experiment conducted with a group of students at the University of Iowa. Half of the students were asked to read Olen Butler's story as he published it, a literary fantasy that features JFK (who did not die in the Texas shooting) attending an auction in which the couple's belongings are sold to the highest bidder after Jackie's death; the other half of the students read a near-identical story, but one in which historical names and events had been replaced with fictional ones. The object of the exercise was to examine to what extent the presence of "real-life characters" in a short fiction text alters the reader's response to generally recognized markers of the short story. These markers Lohafer identifies in part with reference to the formal tradition since Poe (markers of "unity of effect . . . a generative paradox, an epiphanic structure, and a totalizing metaphor"), in part by drawing on the findings of literary empiricism, such as the studies of "storyness" carried out by cognitive psychologists and textual linguists. As the reader of her essay will find out, while the experiment confirmed some of the hypotheses Lohafer had formed about the traffic between tabloid ingredients in short fiction and the traditional markers of the genre, there were also some surprises.

In "Narrative, Lyric, and Plot in Chris Offutt's *Out of the Woods*," John Gerlach takes his cue from Charles May's observation that "from the beginnings as a separately recognized literary form, the short story has always been more closely associated with lyric poetry than with its overgrown narrative neighbor, the novel." Even though the short story is a narrative form, the lyric, paradigmatic tendency of the short story tradition is notable. Gerlach explores how these two tendencies of the short story, narrative and lyric, "are related through the mechanism of plot." Within the genre of the short story, Gerlach suggests, "narrative and lyric . . . may be not so much separate categories as different forms of the same essence." Referring to Paul Ricoeur's term "emplotment," which suggests plotting as process, Gerlach considers plot as "an activity . . . rather than a summary of events." In a critically helpful manner, the concept of emplotment highlights the dynamic aspect of plot, thus also mediating the syntagmatic and paradigmatic, narrative and lyric, qualities of the short story. To substantiate these theoretical notions Gerlach turns to the short fiction of contemporary American short story writer Chris Offutt. Gerlach finds that the plots observable in Offutt's short stories illustrate how closely plot is related to other fictional elements such as diction and character. If, following Ricoeur, we put emphasis on the dynamic aspect of plot and understand it as process, we see more clearly "how it activates our sense of causality." That no causal connection in the text may be apparent does not in itself make our sense of, or search for, causality unimportant or purposeless. Rather, our sense of causality is integral to the process of reading, and it illustrates the close connection between plot, character, and suspense. Gerlach finds that in Offutt's short stories, "emplotment . . . is always at work and can proceed in several directions." Plot, he concludes, has a remarkable power to generate "wholeness, a unified configuration." Thus narrative and lyric may be seen as forming part of the same process. The common denominator is "the writer's strategy of emplotment and the reader's processing of the resulting discourse."

John Gerlach's ideas on short story form figure strongly also in the essay by Per Winther printed here. In "Closure and Preclosure as Narrative Grid in Short Story Analysis: Some Methodological Suggestions," Winther employs Gerlach's *Toward the End: Closure and Structure in the American Short Story* as his starting point. As Winther puts it, Gerlach's 1985 study was the first to develop "a comprehensive system of narrative closural categories for the short story." Demonstrating how anticipation of the ending tends to structure the whole, Gerlach also showed that short story writers of the nineteenth and twentieth centuries took different approaches to closure. This contribution to genre history is noted by Winther, who also comments on the analytical potential of Gerlach study. Winther starts his essay by reviewing Gerlach's signals of closure. He finds that the term "evaluation" can usefully be added to Gerlach's list of closural signals, and he also shows how other items on this list can be revised and refined. For Winther, the most problematic of Gerlach's closural signals is "completion of antithesis." Although Winther does not deny the closural force of short fiction texts distinguished by antithetical structure, he finds that Gerlach defines this term too inclusively, because all the other closural signals also tend to establish conceptual antithesis or polarization. Thus, we need a term capable of distinguishing between the form of conceptual movement Gerlach calls antithetical and those forms implied in his other closural signals: "a suitable new name for this particular form of antithetical narrative movement would seem to be *emotional* and/or *cognitive reversal.*" After having presented an alternative to Gerlach's list of closural signals, Winther notes that these signals are essentially narrative, and that narrative closure is not necessarily the same as hermeneutic closure. Arguing that this is a useful distinction, Winther also proposes a further refinement of Gerlach's conceptual framework by distinguishing between "closural signal" (a textual element that promises a form of closure) and "closural marker" (an element of text that delivers on that promise). Such a methodological tagging of closural signals and markers can, he suggests in conclusion, be hermeneutically productive.

In "The Illustrated Short Story: Toward a Typology," Stuart Sillars focuses on the relationship between text and illustration in popular magazines published in Britain between 1891 and 1900. Exploring this relationship enables Sillars to ask important questions about practices of reading, and attitudes toward the illustrated short story, in a significant and largely overlooked group of the reading public. For largely contextual reasons, turn-of-the-century readers typically looked at the image to assimilate signs of narrative, character, or setting. The reading process had become "a consequence of shifts in patterns of balance between living and working," and an illustrative example of this change is the fact that illustrated short stories were often read on trains. Sillars proceeds to discuss the typology of text and illustration, paying particular attention to the relation it furthers between reader and text and to the specific temporal pattern it establishes. Stating that any typology of illustration must incorporate several dimensions, he suggests, drawing on Roland Barthes's distinction between anchorage and relay and Jacques Derrida's ideas of the image in *The Truth in Painting*, a taxonomy of various aspects of the use of illustration. One striking aspect is that the episodes of the story "almost invariably appear significantly earlier in illustrations than they do in the verbal text." The "visual narrative implication" of this aspect is discussed by Sillars, who, by way of concluding his essay, compares the illustrated short story with two major modernist texts, Joyce's "The Dead" and Woolf's *To the Lighthouse*.

While Sillars considers one particular variant of the short story produced in Britain during a limited period of time, Gitte Mose, in her essay titled "Danish Short Shorts in the 1990s and the Jena-Romantic Fragments," combines a series of text-oriented comments on Danish short stories published one century later with a survey of the genre's characteristics as observable in the context of Danish literary history. Danish literature has traditionally been susceptible to impulses from abroad, and two major Danish short story writers of the eighteenth century, Hans Christian Andersen and Steen Steensen Blicher, were both influenced by German Romanticism. In the early twentieth century a writer such as Johannes V. Jensen—who was influenced by the American tradition of Poe, Hawthorne, and Melville—continued expanding the short story form. The various generic markers of the Danish short story illustrate the problems of classification and terminology pertaining to the short story genre. Taking her cue from the German theorist Walter Höllerer's notion of the short story as a particular form of *Sammelplatz* ("meeting place"), Mose proceeds to discuss a selection of "short shorts," that is, very short short stories whose characteristic traits combine to constitute a generic field distinguished by several of the features mentioned by Höllerer. One collection of "short shorts" is Solvej Balle's *&* (1990), a volume consisting of seventy-one squarelike texts printed on thirty-seven pages. Along with Christina Hesselholdt and other Danish short story writers of the 1990s, Balle was intrigued by Romanticism and especially by the fragments produced by German Romantics such as the brothers Schlegel and Novalis. There are, Mose concludes, interesting affinities between the epic subgenre of the fragment as observable in German Romanticism and the "testing and tentative art of storytelling" practiced by some Danish writers in the 1990s.

Like Gitte Mose, Jakob Lothe is interested in the relationship between the literary fragment and the short story. He holds that the fragment must be seen as related to the genre of the short story and to the modernist short story in particular, and he investigates the function and meaning of the fragment in central modernist texts in his "Aspects of the Fragment in Joyce's *Dubliners* and Kafka's *The Trial*." Lothe claims that several of Mikhail M. Bakhtin's points about the novel's elasticity could be made about the modern short story as well, and he posits a theoretical kinship here between the Russian critic and several of the German Romantics in their deliberations on the aesthetic properties of the fragment, in ways that are "potentially very interesting for critics of the modern short story" (compare with the essay by Gitte Mose). One of Lothe's main points is that the terms fragment and fragmentation might profit from being used together, and that the fragment's unstable generic status is a result of its affiliation with the short story and the novel alike. Lothe combines the definitions of the fragment offered by the *Oxford English Dictionary* and those provided by Gero von Wilpert in his *Sachwörterbuch der Literatur* in his analysis of the use of fragments in two stories by Joyce. While the mysterious phrase "Derevaun Seraun" in Joyce's "Eveline" is seen as an instance of "intended fragment radically detached from the plot," the few lines quoted from "The Lass of Aughrin" in "The Dead" provide an example of an "incomplete fragment" operating in the manner of an ellipsis. Analysis of the use of the fragment in *The Trial* and "Before the Law" is complicated both by the uncertainties surrounding the process of composition as well as the problematic history of publication on the part of the two texts, yet the role of the fragment remains crucial also in sorting out the thematic and aesthetic implications of Kafka's texts. Overall, Lothe finds that "like the short story (which in one sense it metonymically represents) the fragment compresses literary meaning into a short segment of text, yet by doing so it also extends meaning by drawing attention to the incomplete and fragmentary nature of verbal representation."

W. H. New's long and pioneering essay on the Australian tall tale reflects his continued interest in an important though somewhat neglected area of short story theory: the genre as cultural paradigm. In his *Dreams of Speech and Violence: The Art of the Short Story in Canada and New Zealand* (1987), New provided a detailed discussion of the cultural and social parameters of the short story traditions of those two nations; in his essay for the present collection, he adopts a similar focus, discussing the short fiction of yet another postcolonial setting, and his concern is once again with the dialogic traffic between literature and culture/society. The tall tale invited itself as a topic, he says, partly because it is such a recurrent form in Australia, and partly because of the interesting challenges it offered in terms of analyzing the cultural sensibilities that inform the genre and finding an adequate analytical vocabulary to capture its narrative sophistication. Tall tales are found in numerous national literatures, and a common denominator—also applicable to the Australian canon—is that the genre "is one of the voices of marginal protest: it exaggerates in order to refuse the limits of a ruling convention." Though the modern Australian short story is often claimed to have been born in the 1890s with the stories by Henry Lawson, Australian short fiction dates back at least a century before that. An important thematic strand throughout was "consciously contrived nationalism," in preparation for the declaration of political independence, and New argues that the emergence of the tall tale as a prominent public medium in Australia can be fruitfully analyzed in relation to these larger cultural patterns. This involves issues like narrative technique and distinctive "Australian" traits, such as the celebration of the liar and the privileging of male gendered tales. It speaks to the centrality of the tall tale tradition in Australia that it has provoked continued debate, both in terms of a series of tales written in response to earlier tales, as in the many variants of "The Drover's Wife" story, and in the form of a recent series of alternative tall tales authored by women writers out to subvert received notions of genre as well as gender.

A postcolonial focus prevails also in the next essay in the collection. Gerd Bjørhovde looks at the way in which strategies of defamiliarization are used in three Canadian short stories to suggest "the foreignness of the familiar": Ethel Wilson's "From Flores," Mavis Gallant's "The Ice Wagon Going down the Street," and Margaret Atwood's "A Travel Piece." In all three stories everyday items—a red shirt, an ice wagon, lipstick and plastic trays—are introduced in a manner that illustrates the Shklovskyan idea of the quotidian made "unfamiliar." Seemingly one-dimensional narrative elements are thus given thematically significant multiple meanings. In the stories by Wilson and Atwood, the objects become markers of unexpected violence lurking beneath the surface of everyday living, while in the Gallant story the childhood memory of an ice wagon going down a village street triggers questions about the authenticity of adult existence. Bjørhovde finds these three stories to embody a tension inherent in much postcolonial literature, as posited by Atwood in the introduction to *The Oxford Book of Canadian Short Stories in English:* "Canada shares with all of the New World ex-colonies, and with others such as Australia and New Zealand, the historically recent experience of a collision between a landscape and a language and social history not at first indigenous to it, with each side altering the other."

Laura Castor, too, discusses strategies of defamiliarization in an essay titled "Making the Familiar Strange: Representing the House in Sarah Orne Jewett's 'The Landscape Chamber' and Linda Hogan's 'Friends and Fortunes.'" In her collation of stories by Hogan and Jewett, she points to a common denominator in the two stories: the image of the house may suggest something familiar and safe but also may be a space that is strange, carrying the power to frighten. The short story, with its innate capacity for portraying moments of truth, lends itself particularly well to capturing the movement across the border between the familiar and the strange. Drawing on the analytical strategies Gaston Bachelard has developed in *The Poetics of Space,* Castor pits a twentieth-century story by Chickasaw writer Linda Hogan against a largely unknown nineteenth-century local color story by Sarah Orne Jewett. Though there are disparities—explainable in terms of differences in time, social class, and ethnicity—they share a common interest in using the house as a trope for exploring gendered social relations and the relations between humans and landscapes. Both writers, Castor argues, "challenge the Western, dualistic oppositions between man, history, and agency on the one hand, and woman, nature, and passivity on the other."

Several of the essays described above illustrate in one way or another the short story's aptitude for telling several stories simultaneously. Jan Nordby Gretlund makes this focus explicit in his "Architexture in Short Stories by Flannery O'Connor and Eudora Welty." He uses texts by these two southern writers to examine the presence of subtexts that so often are found in literary short stories, making the reading of them all the more rewarding. He borrows the term "architexture" from Gérard Genette and investigates subtexts of a sociocultural order as well as those in which the author comments on her own craft. Gretlund shows that serious commentary on class divisions and inequality in the South can be found in O'Connor's "The Displaced Persons," over and above the religious story that frequently has been privileged in discussions of this text. He finds O'Connor to be pursuing a similarly "dual agenda" in "Parker's Back." Again the effects of the social order are under scrutiny, but in this story a subtext takes on the function of metanarrative, in that O'Connor uses Parker's religious tattoo motif as indirect commentary on her own practices as a creative writer. Dual agendas also dominate in the short fiction of Eudora Welty: "The point is that no matter how unreal, accidental, and indeterminate the fiction, it quickly becomes obvious that there is a reality under the illusion, and this reality is often brought out in subtexts," Gretlund writes. He finds Welty's "Powerhouse" to contain a good example of a subtext that reminds readers of the necessary relationship between the human condition and the nature of fiction. At the same time, indirect comments on the narrator in this story can be read as annotations on Miss Welty's own strategies as a creative writer.

The last four contributors to this collection examine various aspects of the relationship between the novel and the short story. In "A Life Remembered: Store Porch Tales from Yoknapatawpha County," Hans H. Skei discusses William Faulkner's habit of incorporating previously published short stories into his novels, in this case the inclusion of "Fool about a Horse" and "Spotted Horses" in *The Hamlet*. Faulkner's use of the same material in stories and novels challenges commonly held notions about the borderlines between long and short narrative. Both of the stories under discussion in the essay hark back to the very roots of the short story in that they are store porch anecdotes, and as such classic instances of oral storytelling. Whereas Skei finds the incorporation of "Spotted Horses" into *The Hamlet* seamless and successful, in the case of "Fool about a Horse" he balances two seemingly conflicting observations against each other. On the one hand, it can be argued that the integration of short story and novel is not entirely successful in that the essentially comic tale introduces a digression that puts the main narrative somewhat off track; on the other, the anecdote about horse trading serves a necessary function in that Faulkner turns it into a vehicle of characterization. By making V. K. Ratliff the narrator of the novel version (the narrator of the short story is anonymous), Faulkner uses the short story material to establish this character as a watcher of, and counterpart/antagonist to the Snopeses. Also, the funny story helps to establish Frenchman's Bend as a world of "fun and laughter, sympathy and goodwill," which serves as necessary antidote to the brutal realities depicted elsewhere in the novel.

The artistic strategies of southern short story writers figure prominently also in Sandra Lee Kleppe's essay, "Faulkner, Welty, and the Short Story Composite." As her title suggests, Lee Kleppe's discussion taps into the current debate surrounding the hybrid form variously called "short story cycle," "composite," or "sequence," texts positioned generically somewhere between the traditional short story collection and the novel. She discusses Faulkner's *Go Down, Moses* and Welty's *The Golden Apples* in relation to this "new" genre, relying in particular on Rolf Lundén's discussion of the form in *The United Stories of America: Studies in the Short Story Composite*. Lee Kleppe follows Lundén in finding that the theorists of the short story cycle have insisted too much on the unity of the cycles rather than exploring the composites' frequent tendency in the direction of "discontinuity, fragmentation, and openness." She accepts Lundén's labeling of *The Golden Apples* as a composite but feels a need to qualify similar claims made about *Go Down, Moses.* Like Skei in his essay on Faulkner, she draws on Bakhtin's understanding of the novel as a dialogic form and finds that such a conception of the genre accommodates the presence of a so-called fringe story (i.e., "Pantaloon in Black") in Faulkner's text, though she also sees that there may be good reason for calling the book a composite. As a compromise, she introduces the term "Short Story Confederacy . . . a rebellious genre in between the anarchy of the collection and the despotism of the novel."

Axel Nissen examines the relationship between the novel and the short story from yet another angle. One of his points of departure is the observation that the two genres are locked in a binary opposition that is "not innocent." Taking his cue from Mary Louise Pratt's comment that "the short story was often the genre used to introduce new and stigmatized subject matters into the literary arena," and also drawing on aspects of recent queer theory in depicting the short story as a "deviant form," he points out that one instance of a stigmatized subject matter is romantic friendships between men. The short story, he argues, breaks with traditional narrative patterns that represent heterosexual ideologies, or what Judith Roof calls "heteroideology." Nissen's most important question is whether the short story, by virtue of its brevity, has allowed for a "perversion" of traditional narrative patterns. His answer is, basically, yes, and he illustrates this point through a brief presentation of Bret Harte's career and an analysis of Harte's 1897 story, "Uncle Jim and Uncle Billy." Here Nissen finds a superb example of the tradition of romantic love between men, which literary scholarship is only now beginning to recover. It is even a story about "men without women" with a happy ending.

Finally, in "Melville's Stories as Novel Alternative," Hans B. Löfgren brings the debate concerning the relationship between the two genres back to the "birth" of the modern short story during the Romantic period. After commenting on the prominence of the short story and the novella among narratives of Romanticism, Löfgren proceeds to identify and discuss a significant dilemma prompted by the Romantic ideal of the creative process as a dialectical unfolding of consciousness: "the narrator strives to represent a process that is universal and comprehensive, yet the narrative standpoint is itself outside that process." Noting that this Romantic dilemma of narration looms large in nineteenth-century fiction, Löfgren focuses on its resolution in a selection of Herman Melville's short stories. While the narrative contradictions of the Romantic consciousness are conspicuously present in Melville's major novels of the 1850s, his short stories of the same period invent "a particular narrative doubleness that goes a long way toward resolving formal contradictions and enables a more effective treatment of thematic content." Löfgren goes on to argue that Melville's short stories are a "novel alternative" in a double sense: not only providing an alternative genre to that of the novels, they also enable him to construct "an alternative form of the novel that takes the short story form as its basis." One significant aspect of this transformation is the multifaceted shift from a world-representing, mimetically oriented novel to a form of narrative that, in ways that anticipate the narrative experimentation of modernist fiction, tends to foreground its own operations. After having reviewed aspects of narrative method in the two novels by Melville that precede the short stories under consideration, *Moby-Dick* (1851) and *Pierre* (1852), Löfgren turns to "Bartleby" and "Benito Cereno," discussing the ways in which these stories explore "similar type[s] of pseudoresolution and pseudorevelation of truth." For instance, the latter story ironizes the position of a consciousness premised on an idea of racial superiority. When Melville returns to the longer narrative form in order to write the novel *The Confidence-Man* (1857), he adopts and elaborates the double narrative standpoint developed in the shorter fiction. Melville's stories and novels of the 1850s, Löfgren concludes, contain in embryo the characteristics of modern narrative.

Although it was never the intention of the present volume to "prove" the accuracy of the observations about the short story in the Somerset Maugham anecdote, the little lecture attributed to him might in conclusion serve once again as a reminder of the overriding focus on matters of form in the genre debate, the strong interest in the *art* of brevity on the part of short fiction theorists. A skillful master of a certain brand of the short story, Maupassant demonstrated allegiance to aesthetic preferences that many would now consider outmoded. Nevertheless, the keen attention to the importance of artistic technique one associates with his stories remains strong among short fiction writers as well as scholars. Furthermore, T. S. Eliot's general point about the inescapable connection between tradition and individual talent certainly applies also to the genre of short fiction. Awareness also of outmoded genre characteristics will often shed light on later short fiction practices. The essays presented here frequently combine diachronic and synchronic perspectives, invoking a time span that incorporates short fiction practices, on several continents, from the time of myth and oral storytelling, via the aesthetic beliefs of the Romantic Period, the further evolution of the genre in the late-nineteenth and early-twentieth century, all the way to short stories from the 1990s. The approach taken differs from essay to essay, yet these essays cohere in their joint emphasis on *how* stories come to mean what they mean. This is, of course, also very much the province of short fiction theory in general, and it is the hope of the people involved in the Oslo Project that the present collection may serve to stimulate further discussion about the genre and its scholarly methodology.

Oslo, September 2003

Works Cited

Bonheim, Helmut. *The Narrative Modes: Techniques of the Short Story.* London: D. S. Brewer, 1982.

Gerlach, John. *Toward the End: Closure and Structure in the American Short Story.* Tuscaloosa: University of Alabama Press, 1985.

Hanson, Clare. *Short Stories and Short Fictions, 1880–1980.* London: Macmillan, 1985.

———, ed. *Re-Reading the Short Story.* New York: St. Martin's Press, 1989.

Lohafer, Susan. *Coming to Terms with the Short Story.* Baton Rouge: Louisiana State University Press, 1983.

Lohafer, Susan, and Jo Ellyn Clarey, eds. *Short Story Theory at a Crossroads.* Baton Rouge: Louisiana State University Press, 1989.

Lounsberry, Barbara et al., eds. *The Tales We Tell: Perspectives on the Short Story.* Westport, Conn.: Greenwood Press, 1998.

May, Charles E., ed. *Short Story Theories.* Athens: Ohio University Press, 1976.

———, ed. *The New Short Story Theories.* Athens: Ohio University Press, 1994.

———. *The Short Story: The Reality of Artifice.* New York: Twayne, 1995.

New, W. H. *Dreams of Speech and Violence: The Art of the Short Story in Canada and New Zealand.* Toronto: University of Toronto Press, 1987.

Reid, Ian. *The Short Story.* London: Methuen, 1977.

Rohrberger, Mary. *Hawthorne and the Modern Short Story: A Study in Genre.* The Hague: Mouton, 1966.

Shaw, Valerie. *The Short Story: A Critical Introduction.* London: Longman, 1983.

Origins, Development, Substance, and Design of the Short Story

How I Got Hooked on the Short Story and Where It Led Me

Mary Rohrberger

I must say that when I heard that my article was to appear first in the present volume, I was at first somewhat daunted, but then I thought that I may have written, probably did write, at least as far as I know, the first dissertation on the short story as genre. And I thought that some explanation might interest the reader concerning what, at the time, and in the United States even now, seemed to be terribly bizarre behavior. So I will start there and then go on to talk about where it all led me. Please notice that I am starting with the second half of my title as it is printed above. That fact will become relevant later, as you will see.

I completed the dissertation in the academic year 1960–61 and published a somewhat revised version of it, at the invitation of Mouton and Company, in The Hague several years later. How did I come to write a dissertation on the short story as genre? The saga goes something like this. Once upon a time, long ago, there was a graduate student in residence at a well-known southern university in the United States. The chairman of this graduate student's committee was Richard Harter Fogle, who was also chairman of the department and its most respected scholar. Professor Fogle was a specialist in the Romantic period in Britain and America and taught graduate seminars in the British Romantic poets (Wordsworth and Coleridge in one semester, and Shelley and Keats in another). He also taught seminars on Hawthorne and Melville (one in each semester) and, oddly enough, a senior/graduate course on modern poetry. I, for I was that graduate student, of course, took them all.

Of all these writers it was Nathaniel Hawthorne who caught my fancy, especially his short stories, though I had at the time no idea of writing a dissertation on the short story or on Hawthorne. Indeed, there was no academic course on the short story for English majors except one senior-level course taught by the only creative writing teacher on the faculty. As you might guess, graduate students were not encouraged to take it. But one summer I audited the course, doing all the reading and participating in the discussion. It was, by design or chance, an excellent class, and I began to see resemblances among the stories I had never noticed before, a not surprising fact since no one in the upper-division academic program taught a course wherein the form of the short story was examined. One of the resemblances that came to me clearly was that all of the really good stories that we read and discussed were never, upon consideration, what they first appeared to be.

Oh, I had read short stories, a lot of them, in the "Introduction to Literature" course, in which we used the original Brooks and Warren text, by the way, and in survey courses in which there was not time to read a novel, and in which we talked about short stories, but only as examples of certain techniques characteristic of an author's use of them in novels. Short stories as short stories, it seems, were not worth the time of serious academics. Short stories were something novelists tossed off between major productions. They were not really serious attempts at literary achievement. Short stories were for high school students and college freshmen- or sophomore-level "Introduction to Literature" courses. And, strange as it may seem, this situation still obtains in the United States, especially among institutions granting doctorates.

(This is an aside in the nature of an exemplum. When I retired from full-time teaching and returned to my birthplace, I taught at my alma mater the first senior-level course in the short story devised for majors. It was filled with students, three-fourths of whom wanted to be writers, but there was still no creative writing program and still only one creative writing teacher, a poet this time. I taught this course only once. The department was in a crisis, as so many are today. Faculty had decided not to teach composition; their graduate students had been reduced; they were not placing their doctoral students; and they were forced to hire as adjuncts their own former students for additional years. The department had no short story specialists on staff, and undergraduate majors were decreasing, so the course was dropped again to the junior level and assigned to one of their own former students.)

But, back to the main plot, not at the time knowing the probable role of short stories in the English major's curriculum and fascinated by the resemblances among short stories I had noted, I decided to do a dissertation on the short story in an effort to refine the existing definition. I knew that there had to be more to a definition than that which Poe seemed to say in his review of Hawthorne's *Twice-Told Tales*. (I later determined that Poe had said a whole lot more than what was promulgated in the classroom.) What was usually stressed by academics at the time was the notion of necessary brevity and the bit about no word being written that did not contribute to the one preestablished design. My experience reading told me that a unity of effect was possible in novels. I had experienced it over and over. In my mind, emphasis on coherent design did little more than characterize Hawthorne's type of story as a work of art.

I decided to compare major short stories by Hawthorne with a selection of modernist stories by important short story writers, chosen by the frequency of their appearance in major anthologies. Dr. Fogle agreed to chair my committee, and three other members of the department agreed to take a place on the committee. I gave myself three years: one year to take courses, one year to study for and do the comprehensives, and one year to write the dissertation and defend it. I am not sure that any of this is relevant or even interesting, but, pushing right ahead, by the fourth year I had accepted a position at a state university whose faculty did not seem to know they should not be teaching the short story to English majors. I stayed at that university for almost thirty years, spending the first fifteen teaching and the rest mainly in administration.

In the last year of my tenure there, I inaugurated the journal I named simply *Short Story*. The journal is now in its thirteenth year and is under the general editorship of Farhat Iftekharuddin, the dean of the College of Liberal Arts at the University of Texas at Brownsville and a former student of mine. I remain as executive editor. I keep getting off the subject, don't I? In fact, I am not sure I have announced a subject yet. I seem to be telling a story. Well, we will get to the theoretical part. Three years after I arrived at Oklahoma State, Mouton Publishers in The Hague asked me if I would be interested in their publishing my dissertation. It seemed like a good thing to do.

Now comes the first really unfortunate mistake I made. For the published book, I kept the title, only slightly revised, that I had given my dissertation: *Hawthorne and the Modern Short Story*. You can guess what happened. Libraries, apparently most of them, either did not buy it, or lost it, or filed it in their card catalogs under "Hawthorne." And who would look under "Hawthorne" to find out something about the short story? Apparently the book did not fare so badly in Europe, but in the United States, after a few years, the book seemed to me to be gone forever. But not quite. Charles May printed my last chapter, a two-page conclusion, in his *Short Story Theories*, a collection of essays demonstrating, among other things, how little theoretical attention had been paid to the short story. But my last chapter, all by itself, did not begin to encompass all that I attempted in the full manuscript. Nevertheless, some scholars beginning to take an interest in the form of the short story took the part for the whole and thought that my book was a critical study rather than a theoretical one and, moreover, that all I was doing was using a new critical approach, and all I did was point out that the short story was/is modernist in form. But, by far, the strangest charge was that I apparently had the gall to define a genre in two pages.

Now, mind you, I was not really worrying about all of this at the time. I was busy with producing other books and writing articles about a myriad of short story writers, all of whom wrote stories in the modes I had described in the earlier book. I did ask a few publishers about their possible interest in reprinting the Hawthorne book, but all of them said the same thing. They could not afford to reprint a book that had already been printed, and Mouton had stopped doing literary studies and was concentrating on linguistics.

I am going to summarize for you a few of the major points I made in the Hawthorne book because, over time, my thoughts kept building on that base, and along the way, I might even speculate about why I keep referring to that book as "the Hawthorne book" while, at the same time, maintaining that it is really a book about the short story as genre. The first thing I did was to assert that Hawthorne, not Poe or Gogol or Irving or Chekhov or Maupassant, wrote the prototypical short story, each of these authors having been declared, at one time or another, "father" of the form. The next thing I did was to assert that, in spite of what Henry James had said in his book on Hawthorne, the latter did have a literary theory, and what's more, his theory was firmly based in a consistent metaphysic. As a literary theorist, Hawthorne declared that the art form is a closer approximation to reality, as he understood it, than is the extensional world. Simply stated, he believed, as many people do, that there is more to the world than that which is apprehended through the senses. In so saying he fixed the ontological status of the art form as a means of approaching that which is unchanging and real as opposed to ever-shifting matters of fact of the ordinary world of experience. Contrary to Henry James's snide remark that Hawthorne had never heard of "Realism," we can be assured that he had. Not only had he heard about it but also had read Thackeray and Trollope and other British novelists and even declared at one point that he wished he could write like Trollope; but, of course, he could not, not with his aesthetic.

We can also be assured that Hawthorne knew what he was doing. Many prefaces, notes, and sketches attest to the fact that he was aware of the notion of distance, both psychic and physical; he was aware of the need for framing his stories to help the reader get from the world of mundane fact to the world of universals; he was aware of particular devices that would help position readers to take the proper point of view (his actual words) so they might receive his signals, which were—are—mainly the multiple perspective, the allegorical framework of myth, the historical past, and patterns of images creating metaphors, symbolic identifications.

I followed my chapter on Hawthorne's aesthetic theory with an analysis of three of Hawthorne's best-known stories: "My Kinsman, Major Molineux," dated 1832, and the one I identified as the prototypical short story, "Roger Malvin's Burial," another very early story, and "Young Goodman Brown," published in 1840. Next, I did an analysis of both the literary theory and a well-known story by each of the modern writers I had chosen: Conrad, Mansfield, Lawrence, Faulkner, Hemingway, Anderson, and Welty. Then, lo and behold, I found that the hypothesis did seem to fit the facts.

But I knew that there were stories that were different from the ones I had analyzed, and they could not be ignored. These are short stories that are not, except in the broadest sense, symbolic at all. They exhibit all the other characteristics of the short story—brevity, coherence, freedom from excrescence, and so on—but they have no symbolic substructure. Instead, they turn on a single and sometimes a double irony. However, several kinds of short fiction (we have to admit it) have names other than short story. There are sketches, fables, tales, parables, and yarns that are sometimes called "tall tales." So I tried to find a name that would fit the object.

In 1952 Ray B. West had noticed two kinds of short story also, which he differentiated as "realistic" and "symbolic." But what could be more realistic than the surfaces of some highly symbolic stories? Long before West, in the 1880s, Brander Matthews suggested that the new kind of story (whose birth he proclaimed) should be spelled with a hyphen so as to make the distinction; apparently nobody followed up on that proposal. So I did what I thought was at least logical, and I sought a term that was reasonably descriptive. I called this other type of story "simple narrative." Since then several scholars have offered different names for the two types of story: mimetic and lyric, anecdotal and epiphanic, linear and spatial, among others.

Having identified what I considered to be the essential genre characteristics of the short story and the simple narrative, I added, at other times and in other places, secondary characteristics that seemed to distinguish the nineteenth-century short story from the twentieth-century kind. Are you still wondering why I keep referring to the Hawthorne book? Well, because every new idea I had was traceable back to Hawthorne. In the same way that I could not ignore the simple narrative, I could not ignore Hawthorne's distinction between the Romance and the Novel, and that meant I had to admit that simple narrative was, except for length, more akin to novels, and that the short story proper was more like the Romance. The thing is I just could not seem to get away from Hawthorne. Over the years and usually by chance, I reread some of the 1830 pieces that had been classified by older scholars as sketches. "The Hollow of the Three Hills," for example, and I found it to be not a sketch but a fully developed story in the modern mode. Then after I became familiar with postmodern alternate reality stories, I had occasion to reread "The Wives of the Dead," which, surprisingly, turned out to be an alternate reality story. The next thing I discovered came to me in the bright glow of a revelation: Hawthorne's best stories, though following a traditional plot line on one level, on another, clearly ended in epiphany.

Now comes the second half of my paper. It is kind of a summary of the ideas that I developed at various times during my perhaps forty-five years of full-time work. I took these ideas from various sources that I published over the years: articles, monographs, textbooks, encyclopedias, reference books, various introductions. So if you recognize what follows, chalk it up to excellent memory.[1]

Overall, perhaps more is lost than gained if we say a short story is a story that is short, thus separating the elements of the compound noun and pointing the way toward a reduction of story to plot and plot to events ordered both in time (sequentially) and by means of cause and effect relationships (logically). But "story" is more than plot; "short" is more than temporality; and "short story" names a complex entity, perhaps aptly described as "an inseparable web of vibrating energy patterns in which no one component has reality independently of the entirety; and included in the entirety is the observer."[2] Short story theorists beginning with Poe have insisted on the importance of unity of effect and of pattern in the short story and have reserved an essential participatory role for those readers whom Poe insisted act with a "kindred art" (and Aristotle long before called "judicious").

Elsewhere, I and others have argued that the short story proper, as distinguished from the story that is merely short, derives from the Romantic tradition, having its beginnings in myth and legends,[3] wherein a reader is asked to put the extensional world out of mind and deal in and with a kind of underworld, a world of inexplicable strange loops,[4] a mystical world of paradox and ambiguity, of shadows and shifting perspectives governed not by rational order but by intuition and dream logic. Indeed, the very presentation in a short story of potentiality (there is more to the world than can be apprehended through the senses) rather than actuality (matters of fact of the ordinary world of experience) generates for the story an immediate ontology. Moreover, in the hands of master craftsmen like Hawthorne and Poe, the short story became a convincing vehicle for the probing of reality by means of structural configurations where space seemed to slide into time and time into space.

Perhaps more than any other narrative structure, the short story veers toward what Joseph Frank calls "spatial form," a set of narrative techniques and processes of aesthetic perception that works to impede linearity. Frank argues that in certain kinds of modern novels, various signs, referents, and connections are embedded in the text, where they organize and shape Gestalt groupings to which readers respond with a sense of spatial form, though the act of reading takes place over spaced intervals (clock time) and in several sittings. In literary context, spatial form thus became a positive value defined as characteristic of the most exciting novels of the new century. Moreover, in the years since the publication of Frank's article, many a literary critic has located spatial form in use and plainly visible in poetry as well as novels and in periods other than the modern.[5] As is always the case, of course, able combatants arose to challenge the concept of spatial form in the novel in an effort to reestablish the opposite view, that time, not space, is the novel's primary organizing principle.[6]

Beyond a doubt, certain novelists do use technical and stylistic devices to establish a sense of spatial form, but that spatial form seems to me to resonate against the novel's temporal base and not vice versa. The temporal frames of reference that Joyce constructs for *Ulysses*, for example, provide a clear and overriding sense of isomorphic time as it governs the day, as minutes click by in conjunction with clock and calendar. But Joyce also provides symbolic frames throughout the novel that afford a reader a strong though intermittent sense of synchronic time. Perhaps a better example would be a more realistic novel like Honoré de Balzac's *Père Goriot*, a novel generally believed to be firmly based in a plethora of details attesting to the authenticity of the experiential world. But in that novel also, buried beneath the externalities of Parisian social structures and behavior patterns, are ancient taboos against incest and patricide and restagings of primeval battles between gods and devils in shadowy arenas where the combatants are masked. Very likely one could construct a scale along which degrees could be etched to indicate the relative proportion of spatial form and temporality found in specific novels. Nevertheless, for most novels, it does seem that the scale is weighted on the side of everyday reality, measured by means of accumulation of matter-of-fact details within temporal frames.

Surprisingly, with all of the attention paid to spatial form in the novel, little notice has been given to the concept as it operates generically in the short story.[7] Short stories need to be defined in exactly the opposite way, in terms of a synchronic base where elements of the mythic and dreamlike are foregrounded and where sets of internal referents establish a sense of temporality that resonates against the short story's spatial base. In the novel, readers move through time in such a way that it propels them on. Readers desire novels to continue even through successive generations. In the short story readers move in time in such a way that it catapults them from beginning to end and back again, so strong is their desire to reread what is already there.

From the time of their inception, early in the nineteenth century, short stories have exhibited characteristic structures where metaphoric relationships subverted linearity and built to epiphanies. For example, despite surface "once upon a time" beginnings and apparently traditional plots where developing conflicts lead to climax and denouement, Hawthorne's stories exhibit structural underpinnings that tantalize a reader directing attention away from clock time. "Rappaccini's Daughter," for example, offers a first-level conflict, climax, and resolution to satisfy a surface reading of the plot, but an epiphany occurs not at the level of the apparent climax but at the very end of the story, in the last sentence, when Baglioni from a balcony looks with god-like demeanor into the garden to ask, "Rappaccini! Rappaccini! and is *this* the upshot of your experiment!" a question that at once scrambles the characters and the roles they play and causes the epiphanic scene to resonate and alter meaning.

The relationship of the nineteenth-century short story to its more fabulous forebears is easy to see. Peopled with symbolic representations of the gods as well as everyman (and two kinds of woman) characters who undergo patterned adventures both archetypal and pictorial, nineteenth-century stories as a general rule exhibit extraordinary surfaces that call analogues to mind along familiar mythic paths. By the time the century was over, however, a minor revolution was in process, and the "modernist" short story emerged, wherein abrupt in medias res beginnings replaced "once upon a time" starts, wherein characters became everyday and actions were without apparent development, wherein ends were not only foreshortened to meet middles but also paradoxically separated from them by silences that frame epiphanies.[8]

Give or take another fifty years and postmodernism was upon us. Stories became antistories, plots often lost cause-and-effect relationships, "reality" appeared in quotation marks, characters were flattened and artifice foregrounded, and symbols convoluted upon themselves. But through all the surface modifications, basic modalities of the genre remained: an analogical mode defied linearity and arrested time and movement in an eternal and continuous present.

We are, to be sure, circling around the two views of time that Henri Bergson and others grappled with: time defined as succession (clock time, diachronicity) and time as coexistence (*durée*, synchronicity). Bergson argued that the mathematical concept of time is inadequate since it takes no account of "real" time, flux, the stuff of our consciousness that is apprehended by intuition and not through the intellect by means of external references. The apprehension of "real" time is absolute; knowledge of "mechanical" time is relative, Bergson said. He asserted that there are two profoundly different ways of knowing a thing: "the first implies that we move round the object; the second that we enter into it." The first approach is allied with reason, the intellect, and the second with instinct, what Bergson called *élan vital* (1). *Durée* cannot be understood by means of concepts. Analysis can never provide more than an artificial reconstruction of an object. Moreover, Bergson explained, concepts generally go together in couples and represent two contraries that cannot be reconciled logically. Nor can duration be understood through images; but "many diverse images, borrowed from very different orders of things, may, by the convergence of their action direct consciousness to the precise point where there is a certain intuition to be seized" (9).[9] Duration is a succession of states, one merging into another in continuous flux so smoothly that it is impossible to know when one starts and another ends, though consciousness is enriched as present turns into past and announces future.

Duration is characterized by variety, even contraries, since it contains the whole past and present of the person experiencing it—unity and multiplicity. "Seized by intuition we pass easily in many cases to the two contrary concepts; and in that way thesis and antithesis can be seen to spring from reality. We grasp at the same time how it is that the two are opposed and how they are reconciled," Bergson writes (21). As we can see, essential characteristics of *durée* as outlined by Bergson are remarkably similar to essential characteristics of the short story. Bergson's characterization of mechanical time seems to define the novel's temporal base. "Mechanical" time, artificially constructed by the intellect, marks sequential actions and emphasizes externalities. *Durée*, by contrast, seems perfectly fitted to the short story. Synchronicity defines the short story's base. Analogy not only objectifies the moment in space by stopping the clock between ticks but also connects past and future by encompassing successive states, each of which follows and contains that which precedes it. The short story operates in Bergson's "real" time, synthesizing opposites and revealing *élan vital* below the surface of appearances. The short story is characterized by multiple levels generated by substructures that underlie narrative surfaces. Embedded with images forming patterns, metaphoric designs, allusions that resonate, linking small actions or objects in the extensional world with cosmic wholes, short story surfaces occasionally parallel but usually diverge from their substructures, creating tensions, contradictions, ironies, ambiguities, paradox, flux. Clustered about the figure of Goodman Brown, for example, as he stands in the forest at Salem calling out to Faith to resist the "Evil One," are all of his ancestors back to Adam and beyond, all of the lusts and fears and dreams of domination and power in his line. The epiphanic moment—Brown's plea for Faith/faith that is already lost (and, on another level, won, though not by Brown)—is parenthetically enclosed by the story's beginning and end, both of which are implicit in the epiphany and coterminous with past and future, thus providing a sense of clock time (one night's journey) that exists simultaneously with and comments tangentially on the cosmic order.

Paralleling the commanding position held by Hawthorne (and Poe) in the nineteenth-century short story in English, Katherine Mansfield dominates the field in the first decades of the twentieth century.[10] Although the story appeared early in her career, "How Pearl Button Was Kidnapped" is, nevertheless, a virtuoso achievement. Pearl Button is just that—a loose button freed from her moorings, popped off from a dress her mother might be "ironing-because-it's-Tuesday," free to participate in a fantasy journey to the sea in the arms of a Gypsy mother. The story is disconcerting; there is color and movement in abundance but no sound at places where sound would be expected, until the child laughs out loud, a ghostly peal of delight played against the unearthly landscape. The laugh seems a signal of readiness, the seduction strongly reminiscent of the *Erlkönig* who lured children to their death. The journey to the sea is motion without progress. The sea is beautiful. "Lovely," Pearl Button cries out, a call that seems a summons to little blue men who will carry her back to her house of boxes, where time will be rigidly fixed by ticking clocks, and the rescue from the sea will be the real death.

Perhaps Mansfield illustrates her craft best in "Prelude" and "At the Bay." I can here suggest only a few of the ways time and motion are characterized and interact in these brilliant stories. "Prelude" describes a move the Burnell family makes from one house to another. No internal evidence in the story fixes the specific date or geographic location, except that it is not Australia. A general time is fixed by the fact that buggies and candles are used, and the mention of certain plants suggests New Zealand. But although setting is not specific, there is a strong feeling of time and place. There is the time that is measured by the clock and to which the characters respond with daily routines played off against the time of a larger order, that of generations in history; there is time in an even grander sense, the time of nature, of the movement of the planets through the heavens, rotating about the sun. A corresponding sense of place is achieved as the family moves through prescribed paths and areas. The family moves from one house to another, from city to country; the characters move from house to garden and back again to house; they move from family rooms to private rooms, and they move from reality to dream to fantasy in the innermost circle of all.

Time and place interact. The personal time that governs daily activities is ordered by clock time, which, in turn, reflects the movement of the earth around the sun. The planetary motion suggests the larger order of historical time made parallel with the generations of the family delineated in all their tenses. And absolute time transcends planetary motions, extending beyond the finalities of individual life and death and accounting for the characters' attempts to impose structure, order, and meaning on their lives. The past merges in the present moment so that the future is always on the point of becoming one with the present, and sometimes does. The child becomes mother and the mother is child. Generation follows generation in one unbroken sequence. The century plant is coming into bloom and will bloom again in another century as it has bloomed in the last.

Like "Prelude," "At the Bay" is organized around time in all its various tenses, the design of the story functioning symbolically as part of the overall meaning. The story begins at the moment the sun rises over Crescent Bay. Merging images of earth and sea mark the activities of the characters, who are played against a background of the rise and fall of the tides and, as in "Prelude," timed with the movement of the sun and the moon through the heavens. Sequential and nonsequential time move through a montage of images where clock and calendar time, the astrological and the geological, contrast with time as a function of the human mind. Life moves through a path between birth and death and is no more than the rising and setting of the sun; and as the images of sea and earth merge, so life and death are unified into one grand scheme.

This is the accomplishment, perhaps of all great short story writers, the encompassing of time and motion in a present moment while simultaneously suggesting past and future. All of the characteristic devices associated with the short story finally relate to this end: juxtapositions that create montage patterns, the accumulation of details forming networks of images that become metaphors, the layerings of time and place, the meshing of antitheses—joy and sadness, waking and dream, even life and death. Tonal reverberations operate, paradoxically as a means for nonverbal expression, as the painter uses color, texture, and line, as the musician uses notes arranged in patterns along a scale. And, of course, the epiphany, a point of frozen energy resonating just beyond understanding.

Postmodern stories are not different from their precursors. Alain Robbe-Grillet's "The Secret Room," for example, invites analogies with a painting, a series of paintings, or a vast tapestry. The richness of detail, the pictorial intricacy of the patterns, insists that we contemplate form and recognize its beauty even before we apprehend the surreal horror of the scene. The secret room is a dungeon where torture is enacted by men using sacred and sacrificial rites on what may be an infinite series of women hidden in the bowels of the earth as well as eternally in the recesses of the mind. The room is also a place where lusts and fears are played and replayed serially in filmic display, backward and forward, looping through chronomorphic as well as synchronic time.

Basic to the definition of the short story and incorporated into its structure is the metaphysical assumption that there is more to the world than can be apprehended through the senses. Short story writers question the world of appearances and in that questioning cast doubt on the immediately apparent and, at the same time, signify the timeless universals beyond the extensional world. Many years ago I wrote that in the short story, questioning is embodied in technique, what is questioned is embodied in structure, and answers to the questions are inherent in total meaning. Somewhat later, trying to get at the same idea, I wrote that the structure of a story creates metaphors that move to symbolic levels and embody meaning by means of analogies.[11] More recently, in "The Nature of Knowledge in Short Fiction," Charles E. May has addressed much the same set of questions and answers, I think, similarly:

> My assumption is that when we discuss the differences between long fiction and short fiction, we must discuss basic differences in the ontology and epistemology of the two forms. The short story is short precisely because of the kind of experience or reality embodied in it, and the kind of experience we find in the short story reflects a mode of knowing which differs essentially from the mode of knowing we find in the novel. My thesis is that long fiction by its very length demands both a subject matter and a set of artistic conventions that primarily derive from and in turn establish the primacy of "experience" conceptually created and considered; whereas short fiction by its very length demands both a subject matter and a set of artistic conventions that derive from and establish the primacy of "an experience" directly and emotionally created and encountered. (328)

In *The Sense of an Ending*, Frank Kermode makes the point that "spatial form" is a metaphor for "form defined as an inter-connection of parts all mutually implied. A duration (rather than a space) organizing the moment in terms of the end" (57). But in the short story an end does more than complete a pattern and effect closure. The amazing thing about the short story is that beginning and end make a strange loop: beginning is end, and end is also beginning. Epiphany expressed through analogy fuses past, present, and future in a moment of continuous flux. Epiphany encompasses answers to the questions posited by structure, reconciling the contraries inherent in the differences between appearance and reality, on the one hand, and form and content on the other.

Notes

1. See, for example, *Art of Katherine Mansfield* and "Between Shadow and Act."

2. Davies, *Superforce*, 49. I am delighted to have found this definition. Davies is actually describing the universe, but how wonderfully apt the words are with reference to short

stories! Indeed, the book's title is also felicitous, since many think of the short story as super-charged.

3. See, for example, *Hawthorne and the Modern Short Story* and various works by May, such as "Short Fiction Criticism." The short story, May says, "is primarily a literary mode that embodies and recapitulates mythic perception itself."

4. See Hofstadter, *Gödel, Escher, Bach.* Strange loops are discussed at some length through-out. Strange loops are curious tangles; for example, hands drawing hands drawing hands. A strange loop occurs in a hierarchical system when we unexpectedly find ourselves back where we started.

5. See, for example, articles published in Smitten and Daghistany, *Spatial Form.* Location of "spatial form" in other genres is not surprising since all of the so-called linear arts (music, narrative) as well as those arts called spatial (sculpture, painting) finally exist as a construct of the mind. Perhaps the relevant question is where is the art object? Music and poetry are not defined as black marks on a page. But is not a building also a construct of the mind? A viewer can find no one position from which to view a building whole. The perusal of an art object, whatever form it takes—listening to music, reading a story, moving about and viewing a piece of sculpture—occurs in time, step by step, sequentially. In a short story the moment of apprehension of the whole, of unity and multiplicity, is a moment of such intensity that for a reader time slides into space and fuses with it.

6. See, for example, Hutchens, "Novel as Chronomorph." Hutchens denies that the short story shares in the novel's chronomorphism. See also Tobin, *Time and the Novel;* Mendilow, *Time and the Novel;* and Toliver, *Animate Illusions.*

7. This situation is even more surprising when we recall (1) that Poe insisted that the tale (short story) be short enough to be read in one sitting so that there should be no diminution by interruption of the "immense force" derivable from totality and (2) that a distinguishing characteristic of the short story is "epiphany," a point of revelation, of showing forth, the place where everything is seen to fall together. The matter is dealt with in an article by Brown, "'Tess' and *Tess.*" Brown contends that novels can make use of spatial patterns but that short stories deal only in spatial patterns.

8. We needed to learn to read stories by Chekhov, Mansfield, Joyce, and Anderson in the same way that many of us had to learn to read Borges, Barthelme, and Coover.

9. The relationship that Bergson makes between images and intuition seems another way to think of epiphany.

10. Joyce, as came to be usual, was having censorship problems delaying the publication of *Dubliners.* Consequently, *A Portrait of the Artist* demanded attention before *Dubliners* was too much noticed.

11. See my *Hawthorne and the Modern Short Story* and *Story to Anti-Story.*

Works Cited

Bergson, Henri. *An Introduction to Metaphysics.* Translated by T. E. Hulme. New York: G. P. Putnam's Sons, 1912.

Brown, Suzanne Hunter. "'Tess' and *Tess:* An Experiment in Genre." *Modern Fiction Studies* 28, no. 1 (1982): 25–44.

Davies, Paul. *Superforce.* New York: Simon and Schuster, 1984.

Frank, Joseph. "Spatial Form in Modern Literature." *Sewanee Review* 53 (Spring 1945): 221–40; (Summer 1945): 433–56; (Autumn 1945): 643–53.

Hofstadter, Douglas. *Gödel, Escher, Bach: An Eternal Golden Braid.* New York: Basic Books, 1979.

Hutchens, Eleanor. "The Novel as Chronomorph." *Novel* 21, no. 4 (1972): 215–24.

Kermode, Frank. *The Sense of an Ending.* New York: Oxford University Press, 1967.

May, Charles E. "Short Fiction Criticism." In *Short Fiction: 1800–1880, Critical Survey of Short Fiction,* edited by Frank Magill, 153–73. Englewood Cliffs, N.J.: Salem Press, 1981.

———. "The Nature of Knowledge in Short Fiction." *Studies in Short Fiction* 21, no. 4 (1984): 327–38.

Mendilow, A. A. *Time and the Novel.* London: Peter Nevill, 1952.

Rohrberger, Mary. *Hawthorne and the Modern Short Story.* The Hague: Mouton, 1966.

———. *The Art of Katherine Mansfield.* Ann Arbor, Mich.: University Microfilms International, 1977.

———. *Story to Anti-Story.* Boston: Houghton Mifflin, 1979.

———. "Between Shadow and Act." In *Short Story Theory at a Crossroads,* edited by Susan Lohafer and Jo Ellyn Clarey, 32–45. Baton Rouge: Louisiana State University Press, 1989.

Smitten, Jeffrey, and Ann Daghistany. *Spatial Form in Narrative.* Ithaca, N.Y., and London: Cornell University Press, 1981.

Tobin, Patricia Dreschel. *Time and the Novel.* Princeton, N.J.: Princeton University Press, 1978.

Toliver, Harold. *Animate Illusions.* Lincoln: University of Nebraska Press, 1974.

Why Short Stories Are Essential and Why They Are Seldom Read

Charles E. May

I take the first part of my title from the great South American writer Jorge Luis Borges, who once said, "Unlike the novel, a short story may be, for all purposes, essential."[1] I take the second part from the sad fact that, in spite of what Borges says, the short story is largely scorned by agents, editors, readers, and scholars. What I hope to do in this essay is to offer some possible justifications for Borges's provocative remark, provide some explanations for the short story's neglected status, and perhaps suggest how the former is the cause of the latter.

To that end, I wish to examine what I consider to be five of the most significant generic issues that have clustered about the short story as it has developed historically: how the short story deals with the relationship between sequence and significance, how it mediates mystery and pattern, how it constructs character, why its resolution is often metaphoric, and why it shuns explanation.

Sequence and Significance

The basic question that interests me is this: What are the significant theoretical and historical implications of shortness in narrative? If, as Frederic Jameson has suggested, narrative is an epistemological category, one of the abstract coordinates by which we come to understand the world, I want to know if short narratives understand the world differently than do long narratives (95). As Mikhail M. Bakhtin and Pavel N. Medvedev note, "If we approach genre from the point of view of its intrinsic thematic relationship to reality and the generation of reality, we may say that every genre has its methods and means of seeing and conceptualizing reality, which are accessible to it alone" (133). What I want to know is, what methods and means of seeing are accessible to prose fictions that are short?

One of the most helpful discussions of the effect of artistic smallness on the perceiver is Claude Lévi-Strauss's essay "The Science of the Concrete," in which he argues that the reduction of scale or number of properties in an art work creates a reversal in the process of understanding. To understand a real object, says Lévi-Strauss, we tend to divide it and to work from its parts. Reduction in scale reverses this situation. Knowledge of the whole seems to precede knowledge of the parts. Even if this is an illusion, he says, "the point of the procedure is to create or sustain the illusion, which gratifies the intelligence and gives rise to a sense of pleasure which can already be called aesthetic on these grounds alone" (148).

That the short story's shortness creates the illusion that understanding of the whole precedes understanding of the parts was first proposed by Edgar Allan Poe. Indeed, Poe's most significant contribution to the development of the short story as a new genre in American literature was his creation of an alternative definition of "plot." Instead of "simple complexity" or "involution of incident," Poe adapted from A. W. Schlegel a new meaning of the term—"that from which no part can be displaced without ruin to the whole." By this one stroke, Poe shifted the reader's narrative focus from mimetic events to aesthetic pattern. Poe argued that without the "key" of the overall design or plan of a work of fiction, many points would seem insignificant or unimportant through the impossibility of the reader's comprehending them. Once the reader has the overall design in mind, however, all those points that might otherwise have been "insipid" or "null" will "break out in all directions like stars, and throw quadruple brilliance over the narrative."[2]

What Poe's approach to the shortness of story reflects is the basic paradox inherent in all narrative: the writer's restriction to the dimension of time juxtaposed against his or her desire to create a structure that reflects an atemporal theme. The central problem, says C. S. Lewis, is that for stories to be stories, they must be a series of events; yet at the same time it must be understood that this series is only a net to catch something else. And this "something else" has no sequence in it; it is "something other than a process and much more like a state or quality." The result is that the means of fiction are always at war with its end. Lewis says, "In real life, as in a story, something must happen. That is just the trouble. We grasp at a state and find only a succession of events in which the state is never quite embodied" (91).

The problem for the writer is how to convert mere events, one thing after another, into significance. This raises the additional problem that even as writers encourage the reader to keep turning pages to find out what happens next, they must make the poor reader understand that ultimately what happens next is not what is important. This basic incompatibility, which has been noted by many critics, is much more obvious in the short narrative (which, in its frequent focus on a frozen moment in time, seems atemporal) than the long narrative (which seems primarily just a matter of one thing after another).

Ambrose Bierce's "An Occurrence at Owl Creek Bridge" is a particularly clear example of the paradox. At the end of part 1 of the story, when the protagonist looks down at the water below and contemplates how he might escape being hanged, the narrator cues the reader to the story's inevitable artistic distortion of time: "As these thoughts, which have here to be set down in words, were flashed into the doomed man's brain rather than evolved from it the captain nodded to the sergeant. The sergeant stepped aside." This is a self-reflexive reminder that although authors wish to communicate that which is instantaneous or timeless, they are always trapped by the time-bound nature of words. Thus we are shocked to discover what all fictions urge us to ignore in the reading but to be aware of in retrospect: that what seems to be taking place in time is an illusion necessitated by the time-bound nature of narrative language.

Peter Brooks has reminded us that prior events in narrative are so only retrospectively. Brooks says, "In this sense, the metaphoric work of eventual totalization determines the meaning and status of the metonymic work of sequence—though it must also be claimed that the metonymies of the middle produced, gave birth to, the final metaphor. The contradiction may be in the very nature of narrative, which not only uses but is a double logic" (29). The illusion Lévi-Strauss describes of perceiving the totality before perceiving the parts, that is, perceiving the discourse or pattern before perceiving the sequence of events, makes the short story, as Georg Lukács has said, the "most purely artistic form" (51).

Mystery and Pattern

Two basic characteristics of the short story as a universal mode have been recognized by authors and critics throughout the nineteenth and twentieth centuries, both of which are results of the shortness of the form and the tradition from which it derives. They are the story's focus on a basic sense of mystery unsupported by a social framework and its consequent dependence on formal pattern and structure.

Critics of the nineteenth-century German *Novelle*, the precursor of the so-called tale proper for which Poe laid out characteristics in the famous *Twice-Told Tales* review, note that every discussion of that form has some cognate word that suggests strangeness, the unusual, the unexpected, concluding that the "element of the strange, the unheard of" is one of nineteenth-century short fiction's "essential ingredients." This typical short story focus continues in the twentieth century. Flannery O'Connor has said that short stories make "alive some experience which we are not accustomed to observe everyday, or which the ordinary man may never experience in his ordinary life. . . . Their fictional qualities lean away from typical social patterns, toward mystery and the unexpected." The unique problem of the short story writer, says O'Connor, is "how to make the action he describes reveal as much of the mystery of existence as possible" (40, 98).

Terry Eagleton has recently noted that whereas realism, the most common modal perspective of the novel, is primarily a "cognitive form concerned to map the causal processes underlying events, the short story, by contrast, can yield us some single bizarre occurrence of epiphany of terror whose impact would merely be blunted by lengthy realist elaboration." As Eagleton notes, "since realism is a chronically naturalizing mode, it is hard for it to cope with the ineffable or unfathomable, given those built-in mechanisms which offer to transmute all of this into the assuringly familiar" (150).

The short story's focus on mystery and the unfamiliar is partially attributable to the fact that, as Boris Éjxenbaum has pointed out, it is a fundamental, elementary form (81). As a result, the short story has remained closer than the novel to what Northrop Frye has called the primal origin and model of all narrative, the "secular scripture" of the romance. The "strange, unheard-of" experiences of "the ineffable or unfathomable" on which the short story most often seems to focus can best be understood as those moments of crisis and awareness identified by twentieth-century existentialist thought. The ability of the short tale to reflect human reality in moments that cannot be so easily naturalized underlies the distinction between "story" and what Isak Dinesen calls a "novel" art of narration that, for the sake of realism and individual characters, sacrifices story. Whereas the novel, Dinesen says, is a human product, "the divine art is the story. In the beginning was the story." And within our whole universe, she continues, "the story only has authority to answer that cry of heart of its characters, that one cry of heart of each of them: 'Who am I?'" (26). And as Heidegger says, trying to answer the question "Who am I?" by focusing merely on description of everyday existence is bound to be unauthentic (113–16).

The short story's focus on the mysteries of dreams, fears, and anxieties based on experiences or perceptions outside the realm of familiar, everyday life has always been closely related to the formal demands of the genre. What often has been termed the "artificial" patterning of the short story heightens intensity, thus creating the cryptic, elliptical nature of the genre. Let me comment briefly on the title story of Alice Munro's collection *The Love of a Good Woman* as an example of the difference between novelistic elaboration and short story mystery and intensity. The story begins with three boys finding the body of the town's optometrist in his car submerged in the river. Although one might expect the plot immediately to focus on the mystery of the drowned man, Munro is in absolutely no hurry to satisfy the reader's curiosity. She follows the three boys into their individual homes and leisurely explores their ordinary secrets. At the beginning of the next section of the story, Munro leaves the body and the boys altogether and focuses on a cranky dying woman, Mrs. Quinn, cared for by a lonely home nurse named Enid. Mrs. Quinn tells Enid that Rupert, her husband, killed the optometrist when he saw him trying to fondle her. When Mrs. Quinn dies, Enid, who cares for Rupert, decides she must tell him what she has heard and urge him to give himself up. The way she decides to do this, however, creates the open-ended ambiguity of the story: she asks him to row her out on the river, where she will tell him what she knows, also informing him that she cannot swim. At the last minute, she changes her mind but cannot escape the situation. The story ends just before they leave the shore, so the reader does not know whether Enid confronts Rupert and, if she does, whether he pushes her in the river or rows them both back to the shore.

"The Love of a Good Woman" begins like a novel, but instead of continuing to broaden out, as it introduces new characters and seemingly new stories, it tightens up, slowly connecting what at first seemed disparate and unrelated. It is a classic example of Munro's most characteristic technique of creating a world that has all the illusion of external reality, while all the time pulling the reader deeper and deeper into what becomes a hallucinatory inner world of mystery, secrecy, and deception. Unlike the novel, which would be bound to develop some sort of satisfying closure, Munro's story reaches a moral impasse, an ambiguous, open end in which the reader suddenly realizes that instead of living in the world of apparent reality, he or she has been whirled, as if by a centrifugal force, to an almost unbearable central point of intensity.

One of the most significant implications of the compactness demanded of the short story is its need to transform mere objects and events into significance. Whereas the particular can remain merely the particular in the novel, in the short story, Elizabeth Bowen suggests, "the particular must be given general significance" (259). The novel gains assent to the reality of the work by the creation of enough detail to give the reader the illusion that he or she "knows" the experience, although, of course, he or she cannot know it in the same way that he or she knows actual experience. In the short story, however, detail is transformed into metaphoric significance. For example, the hard details in Daniel Defoe's *Robinson Crusoe* exist as a resistance to be overcome in Crusoe's encounter with the external world. However, in a short story, such as Hemingway's "Big, Two-Hearted River," which is also filled with details, the physical realities exist only to embody Nick's psychic problem. As opposed to Crusoe, Nick is not concerned with surviving an external conflict but rather an internal one. In the short story the hard material outlines of the external world are inevitably transformed into the objectifications of psychic distress. Thus, at the end of Hemingway's story, Nick's refusal to go into the swamp is purely a metaphoric refusal, having nothing to do with the "real" qualities of the swamp.

The Problem of Character

In his famous essay "Freud and the Future," Thomas Mann reminds us that life is a "mingling of the individual elements and the formal stock-in-trade; a mingling in which the individual, as it were, only lifts his head above the formal and impersonal elements." Much of the "extra-personal," Mann insists, "much unconscious identification, much that is conventional and schematic, is none the less decisive for the experience not only of the artist but of the human being in general." Mann says the author thus gains a knowledge of the "schema in which and according to which the supposed individual lives, unaware, in his naive belief in himself as unique in space and time, of the extent to which his life is but formula and repetition" (421–22).

Our interest in fictional characters, Mann implies, is, regardless of the events in which they are enmeshed, always centrally located in the process by which they try to find their identity, the means by which they attempt to answer the age-old Oedipal question: Who am I? In such a process the two forces of the subjective and the schematic are decisive. As Robert Langbaum has described it, when you realize that introspection leads to nothing but endless reflection, you see that the only way to find out who you are is to don a mask and step into a story. "The point is," says Langbaum, "at that level of experience where events fall into a pattern . . . they are an objectification of your deepest will, since they make you do things other than you consciously intend; so that in responding like a marionette to the necessities of the story, you actually find out what you really want and who you really are." Echoing Mann, Langbaum says, "psychological interest passes over into the mythical at that psychological depth where we desire to repeat mythical patterns. Life at its intensest is repetition" (177).

However, neither Mann nor Langbaum tells us in what manner a character in fiction pursues his desire to repeat mythical patterns, nor how a psychologically real person can be transformed into a psychological archetype by such a desire. We must assume that as the psychological character, thinking, speaking, acting much like a person in real life, attempts to answer the question—Who am I?—he or she seems to create his or her own individual story. But because story is always schematic and conventionalized, the character is transformed into an automaton-like figure governed by his or her place in the story itself. Thus, the character seems to be the determiner of the schema, which in turn determines the character. The problem for the critic is isolating the specific mechanisms by which the psychological passes into the mythical, that is, the means by which the individual story is transformed into the schematic. This involves finding a way to trace the conventional nature of the story to its source in the desires of the psychological character and then showing how this conventional schema transforms the character into an archetype of desire.

When we analyze a character in a story as if he or she were a real person, we approach the character in terms of the context of the similitude of a real world the story presents; when we interpret a character as an archetype, we must discover the latent structure of the plot, that is, the schema or code that makes the character an archetype by virtue of the position he or she holds in the fable itself. The former is a response to what is individual, subjective, and metonymic; the latter is a response to the traditional, the schematic, and the metaphoric.

To see how metonymic and metaphoric devices interact in a mixed, that is, both realistic and romantic, fiction, it is perhaps best to begin with the extreme form of the metaphoric or romance pole, the allegory. In an allegory, the only way to approach the characters is by reference to their position in a preexistent code. An analysis of the metonymic context leads nowhere. Angus Fletcher suggests the code-bound nature of the allegorical figure when he says that if we were to meet an allegorical character in real life, we would think the person driven by some central obsession (68). The obsessive-like behavior of the character is, of course, a result of his or her actions being totally determined by the position he or she holds in the preexistent code. The difference between an allegorical character and a character in a romance is that the romance figure not only acts as if obsessed because of his or her position in the story but also seems obsessed in reference to the similitude of real life created in the work itself.

This combination seems most effectively achieved when a psychologically real character's obsession is so extreme that he or she projects the obsession on someone or something outside the self and then, ignoring that the source of the obsession is within, acts as if it were without. Thus, although the obsessive action takes place within a similitude of a realistic world, once the character has projected an inner state outward and then has reacted to the projection as if it were outside, this very reaction transforms the character into a parabolic rather than a realistic figure.

The most obvious early examples are those stories by Poe that focus on "the perverse," that obsessive-like behavior that compels someone to act in a way that may go against reason, common sense, even the best interests of the survival of the physical self. In many of Poe's most important stories, the obsession occurs as behavior that can be manifested only in elliptical or symbolic ways. For example, in "The Tell-Tale Heart" the narrator's desire to kill the old man because of his eye can be understood only when we realize that "eye" must be heard, not seen, as the first-person pronoun "I."

Two of Hawthorne's best-known stories—"Wakefield" and "Young Goodman Brown"—also manifest this same mysterious sense of obsessive acts that have no obvious, commonsense motivation. Goodman Brown alternately acts as if he were an allegorical figure who must make his journey into the forest as an inevitable working out of the preordained mythic story of which he is a part, and as a psychologically complex, realistic character who, although obsessed with his journey, is able to question its wisdom and morality. In "Wakefield" Hawthorne is not interested in a man who is realistically motivated to leave his wife because he no longer cares for her, but rather a character who gets so entangled in an obsessive act that he can neither explain it nor escape it.

Melville's Bartleby cannot explain why he is compelled to behave as he does either. He responds to the wall outside his window as if it were not merely a metaphor for the absurdity that confronts him, but rather the absurdity itself and, thus, like Kurtz in Conrad's *Heart of Darkness*, he responds to the map as if it were the territory, kicks himself loose from the earth, and becomes transformed into a character who no longer can be defined within social, historical, or cultural contexts. As a result, the reader is caught in an ambivalent situation of not knowing whether to respond to Bartleby as if he is a character who is psychologically obsessed or an allegorical emblem of obsession. It is typical of the short story that when an obsessed character makes the metaphoric mistake of perceiving a metaphor as real, he or she becomes transformed into a parabolic figure in a fable of his or her own creation.

Metaphoric Resolution

A primary characteristic of the modern post-Chekhovian short story is that stories that depend on the metaphoric meaning of events and objects can only achieve closure aesthetically rather than phenomenologically. James Joyce's stories often end with tacit epiphanies, for example, in which a spinster understands but cannot explain the significance of clay or in which a young boy understands but cannot explain the significance of Araby. His most respected short fiction, "The Dead," is like a textbook case of a story that transforms hard matter into metaphor and that is resolved only aesthetically. Throughout the story the "stuff" described stubbornly remains mere metonymic details; even the snow that is introduced casually into the story on the shoes of the party-goers' feet is merely the cold white stuff that covers the ground—that is, until the end of the story when Gabriel's recognition transforms it into a metaphor that closes the work by mystically covering over everything.

Bernard Malamud is one of the best-known modern writers within this tradition of stories that end with aesthetic rather than dramatic resolutions. Critics have pointed out that although Malamud's manner is that of the teller of tales, his technique or structure is poetic and symbolic. He seems, says Earl Rovit, to "construct his stories backwards—beginning with his final climactic image and then manipulating his characters into the appropriate dramatic poses which will contribute to the total significance of that image." The dramatic action of the story leads the characters into a situation of conflict that is "resolved" by being "fixed poetically in the final ambiguity of conflicting forces frozen and united in their very opposition." Rovit furthermore remarks that "the aesthetic form of Malamud's story rounds upon itself and the 'meaning' of the story—the precise evaluation of forces—is left to the reader." In this way irreconcilable forces are resolved aesthetically (7).

Jonathan Culler has observed that narratives themselves often question the priority of story to discourse. "Positing the priority of events to the discourse which reports or presents them, narratology establishes a hierarchy which the functioning of narratives often subverts by presenting events not as givens but as the products of discursive forces or requirements" (29). The short story, more often than the novel, foregrounds the demands that discourse makes on preexisting story. A narrative, by its very nature, cannot be told until the events that it takes as its subject matter have already occurred. Consequently, the "end" of the events, both in terms of their actual termination and in terms of the purpose to which the narrator binds them, is the beginning of the discourse. It is therefore hardly necessary to say that the only narrative that the reader ever gets is that which is already discourse, already ended as an event so that there is nothing left for it but to move toward its end in its aesthetic, eventless way—via tone, metaphor, and all the other purely artificial conventions of fictional discourse. Thus, it is inevitable that events in the narrative will be motivated or determined by demands of the discourse that may have little to do with the psychological motivation or phenomenological cause of the actual events.

The short story's most basic assumption is that everyday experience reveals the self as a mask of habits, expectations, duties, and conventions. But the short story insists that the self must be challenged by crisis and confrontation. This is the basic tension in the form; in primitive story the conflict can be seen as the confrontation between the profane, which is the everyday, and the sacred, which are those strange eruptions that primitive humans took to be the genuinely real. The short story, however, can never reconcile this tension either existentially or morally, for the tension between the necessity of the everyday metonymic world and the sacred metaphoric world is one of those basic tensions that can only be held in suspension. The only resolution possible is an aesthetic one.

The Refusal to Explain

Walter Benjamin has noted in his essay on the storyteller that the rise of the novel is one of the primary symptoms of the decline of storytelling, for the novel neither comes from the oral tradition nor goes into it. Benjamin says that "information" has come to predominate in the modern world. Whereas the "truth" of information derives from an abstracting effort to arrive at a distilled discursive meaning, the truth of story is communicated by a patterned recounting of a concrete experience in such a way that the truth is embodied rather than explained. The story has a compactness that defies psychological analysis, argues Benjamin.

According to Benjamin, whereas realistic narrative forms such as the novel focus on the relatively limited areas of human experience that indeed can be encompassed by information, characters in story encounter those most basic mysteries of human experience that cannot be explained by rational means. Stories do not demand plausibility or conformity to the laws of external reality, argues Benjamin. What story does is to show us how to deal with all that we cannot understand; it is half the art of storytelling to be free from information. Because the reader of story is permitted to interpret things, story has an amplitude lacking in information (83–109).

Storytellers have often expressed their impatience with explanation and their frustration with listeners who cannot understand the story they are trying to tell. Poe's narrator cannot seem to explain the mystery of Roderick Usher; Melville's lawyer struggles to account for the enigma of Bartleby; Sherwood Anderson laments that it would take a poet to tell the story of Wing Biddlebaum's hands; Chekhov's Ivan feels that he has failed to communicate the secret lives of those who suffer behind the scenes in "Gooseberries." And, in perhaps the most famous example of this frustration of the storyteller in modern Western literature, Conrad's Marlow sits cross-legged on the ship deck and laments, "Do you see the story? . . . Do you see anything? It seems to me I am trying to tell you a dream."

Raymond Carver knew well the short story's tradition of centering on that which can be narrated but not explained; in "On Writing" he accepted Chekhov's demanding dictum: "In short stories it is better to say not enough than to say too much, because,—because—I don't know why." (198). The more recent writer from whom he learned about the short story's shunning of explanation was Flannery O'Connor, who argued that since the short story writer has only a small space in which to work and cannot make use of mere statement, "he has to make the concrete work double time" (98).

"Errand," one of Carver's final stories, is seemingly a straightforward, realistically detailed presentation of the last hours of Chekhov's life. However, what makes it more than a realistic report is the young servant who is asked to bring in the champagne that Chekhov drinks just before his death and Olga Knipper's urgent instructions to the young man at the end of the story. Although the young man sees the body of Chekhov in the next room on the bed, he also sees the cork from the bottle on the floor near the toe of his shoe. The moment is a delicate one, for as the young man awkwardly stands there listening to Chekhov's distracted wife asking him to go get a mortician, the two seem to exist in different worlds.

What Carver brilliantly captures in the story is Olga's storytelling effort to send the boy on his errand. In a manner that is typical in Carver's stories, she repeatedly asks him, "Do you understand what I'm saying to you?" As he grapples to understand, she tells him a story describing his own actions in performing the errand. Because Olga's narrative of what the boy is to do is described as if it were actually taking place, the verb tense of the story shifts from future to present: "The mortician would be in his forties. . . . He would be modest, unassuming. . . . Probably he would be wearing an apron. He might even be wiping his hands on a dark towel." At this juncture, the point of view shifts to present tense: "The mortician takes the vase of roses. . . . The one time the young man mentions the name of the deceased, the mortician's eyebrows rise just a little. Chekhov, you say? Just a minute, and I'll be with you." However, as Olga urges the waiter to perform his important errand, the young man is thinking about the cork at the toe of his shoe. And just before he leaves, he leans over without looking down and closes his hand around it—an embodiment of those seemingly innocuous but powerfully significant details that constitute the true genius of Chekhov's art. It is the most poignant example in Carver's fiction of his understanding of his Chekhovian realization: "It is possible, in a poem or a short story, to write about commonplace things and objects using commonplace but precise language, and to endow those things—a chair, a window curtain, a fork, a stone, a woman's earring—with immense, even startling power."[3]

Conclusion

The very shortness of the short story, as well as the necessary artistic devices demanded by this shortness, force it to focus not on the whole of experience (whatever that is) in all its perceptual and conceptual categorization, but rather on a single experience lifted out of the everyday flow of human actuality and active striving, an experience that is lifted out precisely because it is not a slice of that reality, but rather a moment in which "reality" itself is challenged. The novel, by its very length, regardless of how many crisis moments it may present, still must in some way resolve them, cover them over, conceal them by the very bulk of its similitude to the ordinary flow of everyday experience. The short story, standing alone, with no life before it or after it, can receive no such comforting merging of the extraordinary with the ordinary. For example, we might hypothesize that after Miss Brill has been so emphatically made aware of her role in the park each Sunday, she will still go on with her life, but Katherine Mansfield's story titled "Miss Brill" gives us no such comforting afterthought based on our confidence that "life goes on," for it ends with the revelation.

The question of the short story's form being true to reality or false to it, of being a natural form or a highly conventional one, requires a reevaluation of what we mean when we say "reality" or "natural." If we assume that reality is what we experience every day, if we assume that reality is our well-controlled and comfortable self, then the short story is neither "realistic" nor natural. If, however, we feel that beneath the everyday or immanent in the everyday there is some other reality that somehow evades us, if our view is a religious one in its most basic sense, that is, if we feel that something is lacking, if we have a sense of the liminal nature of existence, then the short story is more "realistic" than the novel can possibly be. It is closer to the nature of "reality" as we experience it in those moments when we are made aware of the inauthenticity of everyday life, those moments when we sense the inadequacy of our categories of perception. It is for these reasons, I think, that short stories are essential and yet seldom read.

Notes

1. Quoted by Halpern, *Art of the Tale*, v.
2. Quoted in May, *Edgar Allan Poe*, 121.
3. "On Writing," 275.

Works Cited

Bakhtin, M. M., and P. N. Medvedev. *The Formal Method in Literary Scholarship*. Translated by Albert J. Wehrle. Baltimore: Johns Hopkins University Press, 1978.

Benjamin, Walter. "The Storyteller: Reflections on the Works of Nikolai Leskov." In *Illuminations*, translated by Harry Zohn, 83–109. London: Jonathan Cape, 1970.

Bowen, Elizabeth. "The Faber Book of Modern Short Stories." In *The New Short Story Theories*, edited by Charles E. May, 256–62. Athens: Ohio University Press, 1994.

Brooks, Peter. *Reading for the Plot.* New York: Knopf, 1984.

Carver, Raymond. "Errand." In *Where I'm Calling From,* 381–91. New York: Atlantic Monthly Press, 1988.

———. "On Writing." In *The New Short Story Theories,* edited by Charles E. May, 273–77. Athens: Ohio University Press, 1994.

Chekhov, Anton. "The Short Story." In *The New Short Story Theories,* edited by Charles E. May, 195–98. Athens: Ohio University Press, 1994.

Culler, Jonathan. *The Pursuit of Signs.* Ithaca, N.Y.: Cornell University Press, 1981.

Dinesen, Isak. "The Cardinal's First Tale." In *Last Tales,* 3–27. New York: Random House, 1957.

Eagleton, Terry. *Heathcliff and the Great Hunger: Studies in Irish Culture.* London: Verso, 1995.

Éjxenbaum, B. M. "O. Henry and the Theory of the Short Story." In *The New Short Story Theories,* edited by Charles E. May, 81–88. Athens: Ohio University Press, 1994.

Fletcher, Angus. *Allegory.* Ithaca, N.Y.: Cornell University Press, 1964.

Frye, Northrop. *The Secular Scripture: A Study of the Structure of Romance.* Cambridge, Mass.: Harvard University Press, 1976.

Halpern, Daniel, ed. *The Art of the Tale.* New York: Penguin, 1986.

Heidegger, Martin. *Sein und Zeit.* Tübingen: Max Niemeyer Verlag, 1957.

Jameson, Frederic. *The Political Unconscious: Narrative as a Socially Symbolic Act.* Ithaca, N.Y.: Cornell University Press, 1981.

Langbaum, Robert. *The Modern Spirit.* Oxford: Oxford University Press, 1970.

Lévi-Strauss, Claude. "The Science of the Concrete." In *European Literary Theory and Practice,* edited by Vernon W. Gras, 133–63. New York: Dell, 1973.

Lewis, C. S. "On Stories." In *Essays Presented to Charles Williams,* edited by C. S. Lewis, 90–105. Grand Rapids, Mich.: William B. Eerdmans, 1966.

Lukács, Georg. *The Theory of the Novel.* Translated by Anna Bostock. Cambridge, Mass.: MIT Press, 1971.

Mann, Thomas. "Freud and the Future." In *Essays of Three Decades,* translated by H. T. Lowe-Porter, 411–28. New York: Knopf, 1947.

May, Charles E. *Edgar Allan Poe: A Study of the Short Fiction.* Boston: Twayne, 1991.

Munro, Alice. *The Love of a Good Woman.* New York: Knopf, 1998.

O'Connor, Flannery. *Mystery and Manners.* Edited by Sally and Robert Fitzgerald. New York: Farrar, Straus and Giroux, 1969.

Rovit, Earl "The Jewish Literary Tradition." In *Bernard Malamud and the Critics,* edited by Leslie A. Field and Joyce C. Field, 3–10. New York: New York University Press, 1970.

Writing Short Stories

My Double Story, with Reflections on Occasion, Tonality, and Direction

Andrew K. Kennedy

Two persons are trying out an inner dialogue in this discussion: the first, the writer of stories working intuitively, groping toward narrative targets from a mind more or less successfully purified of the buzz of abstractions, against the second, the literary critic and teacher, tolerably well informed about some questions of narrative theory but certainly not a contributor to this "field." It must be said (who is saying this?) that these two persons do not always communicate well with each other, frequently ignoring each other's competence altogether.

If this sounds like a precariously schizoid condition, I am now taking the opportunity to seek therapy, through bringing the two polarities—of writing and theorizing—a little closer, paying conscious attention to half-conscious or at best implicit theorizing under the act of writing and doing a certain amount of post hoc "narratology." I would situate this position somewhere between two extremes: between the complete interplay of writing and criticism (as in the supreme modernist synthesis of Eliot) and the complete separation of writing and criticism. (Witness David Storey, novelist and dramatist, who once told me in conversation: "These two activities have nothing to do with each other, nothing!"[1])

Between these polarities is a middle ground where the writer is constantly being challenged by critical thinking: about the short story as a distinct and specific genre with intrinsic and peculiar pressures in shaping the language of this or that precise story to be told, here and now, unique in the sense of never before like *this*, in two centuries of a "great tradition." In the moment of writing, the choices to be made—in narrative and language—begin to be felt as finite. Then the infinite-seeming potentialities conjured up by the imagination are discarded, the invention-hungry mind is pruned, drafts and notes are canceled. For every single choice in writing (as in decision making in life) will exclude other ways of doing it, and these choices are made by the critical faculty. I have never believed in anything approaching automatic writing or dictation from the spirit world, nor do I find that stimulants, wine or even espresso, are good for writing. There is no substitute for clarity, and that necessarily involves reflecting on what one is constructing.[2] Writing for me is reflexive in the sense that it constantly points back to the act of writing, whether or not that kind of form consciousness can be traced in the final form of the work.

Perhaps I can track down certain stages in the act of writing, as experienced. I nearly always start thinking toward a short story (often marked "perhaps" after a title in a notebook) from a situation fairly clear in outline if not in detail. I will call this the stage of finding an *occasion* for writing (in Whitehead's sense of occasion[3]). The chosen occasion provides not only a starting point but also a kernel that remains fairly steady throughout all the many variations of narrative and style in the writing, rewriting or re-rewriting. Such an occasion may suddenly present itself out of the past, especially in the more personal stories—personal, *not* directly autobiographical. Thus, a walk may release the troubled core experience of another walk at the end of the Second World War, and that memory is then expanded and transformed into fiction. One of my stories, "Learning, Learning,"[4] was prompted by the old domed Reading Room of the British Library in remembrance of clearing out the rubble of war in my school library in central Europe. Around that core experience everything else in the story is invention: the narrative sequences, the characters (a teacher of German and a Christian teacher of religious knowledge), their attitudes and tones and their dialogue with the boy, including a load of ambivalence toward German culture and Jewishness. In other words, the narrator's personality is also invented or constructed according to the requirements of the story. The advantage of starting from an *occasion* is, then, a simultaneous emotional and structural center that is given—a gift. With luck, all the other elements of the story will begin to radiate from that center, or else, to change the metaphor, the pieces of the jigsaw puzzle can be placed around that one big piece.

The choice of the narrator is fundamental: who is going to tell this story, in what person, what tone, from what *point of view?* That is good, familiar, even hackneyed critical terrain, yet in every new act of writing, the choice is new and crucial. For example, in the three personal stories just referred to (placed first in *Double Vision*), a third-person narrator tells the story of a boy—aged about twelve to fourteen, the chance survivor of Nazi slave labor—from a detached point of view. A first-person narrative would turn the stories into a confessional, or a fragment of a memoir, and would have to re-create the very young voice. (Remember, Dickens, in *Great Expectations*, could not quite achieve that, perhaps did not want to.) But given the subject —the terror of war and Nazi deportation—total detachment or anonymity would be impossible and probably undesirable, in writerly terms.[5] On reflection, I chose a detached descriptive opening: "He found himself outside the bleak transit station, an incomplete block of flats hastily converted to receive the survivors" ("Wine," in *DV*, 9). This is followed by a series of episodes—suggesting confusion, and a sense of unreality —ending ironically with the sick and almost sleepwalking boy drinking red wine from his hands in the midst of a victory celebration by Russian soldiers. The fairly detached narrative voice is sustained throughout the story but is interrupted by memory flashbacks like "Women searching excrement for something to eat" (13). The horrors of war are recorded in a bare, plain prose, in keeping with the narrator's style, but the shift to the past is also a shift into the boy's mind. The writer/critic then asks, Is this shift of focus justified? How can the narrator, a limited (not omniscient) observer, suddenly enter the inner thoughts of a character? Well, it is supposed to be connected, by the reader, with earlier entries into the boy's consciousness: "To celebrate what? Another sham release? Fatuous self-appointed prophets would intone, 'The war is over, we are free!' He had heard it all before and wished that *they* were dead with the rest. His parents . . . " (10).

So a measured dose of stream of consciousness flows into the "external" narrative, and the flashback (printed in italics) falls into the stream. (I know Joyce did something like this in "The Dead," but if that is an influence it was indirect or unconscious). The first-person narrator in "Learning, Learning"—the story in two libraries, one in ruin, the other splendidly domed—is a pseudoscholar meditating on the uselessness of books both at the beginning and the end, providing an ironic frame story, says the critic.

By contrast, the narrator of a novella-length story in "Letter on Fidelity" is far from detached. He is writing a long monomaniac letter to his wife (though trying to engage her in a dialogue) in aesthetically impassioned but ethically ambivalent rhetoric, confusing art history with the pursuit of love, reality with illusion. He starts like this: "Dearest—Now that our married love has reached this state—we can be single in union, free in dependence, held together as a balance of opposites in one design" (*DV*, 73). In one episode, sitting in a runaway taxi with the temptress, the female art student accompanied by a boyfriend, the narrator reflects on why he is unable to respond to the girl's remark about teenage experience: "For to say 'I've never been a teenager' might have sounded insipid; and to have added 'of your sort' might have been interpreted as a snub. It might have opened a social gulf between the two of us, just as we seemed, if only for one moment, to be drawn into aesthetic closeness, once more" (100). In other words, the narrator is a persona and his tone includes chunks of parody and pastiche, says the critic. Nevertheless, a first reader—my then seventeen-year-old daughter—thought that the narrator was writing autobiography, supporting this opinion with, "All academics talk like that!" Later, a reviewer of that story in the *Times* was reminded of Nabokov—a compliment of sorts, except that I have read *Lolita* only in haste when it first came out, unaware then and to this day of any influence.

I next tried something new to me, and I am not sure whether it has been done by anybody else: a *critical* narrator, who is ambivalently reluctant to engage with the problems of his characters. For example, one narrator attempts to distance himself from his own potential involvement in the life and the confessions of a young woman and her boyfriend (in "Reading the 'Princess and the Peas'"), and another narrator tries to dedramatize the confused erotic fantasy of a melancholy thinker (in "Cliffs of Fall"). This variation on the first-person narrative was given a further twist in a long story ("The Speechmaker") that turns on a full-circle shift of sympathy on the part of the narrator: from antipathy toward a fellow convalescent who cannot stop talking (an acute case of logorrhea) to deepening empathy when that patient's vocal cords are damaged by disease to the point of perpetual silence. It took years to develop that particular shifting narrator, with many drafts and versions, and it was not at the time accepted by my editor, who called it "brain music." (She preferred and published other stories, with less complex narratives.) I mention this only to remind you, and myself, that there is a risk in experimenting with a first-person narrator—whether he or she assumes a neutral, an impassioned, a critical, or a sympathetic persona.

Under the heading of "point of view," I have really started to talk about choosing a particular language and tonality for the narrator. What I call *tonality* involves controlling the voices—of narrator and characters—in something like a verbal score. The precise choice of words—yes, the old Flaubertian *mot juste*, no substitute for that—should create a precise notation for each voice, that is, contrasted voices in polyphony, as in a chamber opera. (In stylistics this may be called finding the right style register or the speaker's ideolect.) Clearly, a short story can accommodate a limited number of tones, but I want to avoid monotone. Variety and counterpoint are to me important: a character should, ideally, be quite distinct in vocabulary, syntax, and rhythm; and a narrator should vary his textures and tempi and sometimes his modes of address as well. For example, the narrator of "Letter on Fidelity" puts together a whole gamut of texts—lecture notes, a letter addressed to a vanished lover included within the letter to his wife, a medical diagnosis of toxemia of pregnancy, extracts from a journal, and quotations, sometimes in Italian, as the narrator is steeped in the history of art. Elsewhere, I have also used preexistent texts—for example, an extract from the fairy tale "The Princess and the Pea," a travel guide book, rules for Trappist monks, and, again, parody and pastiche.

Nevertheless, the various styles are supposed to be held together by the score, not by absolute "unity," the famous criterion of Poe and his followers, but by what I would call a sense of *direction*. With luck, the direction is also given by the germinal occasion, and then the end is foreseen from the beginning—end as closure and as purpose. An end image will probably arise quite early in the writing (as in my earlier example, the war-shaken boy drinking wine from his hands in the street), but the shaping and the wording of such an end scene have to be worked on and reworked with a mixture of improvisation and experiment. Ideally, the ending should be sufficiently sharp and resonant to call for a rereading or at least a rethinking of the whole story. It is quite possible for a sharply etched ending to coexist with an open ending:

the words are precise but the action remains indeterminate. Or else the ending is ironic, like putting a question mark after the whole text.

An equally strong marking and resonance is needed for the opening sentence(s)— but this is too large a subject for now. Did Chekhov really suggest that the beginning and the ending of a story should be cut?[6] It is not a method I could follow. For my part, I would rather discard the middle. Seriously, I think of the opening and the ending of a story as carrying an extra load of information and implicit meaning, in letters carved as it were in stone, an epigraph and an epitaph.

I do not think of myself as some kind of unreconstructed realist. But rumors of the death of realism have been exaggerated, as Mark Twain thought of rumors of his death. However, a true realist would hardly recognize the element of realism in my stories—I know this from actual reader responses. I do not write toward a plot but, as suggested, from an occasion and along a direction that is not arrowlike but zigzagging. I seldom give exact time and place for the setting of a story, but just provide reasonably clear hints, for geography and history do matter to me, inescapably. The personal stories come from the shadows of the Holocaust and must have a degree of documentable authenticity; but sheer invention still needs to be related to a core of experience, to something "felt upon our pulses," in Keats's phrase. Sometimes there is pseudoaccuracy, as in "Letter on Fidelity," which carries an exact date and a London address. My aim is to give the reader certain points of reference across a distant view, without fixity or excess topography.[7]

There is, then, a fusion of moods and modes in most of my stories, probably inevitable for someone arriving in the violently turbulent late modern scene with atavistic memories of the Enlightenment. Of course, I am aware that this kind of doubleness runs the risk of not pleasing either the traditionalist or the avant-gardist. The former objects to episodes deliberately blurred, even when a character is wrestling with a hallucinatory experience or suffering a virtual nervous collapse. As for experimental writing, the fashion now is for hotter stuff, immersed in the messiness of contemporary living, or else a radically nihilistic parody, since, as a young writer informed me in private conversation, all writing is pastiche and the pursuit of an authentic core is naive.

On a lighter note, I can still hear the voice of Isabel Allende telling us—with an energetic and erotic gesture—that storytelling is like making love. I did not know that. But if I had known it, before I started on my present reflections, I would not have known how to begin.[8]

Notes

1. Talking to David Storey while he was rehearsing his play *Cromwell* at the Royal Court Theatre, London, in 1973.

2. Jorge Luis Borges, among the most challenging twentieth-century short fiction writers, stressed that "the art of writing was mysterious," not an "act of intelligence." Foreword to *Dr. Brodie's Report* (1970), 12; quoted in Shaw, *Short Story*, 255.

3. I tend to associate "occasion" with Whitehead (first read when I was a student of philosophy). In a complex, sometimes overabstract definition, "an occasion of experiencing" is said to arise not out of a passive situation but, on the contrary, from an "initial situation [that] includes a factor of activity" Whitehead calls "Creativity." "The initial situation with its creativity can be termed the initial phase of the new occasion," he writes (208–9).

4. Reprinted from *Stand* magazine in *Double Vision* (after initial reference abbreviated as *DV*).

5. Hemingway presented war experiences in an "anonymous," cool prose style and flat tone. It is interesting to recall that a writer as different as Woolf also praised anonymity: "The beauty is in the statement, not in the suggestion. . . . The world is seen without comment" (Brenda R. Silver, ed., "'Anon' and 'The Reader': Virginia Woolf's Last Essays," *Twentieth Century Literature* 25 [1979]: 384; also quoted in Shaw, *Short Story*, 237.)

6. I cannot trace the letter in which Chekhov is said to have made this remark. Contrast with this quotation: "The beginning of my stories is always promising and looks as though I were starting on a novel, the middle is huddled and timid, and the end is, as in a short sketch, like fireworks" (Chekhov, *Letters on the Short Story*, 11; quoted in Shaw, *Short Story*, 122.).

7. From "the intentional fallacy" on, any remark made by an author about, yes, some kind of intention has been critically suspect. However, I have given myself permission to report that in writing I do have aims that are comparable to preparing some nonverbal activity, on some level.

8. Additional note: Since writing this essay I have received the following statement in a letter (dated May 15, 2001) from my former editor at *Stand* magazine, Lorna Tracy, herself a short story writer, at one time highly praised by Angela Carter: "I've always dealt with theory by the simple expedient of having no truck with it. Like the subject of economics, I cope with it by abolishing it."

Works Cited

Kennedy, Andrew K. *Double Vision*. Cambridge, U.K.: Meadows Press, 1999.
Shaw, Valerie. *The Short Story: A Critical Introduction*. London: Longman, 1983.
Whitehead, A. N. *Adventures of Ideas*. Harmondsworth, U.K.: Penguin, 1948.

Real-World Characters in Fictional Story Worlds

Robert Olen Butler's "JFK Secretly Attends Jackie Auction"

Susan Lohafer

Imagine a tale that begins: "Facing his inquisitors, Peter Smith knew they had already judged him guilty of blasphemy." Who is Smith? Who cares? We are interested in the predicament. Has innocence been wronged? We read to find out. If it is a narrative we can read in one sitting, if it shows us a fabricated world with a character at risk, if it gives us an outcome that is humanly significant, we can be reasonably sure we are reading a short story.

Here is another beginning: "Facing his inquisitors, Galileo knew they had already judged him guilty of blasphemy." Now the words are concrete. We can name the inquisitors.[1] We know what was blasphemous: the earth's revolution. We read to know more. If there are claims to truth-value, if every assertion is marked as either factual or speculative, if differing viewpoints are contested or revised, we are likely to be reading a historical account.

Finally, consider a third beginning: "Facing his inquisitors, John Lennon knew they had already judged him guilty of blasphemy." The terms are metaphoric again, but more pointed than they were in the line about Smith. I have heard of the Beatles, and no doubt you have too. We have heard the stories about Lennon: about how he ran afoul of the American establishment for his pacifism during the Vietnam War; about how he was assassinated, though not directly for *his* theory of "Revolution." While some of us may be acquainted with the historical record, such as it is, the great majority of us "know" only the celebrity, the image made by newspaper stories, album covers, TV appearances, films, articles, books, and, of course, music — in other words, the verbal, visual, and aural information that has found its way into our collective memory.

With a bit of license, I might imagine a composite tabloid feature story the public has internalized. Slanted toward mass-audience appeal, such a story would encode themes like the Liverpool friendships, images like John and Yoko in bed, and a shifting assortment of factoids. The John Lennon most of us know is neither a real man nor a fiction. He is a celebrity.[2] If we were to read a short story about a British rock star named Peter Smith who had an affair with a Japanese artist, we might say, "A-*haaa!* Smith is an analogue for Lennon." However, if the character were *named* John Lennon, what then? Even if the short story sent its Beatle to the moon—in other words, even if the narrative were clearly a fantasy—the historical record and the tabloid scenario would still impinge on our reading of the text.

Would these back stories be external competitors for the reader's attention? Would they be hidden layers of the fictional story? Would they blur the line between narrative nonfiction and the short story genre? That last question is the theme of a larger project on which I have been working. I have considered the inroads of "creative nonfiction" on the territory of short fiction, and now I will be considering the effect of nonfictional characters in a fictional story world. Specifically, I will be asking whether a celebrity protagonist, trailing clouds of nonfiction, alters our response to markers of the short story.

These markers derive from, or point to, a model of the genre, so what may really be at stake is the value of such a model and, perhaps, of genre-based criticism and pedagogy. The most familiar markers are those identified by Edgar Allan Poe: the one-sitting length, the "single effect." Markers dear to formalists include a generative paradox, an epiphanic structure, and a totalizing metaphor. Other markers I have been working with over the years include strong closural signals, preclosure patterns, and other evidence of cognitive strategies for chunking experience into memorable units.

Many of my terms come from a formalist tradition, but some of my methods come from literary empiricism. Most people who use words like "cognitive" and "empirical" are psychologists or textual linguists, and I must stress right away that nothing I do is scientific or intended to be. It is, however, grounded in what I call reading experiments, from which I gather my equivalent of "data." These experiments are greatly influenced by the work of cognitive scientists like Perry Thorndyke in the 1970s and William F. Brewer in the 1990s, and yet my interests and principles are literary. I simply ask a group of readers, usually the students in my own or a colleague's classroom, to read texts and answer questions about them, and then I look for patterns in the answers, using them to help me understand the nature of storyness in general and the artistry and meaning of some story in particular.

That term "storyness" will be important in my discussion of celebrity protagonists, so let me explain what it means to me. I became interested years ago in the work of psychologists for whom storyness is a matter of narrative grammars, goal-outcome relationships, or standardized scripts.[3] Most models of storyness posit a location in the world, a goal-seeking agent, and a humanly significant outcome. Kernel event-sequences generally have a three-part structure, as theorists like Gerald Prince and Tzvetan Todorov have claimed. The British psychologist R. L. Gregory has suggested that we learn what a story is from the way neurons code information about a brand-new environment. In other words, what nurtures and what harms us is "remembered" by our body in the form of a neurological "plot." Here is one version of it: (1) "What's this?" (2) "Let's see." (3) "Ouch!" or "Ooooh!" That plot is instantiated over and over again, with infinite variations and complications. I believe it is consistent with all we have been hearing about the mystery at the heart of the short story, because we must have a script for knowability before we can feel the ache of *un*knowability. Our primal learning curve underlies the wheel of fortune and the cycle of yearning and loss, sometimes with recoveries or discoveries, that structures so many short stories, including the one I will be discussing.

Let me continue to set the stage for that discussion. Everyone agrees on the end directedness of this genre, but for me that fundamental marker becomes even more important when I consider the relationship between the sophisticated literary form and its primal origins. My reading experiments have taught me that a distinctive feature of nineteenth- and twentieth-century short stories is the embedding within them of shorter, "putative" stories that urge the text onward. With respect to the entire text as written, the endings of these embedded stories constitute preclosure points. To recognize them, we need an internalized sense of storyness—exactly what I am positing. My experiments are simply ways of tapping into that inheritance, and for my purposes it does not matter—in fact, it is necessary—that the readers I use are *not* trained critics, but a mix of the dull and the bright, the interested and the bored, the caring and the callous. When called on to exhibit their ingrained sense of storyness, they are, as a group, wiser than Solomon.

The story I chose for my test case is Robert Olen Butler's "JFK Secretly Attends Jackie Auction." The title identifies two famous people known to most Americans and to many people around the world: John Fitzgerald Kennedy, thirty-fifth president of the United States, and his wife, Jacqueline Bouvier Kennedy. This much-photographed, much-written-about couple have been ardently admired and just as vehemently criticized, but they have provided the American imagination with an ideal, however dubious, of physical beauty, social charm, and well-bred style. Competing images of a philandering husband and a jet-setting widow are part of the picture too. The enduring power of these images may be due to the national trauma of Kennedy's assassination in 1963 and, more recently, to the death of his wife in 1996.

After she died, many of her own and the former president's personal effects were displayed and then auctioned off by Sotheby's in New York City. Both tabloid and legitimate news media, as well as the Internet, ran stories about this high-profile event, highlighting such memorabilia as Jackie's three-strand pearl necklace, made famous in a photograph of her baby son playing with that same necklace on his mother's neck. Although the pearls were fake, they sold for $211,500. JFK's golf clubs, the woods only, in a monogrammed golf bag, went to Arnold Schwarzenegger for more than three times that amount ($772,500).[4]

Butler's story includes a fictional visit to this very real, highly publicized event. However, the story focuses on JFK, acknowledging the historical event of his assassination but creating an alternative and fantastic scenario that goes as follows: the bullet did not kill Kennedy but destroyed the "editor" in his brain, causing him to speak freely and truthfully about classified information. To prevent him from revealing state secrets, the Central Intelligence Agency allowed the public to believe he had died in Dallas. Instead, he was transported to a secret CIA compound in Virginia, where he has been spending his days playing golf, occasionally bedding female agents supplied for this purpose, and remembering the past. Now, by special dispensation, and because it is felt that no one will recognize him anymore, he is allowed, under CIA guard, to attend the auction of his own and his wife's belongings.

At the auction Kennedy is dismayed to see several women dressed as replicas of his wife. The pillbox hat, the bouffant hair, the boxy suit were icons of style; the image they created was a popular fetish. Kennedy's mind is flooded by memories of the women in his life, and especially of Jackie. In a vividly remembered love scene, he recalls her naked body adorned only by the pearls that are soon to be auctioned. The "things" on sale become touchstones of memory, as do the look-alike wives who churn his emotions. But when one of them finally addresses him, it is because she mistakes him for another famous person, the actor Henry Fonda. The moment is a classic turning point, jolting the character into an ironic self-awareness. The story ends with an interior monologue, a meditation on the human need to touch objects and bodies in order to reify memory and keep death at bay.

Butler has said that all short stories express "yearning";[5] this is the essential human experience, the driving force behind the highest art and the lowest journalism. His fantasy about JFK is collected in a volume called *Tabloid Dreams*, in which every tale is a reinvention of the bizarre yet poignant stories that greet us on the newsstand. In the one I have chosen, Butler is invoking the golden-boy image, the political charisma, the sexual profligacy, the glamorous marriage, and the Dallas tragedy that created a tabloid legend. How does our knowledge of that legend affect our reading of the short story?

To find out, I prepared two texts with the title and the author's name removed. One was Butler's original story with some omissions summarized in brackets to shorten the reading time. This I will call the Kennedy text. The second was a variant text in which I changed JFK to an entirely fictional character named Harry Osborne. This is the Osborne text. I made the protagonist a famous writer, a sort of Hemingway figure who had been an unofficial observer during the Vietnam War. Later, he was presumably killed in a plane crash, but—you guessed it—he did not really die. Only his mental "editor" was destroyed, letting him talk freely about what he had seen in South Asia. An embarrassment to his country, he was spirited away by the CIA and hidden for decades. A flagrant womanizer, he had been married to a movie star who wore denim and mohair.

If you are not laughing at me, you should be. My pseudostory is even less plausible, and far more awkward, than the original. However, the point was to create an obviously fictional character and story world while retaining as much as possible of the original wording. The original abridged text was 2,200 words, and I changed or added 236 words, or almost exactly 10 percent. Many of these changes were simply name substitutions, Osborne for Kennedy, Sally for Jackie. Overall, 90 percent of the original text was retained verbatim. The sentences in both texts were numbered and matched line for line. Each text was followed by the same set of questions.

My readers were the students in an entry-level course on the reading of short stories, taught by a colleague of mine at the University of Iowa.[6] On the day I visited, twenty-four students were in the room, and I asked half of them to read and respond to the Kennedy text and half to read and respond to the Osborne text. Overall, the ratio of female readers to male readers was two to one. Members of this class had had no direct contact with me before and were told nothing in advance about my theories or the experiment.

What I am describing in this essay is, of course, only a pilot study. The sample is extremely small, but as I mentioned before, these reading experiments are not scientific. They are merely heuristic devices, ways of generating responses, in a fairly systematic way, from readers whose great virtue is that they are not Susan Lohafer. I can shape the questions, even prompt, unintentionally, the answers—but I can never completely control or predict the results. Therefore, they have a degree of objectivity I cannot achieve on my own. Naturally, when I begin interpreting the results, I reenter the picture, but with checks on my theorizing.

Here is what I expected to find: (1) that responses to the Kennedy text would reveal more interference from tabloid signifiers, and (2) that responses to the Osborne text would reveal more sensitivity to markers of the short story. Such findings seem obvious, but here are some implications: first, that the kind of storyness I am positing for the short story requires the relatively self-sufficient, surrogate world of fiction and is less prominent in short narratives that announce themselves as hybrids of fact and fantasy; second, that readers respond less sensitively to the *same* short story markers when a recognizable name leads them to index, instead, the external narratives of the historical record or its tabloid expression. Along the way, I hoped to show how these experiments, regardless of their outcome, give the teacher and critic new leverage on any story.

And so I ran my reading experiment. One question had to do with types of audiences likely to enjoy the story. To my surprise, over half of both groups of readers thought daydreamers would like the story better than conspiracy theorists would, and exactly 92 percent of both groups thought romantics would like it better than would cynics. When given several options and asked to choose the best title for the story, 75 percent of both groups chose "The Pearl Necklace." This parity helped assure me that the stories were comparable.

Looking at the other suggested titles, I noticed that the remaining 25 percent of the readers had divided their choices in an interesting way. Only readers of the Kennedy text chose "Covert Operations Revealed" or "Dead Celebrity Attends Auction." These headline-style titles focus on paranoia about the CIA and fascination with celebrities—two staples of the tabloid imagination. Another title option was "Free at Last." Since the wording invokes the rhetoric of the American civil rights movement in the 1960s, and hence the era and context of the Kennedy administration, I had thought that at least some readers of the Kennedy text would choose it. None did. However, a quarter of the Osborne text readers *did* choose it. Why were they drawn to "Free at Last," when they, too, had read a story about covert operations and a dead man at an auction? Was it because they had *not* been influenced by the Kennedy name, but by the *genre's* penchant for universal themes?

I decided then to look at the way my readers had indexed the image of the pearl necklace, which had attracted so many of them as a title for the story. I had asked them to pick the four most important connotations they associated with this image. Some of the options were "sexual pleasure," "purity of heart," "wealth and position," "high-class taste," "true love," "Fifties' decade," and "essence of femininity." Readers of the Kennedy text were four times more likely than readers of the Osborne text to associate the necklace with "wealth and position." They were also twice as likely to index "high-class taste" and "Fifties' decade." The influence of the real-life Kennedys was obviously at work. As I expected, a much smaller number—only one—of the Osborne readers chose the "wealth" connotation. But 75 percent of them chose "true love"! Why? The experiment will eventually tell us.

I also asked my readers what *they* wanted to know more about. It seemed logical to expect that the Osborne readers would more often focus their curiosity on omissions or ambiguities within the story world, while the Kennedy readers would more often ask questions that could be answered only by referring to the "real" world. Theoretically, such questions are unlimited, once the boundaries of the story are overstepped. How did the CIA function in the 1960s? What were the state secrets Kennedy might have known? Was Jackie *really* an expert on ancient Greek pottery? The sphere of what can be known about any subject, or of what we might want to know, quickly expands beyond our grasp, as Alexander Gionis explains.

Writing about another hybrid short story, Donald Barthelme's "Robert Kennedy Saved from Drowning," Gionis speaks of "information entropy." Our powers of discovery and assimilation can never keep up with the exploding universe of information. Thus, as he reminds us in his title, "The more we know, the less we know." For example, the more we know about a historical figure, the less coherent and reliable is *any* representation of that figure—historical, tabloid, or fictional. Therefore, in his view, the historian and the fiction writer may use many of the same signifiers, such as the proper names of famous people, with equal authority, regardless of genre. I grant the fiction writer's authority, but I believe that genre markers affect the way we will process identical or closely related signifiers.

So I asked my readers to tell me very briefly what they wanted to know, and then I distributed their questions into the following categories: information needed for internal story sense, information about the world outside the story, and information needed to understand a specific character. Of course, only the Kennedy readers mentioned JFK or Jackie by name, but curiosity about the lead characters was about the same for both sets of readers. Contrary to my expectations, about the same number of Kennedy and Osborne readers (six and five, respectively) wanted to know more about the world outside the story. A Kennedy reader asked, "Where exactly is the auction?" revealing that she had never heard of Sotheby's. Rather plaintively, an Osborne reader said, "I wish I could know more about those covert operations." However, by five to two, readers of the Osborne text asked more questions about the logic of the story world. For example, "Why didn't the CIA just kill him?" or "What, besides sex, did Sally and he share?" These questions would never have occurred to a Kennedy reader, who might guess, from tabloid scenarios, that the CIA spared Kennedy because he had worked hand-in-glove with them and was one of their heroes. A Kennedy reader would have known, too, that JFK and JBK belonged to prominent families and were drawn to seats of power.

I am going to turn now to the preclosure part of the experiment. As I have been doing for years, I asked my readers to identify sentences where they thought the story *could* end, although the author kept going. Under ideal conditions, these choices reveal where the reader's sense of storyness kicks in, educated from the nerve ends on up through fairy tales to sitcoms to, if we are lucky, Hawthorne, Joyce, Borges, and beyond. Unfortunately, the bracketed summaries used to abridge the stories created a visual break that affected the preclosure choices. However, since these disruptions occurred at the same points in both texts, I could still compare the data.

When I did, the stories opened up to me. I will start with the Kennedy text. The earliest sentence to be chosen by more than one reader is number seventy-two. It comes right after Kennedy remembers Martin Luther King, a famous black civil rights leader who was also assassinated in the 1960s. The ex-president ruefully acknowledges the insight the two of them might have shared, had they confided in one another. In the Kennedy text, the sentence reads, "We could have told each other so many things we never had sense enough to talk about when we were living our public lives."[7] It is a sad and funny thought, with a kind of didactic wistfulness: leaders could do so much more if they would only *talk* to each other. The story that ends here is a wry anecdote, with a twist of historical hindsight.

The next sentence to be chosen by more than one reader is number eighty-six, occurring after the main character has entered the auction room and seen so many of the objects he has never forgotten. The sight of them moves him deeply and leads him to confess, "Jackie has been with me, as well, all these years" (178). In earlier experiments, I have found that one of the most common closural signals is repetition of a key word—such as a proper name—that has acquired special significance in the discourse of the story.[8] Another lexical signal is a verbal absolute, such as "all" in "all these years," especially if found in a declarative summary, such as "Jackie has been with me . . . all these years." I am not surprised that this sentence was favored as a pre-closure point, but what does it close? Here, in this one sentence, all the pseudo-historical drama of sexual and political intrigue changes key, resolving into a simple statement of fidelity to a memory.

Sentence number 108 is next in line as a preclosure point. It identifies the moment when JFK notices that a clone of Jackie is "in the aisle seat directly across from me and she is looking at me intently" (181). The story that ends here looks suddenly like a thriller about hiding in plain sight, about dodging detection. For me, however, there is far more closural force in sentence number 137, which was the favorite preclosure point for my readers. It occurs right after a moment of crisis. That eagle-eyed wife impersonator has caught up with the narrator, who is trying to escape. She apparently *has* recognized him—an outcome he both fears and desires—but her words betray a comical mistake: she thinks he is Henry Fonda. Relieved but also disappointed, he speaks to the woman kindly yet dismissively, with inner resignation, saying, "'You must buy some of Jackie's pearls'" (183). Why did this sentence halt so many readers?

Once again, key words are present: the wife's name *and* the signature pearl neck-lace. The syntax is simple, the verb is imperative. In both the actions and emotions of the main character, this is a turning point. After this moment he will slip out a side door, evading his guards, and walk into the city. "Free at last." Already, he is relin-quishing the fear and the hope of being once again the center of attention. When he tells the faux wife to get herself some pearls, he rounds out an object lesson in the irony of fame.

But there is more to the story. The Kennedy readers found another preclosure point. It comes after the narrator's address to the fake wife and before his meditation on memory. JFK rhapsodizes about his real wife: "I love Jackie. I know because inside me I have her hands and her hair . . . and her toes and her bony elbows and her knees and her shoes and belts and scarves and her shadow and her laugh and her moans and her simulated-pearl necklaces. . . . *And somebody has my golf clubs*" (184; italics mine). That final clause stopped two Kennedy readers. After the litany of "hands" and "toes" and "scarves" and "moans," the remark about the golf clubs is surprisingly flip-pant, and it cuts both ways. Does he mean that some lucky buyer can showcase those clubs, and just the sight of them will keep alive the man who once used them? Or does he mean that he himself is just a collector—that the "moans" and the "scarves" that he remembers are just the trophies of a sexual Schwarzenegger?

Perhaps the sentence stood out for Kennedy readers because they had heard of the golf clubs, but there *is* a story that ends here, and it is a cautionary tale with a dubi-ous tone: yes, in the great auction hall of life, we can all have a piece of Jackie to prove that we loved her, but we are just as liable ourselves to be sold off to strangers. *I want her pearls, you want my golf clubs. Are we links in a circle of love, or scavengers* of glamour and fame? The story that ends with the golf clubs is either gushy or cynical.

And so we come to the actual ending. First, Kennedy becomes a philosopher: "In a world where we don't know how to stay close to each other, we try to stay close to these things. In a world where death comes unexpectedly and terrifies us as the ultimate act of forgetting, we try to remember so that we can overcome death" (184). Then he slides into a parody of public address: "And so we go forth together in love and in peace and in deep fear, my fellow Americans, Jackie and I and all of you. And you have my undying thanks" (184). Period. Blank space. To my taste, this closure is both arch and naive, but it captures me. Butler has a genius for crossing the trashy with the tragic with panache and poignancy. The story that ends here—that is to say, the story Butler actually wrote—is about "yearning" and about the only solace we have: humans touching humans in the flesh, in memory, and in speech. It ends in a rallying call for support ("And so we go forth together. . . . And you have my undying thanks"). Out of political speechifying and the tabloid imaginary, Butler creates a sentimental parable.

By now it should be clear that the Osborne text is not the same thing at all, despite the overlap in wording. The Osborne text is the Kennedy text manqué, but it is also a text that is, generically speaking, more naked. Except in relation to secondary characters and events, this is a story without tabloid interference. And so, before considering which sentences the Osborne readers chose as preclosure points, it is important to notice which ones they did *not* choose. They did not choose the sentence about sharing stories with Martin Luther King. They did *not* choose the admission that "Sally has been with me, as well, all these years."

Neither did they double up on a number of options, diluting their first choice. No, the Osborne readers chose only one sentence more than once, and they chose it repeatedly: "You must buy some of Sally's pearls." This is, of course, the mate of the favored preclosure choice in the Kennedy text, but it was even more popular with the Osborne readers. Is the story that ends here still an object lesson? Perhaps, but again, there is a shift in meaning because Sally is not Jackie. She is a movie star, but that information has not been dramatized, nor substantiated by knowledge from outside the story. Sally, for example, is not Sally Field. As a signifier, she is primarily "wife," and so Osborne's remark to the wife impersonator—"buy those pearls"—is above all the response of Sally's husband. Is he touched, finally, by the innocent devotion of the woman—*all* the women—dressed as his wife? Does he see, finally, that the pearls are a kind of currency that gains value when circulated? Or is he realizing that fake pearls are just right for impersonators—including, perhaps, the original Mrs. Osborne? Any and all of these interpretations are possible, and they all suggest that he is no longer there to buy, but to reflect. Perhaps this is not an object lesson so much as a consciousness raising.

For Osborne readers, no preclosure occurs when the narrator shifts from a catalog of his wife's attributes to an item on the auction list. Perhaps that is because I changed the famous golf clubs to a fictional pen case, but it may also be because the two stories leading up to this point are so different. The Kennedy text is about a man we thought we knew, whose inner life is revealed in a touching confirmation of what we have wanted to believe all along—that Jack loved Jackie. It is a soothing idea that is exploded or revised by the remark about the golf clubs. The Osborne text is more simply about a man awakening to thoughtfulness. In the shift from Sally's attributes and possessions to the remark about the pen case, there is no terminal flash of dark humor.

The actual ending of the Osborne text is virtually the same as in Butler's story. Like the celebrity politician, the famous novelist has learned from personal experience that we are all shadowed by death, clinging to the bodies and the objects that furnished our lives. In the end, we are clones of each other, celebrity and fan, bound by the same "deep fear" of death and needing to "go forth in love and in peace." The same last words close both texts, but, of course, they resonate differently.

Let me review the preclosure points in each story. Readers of the Kennedy text found endings to the following embedded stories: a somewhat righteous historical anecdote about famous men who do not talk to each other; a rather self-congratulatory love story about memories held in trust; an ironic object lesson in the auction hall of life; and finally, a testimony with a self-mocking wisdom and a wisecracking moral: touch, love, and remember, for tomorrow we die. Perhaps none of the internally unfolding stories invalidates the others, but neither do they depend on each other. They scatter interpretations, as do the myriad tabloid stories that are both true and not true of John Fitzgerald Kennedy. Giving Butler's work its due as a postmodern satire, we may praise a sort of entropy of interpretation. The more we look at the story, the more senses it has and the less it *makes* sense.

In the Osborne story, readers found only one significant preclosure point, suggesting that their reading experience was more simply structured. The sentence they chose is the combined invitation and command to go buy those pearls. It is a first gesture toward another human being, and it centers the story on Osborne's new perception of audience. The whole story ends, just as the Kennedy text does, with some final words about "love" and "peace" that echo 1960s' sentiments, Christian rhetoric, and Butler's humanism. Yet in the Kennedy story, they come from a politician who has had his finger on the nuclear button and has addressed the world before, while in the Osborne story, they come from a novelist who has never had such power but is now approaching it.

The pattern of preclosure choices tells us that the Osborne story pivots on the inner change that allows him to relinquish the pearls. Perhaps he is realizing that his love for his wife both embodies and transcends the material and the personal. This is a love story moving from *eros* to *agape*. I think that is why so many of the Osborne readers linked the pearl necklace with "true love," while none of the Kennedy readers did.

In the end, what the Kennedy readers found is the sentimental parable that reclaims a culture hero and the rhetoric of his era. What the Osborne readers found is the initiation story of a man who once knew too much, then not enough, and then what was needed—perhaps the normative curve for a secular prophet or a late-blooming author. Is Osborne a Butler impersonator?

If so, he is a better one than I am. The story I concocted was far fetched, as many readers noticed, but they took it seriously enough for the experiment to work. Without interference from the historical record and the tabloid scenarios, responses to Osborne's story gravitated toward, and conformed more closely to, those predicted by the genre model. The same markers are present in the Kennedy text, but they have less control over the reading experience. There is too much excess information already in place, coming from tabloid scenarios that are fictions too, perhaps, but follow different rules. Far from devaluing Butler's achievement, the experiment helps us understand it. The celebrity protagonist creates interference that is highly productive, not because it suppresses the genre model—which it does—but because it meaningfully contends with it, threatens to overwhelm it—as we have seen by comparison with the Osborne story—and yet never quite does. That, rather than JFK's resurrection, is the miracle of Butler's tale.

I would like to say a final word about reading experiments. I have argued elsewhere that they are a way of short-circuiting some of today's ruling ideologies.[9] That is not to say, however, that reading experiments ignore social relevance. On the contrary, their results give a more objectively earned perspective on, for instance, the popular culture of celebrity auctions. Nor would I claim that story competence manifests itself in the same form in all populations of the world—only that triggering that competence will always be instructive. Finally, of course, I realize that no two groups of readers will provide the same preclosure evidence, nor will any two scholars draw the same conclusions from that evidence. I claim no more authority for my reading of Butler's story than any other scholar might claim for his or hers, but I do see the reading experiment as a pathway to insight.

My test has helped me to see the cognitive primacy and efficiency of the short story and to understand why this genre is a hedge against "information entropy." In postmodern times, that is a stance so conservative as to approach the blasphemous. Yet I believe we have not yet outgrown that primal, neurological plot. When we do, we can forget about genre distinctions. We will have no need for short stories.

Notes

1. Sobol, *Galileo's Daughter*, 244.

2. See, for instance, Coombe, "Celebrity Image and Cultural Identity." Other articles of interest include Margolis, "Public Life"; and Wicke, "Celebrity Material."

3. For a survey, see Yussen, "Map of Psychological Approaches."

4. Gray, "What Price Camelot?" 70.

5. Statement made during a panel discussion at the Sixth International Conference on the Short Story, October 12–15, 2000, in Iowa City, Iowa.

6. I am indebted to the generosity of Dr. Rebecca Clouse, who, for the purposes of the experiment discussed in this paper, allowed me to borrow the students in her class on "Reading Short Stories" in the English Department of the University of Iowa. I am deeply grateful to her and to the students who gave me their valuable and indispensable help on February 22, 2001.

7. Butler, "JFK," 176. Citations will be followed by page numbers from this text; however, please note that the "sentence numbers" used to identify preclosure points refer to locations in the abridged version used for the experiment.

8. Lohafer, "Cognitive Approach to Storyness."

9. Lohafer, "Why the 'Life of Ma Parker.'"

Works Cited

Butler, Robert Olen. "JFK Secretly Attends Jackie Auction." In *Tabloid Dreams*, 169–84. New York: Henry Holt, 1996.

Coombe, Rosemary J. "The Celebrity Image and Cultural Identity: Publicity Rights and the Subaltern Politics of Gender." *Discourse* 14, no. 3 (Summer 1992): 59–88.

Gionis, Alexander. "'The More You Know the Less You Know': Ronald Sukenick's 'What's Watts' and Donald Barthelme's 'Robert Kennedy Saved from Drowning.'" In *Revisioning the Past: Historical Self-Reflexivity in American Short Fiction*, edited by Bernd Engler and Oliver Scheiding, 285–86. Trier: Wissenschaftlicher Verlag, 1998.

Gray, Paul. "What Price Camelot?" *Time*, May 6, 1996, 67–73.

Gregory, R. L. "Psychology: Towards a Science of Fiction." In *The Cool Web: The Pattern of Children's Reading*, edited by Margaret Meek, Aiden Warlow, and Griselda Barton, 393–98. London: The Bodley Head, 1977.

Lohafer, Susan. "A Cognitive Approach to Storyness." In *The New Short Story Theories*, edited by Charles E. May, 301–11. Athens: Ohio University Press, 1994.

———. "Why the 'Life of Ma Parker' Is Not So Simple: Preclosure in Issue-Bound Stories." *Studies in Short Fiction* (Special Number on Short Story Theory) 33, no. 4 (Fall 1996 [printed Spring 1998]): 475–86.

Margolis, Stacy. "The Public Life: The Discourse of Privacy in the Age of Celebrity." *Arizona Quarterly* 52, no. 2 (Summer 1995): 81–101.

Prince, Gerald. *A Grammar of Stories*. The Hague: Mouton, 1973.

Sobol, Dava. *Galileo's Daughter*. New York: Penguin, 2000.

Todorov, Tzvetan. *The Poetics of Prose*. Translated by Richard Howard. Ithaca, N.Y.: Cornell University Press, 1977.

Wicke, Jennifer. "Celebrity Material: Materialist Feminism and the Culture of Celebrity." *South Atlantic Quarterly* 93, no. 4 (Fall 1994): 751–78.

Yussen, Steven R. "A Map of Psychological Approaches to Story Memory." In *The Tales We Tell: Perspectives on the Short Story*, edited by Barbara Lounsberry et al., 151–56. Westport, Conn.: Greenwood Press, 1998.

Narrative, Lyric, and Plot in Chris Offutt's *Out of the Woods*

John Gerlach

"From the beginnings as a separately recognized literary form," Charles May observes, "the short story has always been more closely associated with lyric poetry than with its overgrown narrative neighbor, the novel."[1] The short story, he says, has historically pursued a "movement away from the linearity of prose toward the spatiality of poetry." Critics have used various terms to describe the relationship between lyricism and narrative within the short story tradition. The extremes of the scale could be termed "syntagmatic" or "paradigmatic"; stories work both through the forward direction of linear narrative as well as an all-at-onceness, a lyric quality, and stories may slide to one or the other end of this scale. Critics have created names for the lyrical, paradigmatic tendency of the short story tradition: for Suzanne Ferguson it is the impressionist story, for Eileen Baldeshwiler it is the lyric short story. In my own book, *Toward the End*, I came up with imagistic form and compressed form. What I want to explore here, however, is how these two tendencies, narrative and lyric, are related through the mechanism of plot. Narrative and lyric within the short story may be not so much separate categories as different forms of the same essence. Matter from one perspective, energy from another, or perhaps more accurately, time from one perspective, space from another. I propose that we can see in plot the tendencies that can easily lead from the syntagmatic to the paradigmatic.

Plot could simply be defined as the concatenation of actions, which is more or less what is popularly meant by recounting the plot of a book or a movie, but no theorist rests there. One point those who write about plot more or less agree on is that it is not separable from other elements such as theme, diction, and character. The briefest, perhaps most famous quotation comes from Henry James in "The Art of Fiction." Responding to an essay by Walter Besant, James rejected Besant's claim that composition consisted of separate layers of technique, a "series of blocks." "What," James asked, "is character but the determination of incident? What is incident but the illustration of character?" (597). Focusing more exclusively on the term "plot," R. S. Crane contended that it correlates such variables as our estimate of the moral character of the hero, judgments about the painful or pleasurable consequences of events for the hero, and opinions about the hero's responsibility for what happens—plot is a kind of controlling frame for reading the story (632). Considering the difference between fabula and sjuzet (i.e., between incidents in the story arranged chronologically and incidents as actually sequenced within the text), Peter Brooks attempted to decide which should be identified as the plot; he ultimately decided plot is really the relationship between fabula and sjuzet: plot "could be thought of as the interpretive activity elicited by the distinction between *sjuzet* and *fabula*, the way we *use* one against another" (13). James Phelan, too, wanted to separate plot from character but conceded that he could not (ix). Perhaps we could simply conclude we do not know how to define plot at all, since it is both itself and everything else, but I do not think that is the fault of indecisive or contentious critics. From Aristotle through E. M. Forster, plot has been analyzed as a comprehensive feature of narrative.

Plot could best be regarded as an activity, from the perspective of the writer or the reader, rather than a summary of events. Paul Ricoeur uses the term "emplotment," which suggests plotting as process. As Ricoeur explains, "to make up a plot is already to make the intelligible spring from the accidental, the universal from the singular, the necessary or the probable from the episodic" (41). Emplotment is the "operation that draws a configuration out of a simple succession" (65). Ultimately, plot "transforms . . . elements into a story." Using plot in that sense, in conjunction with some of Gérard Genette's terms for narrative structure, in particular order, frequency, and voice, provides a systematic and reliable way of describing how the syntagmatic and paradigmatic, narrative and lyric, are mediated by emplotment.[2]

I have chosen to draw my examples from a contemporary short story writer, Chris Offutt, because he writes consistently about his own home territory, Kentucky, within a traditional tale-telling culture, using both the syntagmatic tradition and a lyrical mode. His first collection, *Kentucky Straight*, is dominated by what seem like obligatory *Field and Stream* topics, such as poker ("Smokehouse") or pool ("Nine Ball"), stories in which the narrative progression is shaped by the games themselves. The collection also contains legends like "The Leaving One," in which the spirit of a grandfather passes into a son, or "Aunt Granny Lith," about a spirit midwife, or "The Old of the Moon," about a quest to recover a child's head from a bear's stomach. These supernatural tales still feature linear narrative, and they could be analyzed as folktales in the fashion of Vladimir Propp, with an analysis that stresses syntagmatic qualities. Offutt's second collection, *Out of the Woods*, is about Kentuckians sometimes out of the woods, out of trouble, but, of course, the title is often ironic. These are characters who are either trying to get back into the woods, or they are not out of the woods at all, but into more trouble. These are stories about people trying to find themselves, to define themselves outside of Kentucky. They are still people of the code, people for whom "honorable" behavior is essential, though it may sometimes be brutal or unkind behavior. To tell their stories Offutt sometimes adapts more flexible plot strategies, transforming plot so that lyrical elements predominate. I will limit myself to the three of the first four stories, the title story, "Out of the Woods"; the fourth, "Two-Eleven All Around"; and the third story, "Moscow, Idaho." "Out of the Woods," which I will analyze first, is a conventional linear story that nevertheless demonstrates paradigmatic elements observable in virtually any linear tale; "Two-Eleven All Around" and "Moscow, Idaho" are more clearly variants of lyrical/spatial stories, generated by the manipulation of frequency, order, and voice.

Plot in the title story, "Out of the Woods," assumes the form of a quest, a syntagmatic linear form, but within syntagmatic form we can detect paradigmatic tendencies. Look first at the linear elements: the protagonist, Gerald, takes on the task of bringing his brother-in-law Ory from a hospital in Nebraska, where he is recovering from a gunshot wound, back to Kentucky. We could map out the sequence in the fashion of Vladimir Propp, Claude Bremond, Gérard Genette, or Tzvetan Todorov, defining plot as a kind of grammar of quantifiable elements. Gerald is dispatched by the Gowan family, Ory's brothers, who are now Gerald's brothers-in-law—he has married Ory's sister Kay. The members of the Gowan family are the Proppian donors, setting the quest in motion. Gerald's first helper in Nebraska is Dr. Gupte, who informs Gerald of his first obstacle in reaching the sought-for person. Ory is dead. This discovery does not diminish the forward thrust of the plot: Gerald can still bring Ory back, just a dead Ory. Sheriff Johnson is his next helper, ready to help Gerald deal with the next obstacle: Ory owes back rent, hospital bills, and the cost of a funeral.

Gerald's subsequent step is not a direct one, but it is not arbitrary, either. To learn what happened to Ory, he visits the woman who shot him—Melanie, Ory's girlfriend—in jail. Melanie is wearing an orange jumpsuit and a gold ring in her left nostril and has dark purple hair. He does find out what happened: she shot the raging, drunken Ory when he angrily demanded the return of the blonde wig he had given her. When she offers Gerald both a drug deal and herself, Gerald stomps out and cuts his own deal with the sheriff to get Ory's body back, selling the sheriff Ory's car to cover the debts. The sheriff sees the deal only as payment to help Gerald pay Ory's funeral expenses, but Gerald does not have a funeral in Nebraska in mind. He steals the body and takes off for Kentucky. The journey back to Kentucky owes a good deal to conventions of southern storytelling, reenacting Faulkner's As I Lay Dying. Grotesquely comic business ensues, but ultimately Gerald completes his journey, returning to his mother-in-law's house, and the family and Kay join him. Ory's body is returned. Mission accomplished. This linear recounting, however, leaves out anything beyond farce and in itself is a good illustration of the insufficiency of the popular definition of plot as a mere sequence of events to provide a clear sense of the dynamics of a story.

When we understand plot as a process, as a connecting device, we begin to see how it activates our sense of causality. We want to know not only what happens next to Gerald but also why he is doing what he is doing—assumptions that R. S. Crane has posited in his definition of plot. We want to know if Gerald might succeed, we want to know what success will mean in moral terms. The why, Gerald's reason for undertaking the quest, is the distance he feels from the family he is married into: "He still needed to prove his worth" (20). He needs to prove himself to his wife, Kay, for reasons both high and low. Hearing what has happened to her brother, Kay is concerned, hugging her knees, biting her thumb, high reason for a hero to assist a damsel in distress. The fact that she is "gasping in a throaty way that reminded him of the sounds she made in bed" (20) suggests a lower reason. If he wishes to continue to enjoy her sexual favors, he had better go questing for Ory. She knows that too, and once he has agreed to the task and is ready to depart, "she snuggled against him," and when he "opened the front [of her robe] . . . she pushed against his leg" (21).

Melanie, Ory's girlfriend, we may realize, reactivates the theme introduced by the scene with Gerald's wife, Kay. Melanie is a new sexual temptation. Melanie and her blonde wig remain only isolated thoughts for Gerald as he resumes his journey with the body back to Kentucky, and the wig occasionally appears extraneously, part of Gerald's reflection, not yet at the level of generating a substory. On his way back, as he passes through Illinois, "he stopped and lay down beside the truck. Without the blanket he was cold, but he didn't feel right about taking it back from Ory. Gerald thought about Ory asking Melanie to wear the blond wig. He wondered if it made a difference when they were in bed" (32). That theme remains suspended, briefly alluded to subsequently, until its resolution in the ending. Plot activates the reader's attempt to paradigmatically stack thematic concerns that arise from the concatenation of syntagmatic elements—the *why* rather than the *what next*. Even so, we will still perceive a story like this one as linear, primarily narrative rather than lyrical.

The tendency of plot to become episodic, to fragment momentarily into nearly or completely independent incidents, can also generate paradigmatic elements. As Ricoeur's analysis of Aristotle indicates, episodes are not all undesirable, as long as they are controlled by plot: episodes are "what give amplitude to the work, and thus a 'magnitude'" (42). As long as an episode coheres within the larger progression of emplotment, we begin to recapture this centrifugal energy in paradigmatic terms, again to understand character in the case of this story. Take, for example, Gerald's meeting with Dr. Gupte. It is borderline episodic—it is brief and reveals essential information, but Gerald's tendency to drift out of focus and the enclosed nature of the scene push it toward the episodic:

> "I am Dr. Gupte. You are with the family of Mr. Gowan?"
> "You're the doctor?"
> "Yes." He sighed and opened a manila folder. "I'm afraid Mr. Gowan has left us."
> "Done out, huh. Where to?"
> "I'm afraid that is not the circumstance."

"It's not."

"No, he had a pulmonary thromboembolism."

"Is that American?"

"I'm afraid you will excuse me."

Dr. Gupte left the room and Gerald wondered who the funny little man really was. He pulled open a drawer. Inside was a small mallet with a triangular head made of rubber, perfect for nothing. A cop came in the room, and Gerald slowly closed the drawer. (23)

Within this enclosure, the doctor opening a manila folder and Gerald closing the drawer, the reader, be he or she superreader, model reader, or competent reader, is likely to respond to distinctive language—"is that American," and the little mallet "perfect for nothing" of this momentary interlude. Readers will have different interpretations: Charles May notes that "Gerald makes some common-sense arrangements and a few man-to-man deals with authorities and heads back to Kentucky with his brother-in-law's body in the back of the pickup."[3] In May's view, Gerald's approach to his situation makes the best of a difficult situation. While I agree in general, in the case of Dr. Gupte, Gerald reveals some of his smugness, the country boy superior to anything foreign, so clever he might outclever himself, be caught the next time before he can metaphorically close the drawer. In this scene, he is really the funny little man, not the doctor. Whatever our interpretation of this scene, however, interpretation has been prompted by a break in continuity, something pointing beyond linearity to a puzzle. Writers trust the human desire to recuperate diversion or interlude within a controlling pattern. This borderline episode creates a paradigmatic emerging picture of who Gerald is within the context of what he does. Put another way, the emplotment creates coherence as well as diversification and amplitude. An enclosed and almost independent episode, if properly constructed, generates reflection and coherence without dispelling the illusion of syntagmatic orientation.

More clearly tangential episodes are also interpreted paradigmatically: we are forced to seek the significance of individual strands of action within the plot as a whole. During the return, Gerald, like Faulkner's Anse Bundren, is plagued by a buzzard attracted to the cargo in his truck. His solution is to pile on some dirt from a plowed field. He is not entirely successful—when he stops at a gas station he discovers a dog "in the back of his pickup, digging" (34). Gerald can get rid of the dog but not its owner. Fortunately for Gerald, he need not act or explain, for the man has developed his own explanation, and Gerald merely needs to keep his mouth shut. The man asks:

"Did yours up and not eat, then lay down and start breathing hard?"

"More or less."

"It's the same thing. A malady, the vet called it."

"A malady."

Gerald got in the truck and decided not to stop until he was home. (35)

Once again Gerald can get away with merely closing a drawer, so to speak. We have not learned more about him, other than that he is lucky. The episode may seem nothing more than farcical, action for action's sake, episode without purpose, but the episode does create suspense—just how lucky can Gerald be? Will he always be so lucky, or will he ever have to explain himself, find his own way out?

Soon enough he is called on to explain himself, creating a substory virtually rivaling the whole story itself, an imaginative recasting that Gerald hopes will replace what's actually happened. Here is the story, virtually a summary, that Gerald plans to tell on his return to Ory's family: "Ory had quit drinking and taken a good job as manager of a department store. He'd gotten engaged to a woman he'd met at church, but had held off telling the family until he could bring her home. She was as nice as pie, blond headed. He was teaching her to shoot a pistol and it went off by accident. She was tore all to pieces about it. He'd never seen anyone in such bad shape. All she did was cry. It was a malady" (36). If he cannot bring back a live Ory, he can at least return with an acceptable memory. Ory was gainfully employed, absorbing religion, had chosen a wife with hair of the culturally approved color, blonde, not Melanie's purple, and has suffered accidental death. Ory has been appropriately grieved. In Charles May's view, "In this carefully controlled account of a simple man's homey, heroic management of an extraordinarily ordinary situation, Gerald's final gesture is to tell a public lie—that Ory was accidently shot—for the sake of his in-laws" (602). In my view, there is a limit to the extent that Gerald can lie to himself. Gerald is again showing himself inventive, preparing to deadpan his way out, but this may be a drawer he cannot close, a stinker of a lie that he cannot pile dirt on, a malady that will not go away.

As Gerald returns, the family appears, and more dogs, more people look for Ory. We anticipate the moment of discovery, but Gerald is strangely abstracted, absorbed in a Melanie fantasy—wondering how his wife Kay would look in the blonde wig. At one level he is falling into old habits, reexperiencing Kentucky: "The smell of the woods was familiar. It would be this way forever." But there is one more sentence, the final sentence of the story: "Abruptly, as if doused by water, he knew why Ory had left" (37). Different readers will continue the story in different ways. Perhaps Gerald's epiphany initiates his new understanding of Ory. In my view, Gerald is beginning to understand himself, beginning to realize that he has the same desires Ory did and is no longer a man at home in Kentucky. He has become an ironic Jamesian ambassador who, instead of bringing back the man who wandered off, becomes himself the man he sought, eager to see his wife in a blonde wig—overwhelmed by a transformation of the very sexual drive that first compelled him on his quest. Whichever approach readers take, they are still likely to regard "Out of the Woods" as a conventionally plot-driven story, a tale; we expect endings to be paradigmatic, and that does not change our perception of linearity. My point, however, has been to illustrate linear plot in the process of conventionally evolving into character and theme, as Crane, Brooks, and Phelan have argued, and to suggest the role that stories embedded within the action, a natural property of emplotment, have in shaping what we will consider as a conventional linear tale.

The fourth story of the collection, "Two-Eleven All Around," does not develop in linear fashion. When there is a significant disjunction in what Genette terms order (i.e., disjunction between the chronological sequence of events and the actual telling), or disjunction in frequency, the number of times an event is told, emplotment generates a more paradigmatic perception. The increasing presence of embedded elements (flashbacks, or in Genette's terminology, analepsis) can generate a more paradigmatic sense of all-at-onceness, of lyrical spatiality. Analepsis minimizes the effect of chronological time in favor of perceived time, time in human memory; diversions from the default one-to-one telling to event ratio also diminish linearity. Ralph Freedman has made a useful point about what he has termed the lyrical novel, a point that can also be applied to the short story. Lyrical novels mimic narrative structures; the syntagmatic element (he calls it "consecutiveness") "is simulated by lyrical language: its surge toward greater intensity reveals not new events but the significance of existing events" (8). Put another way, "the lyrical novel absorbs action altogether and refashions it as a pattern of imagery" (2).

Stories we are inclined to classify as lyrical immediately signal a lower reliance on linear structure. The initiating situation in "Two-Eleven All Around" is exposed in the first sentence: "When she locked me out I didn't mind that much because things were drifty from the start" (79). There is not much forward impetus—if the character does not mind much being locked out of the house by his girlfriend, there is no clear next step, or even the energy to take one. We do not expect much of a linear plot. If there is a story here, the first-person narrator is mostly interested in telling us how he got locked out, not what he will do next. First-person narration can easily lend itself to what seems a "plotless" approach. A seemingly artless narrator tries to figure out what his story is and how to tell it.

Emplotment nevertheless is always at work and can proceed in several directions. While explaining to us what his situation is, the narrator suggests one kind of plot, a plot of a secret about to be revealed. In this plot the narrator lost out to a rival, someone whom his girlfriend prefers to the narrator, someone she will lock herself in with. A plot of this sort would organize for the reader a kind of chronology, a situation that accounts for the narrator's current predicament on the porch. The initial twist to this theoretical plot is that the someone is in fact an object: a police scanner. The narrator reacts as he would to a rival: he is "jealous of men who would never touch her. Jealous of voices in the dark" (82). Character here is harder to assess than in "Out of the Woods"—we see that our narrator enjoys expanding the irony of his predicament, but we do not know whether that is wisdom or self-deception. He admits she has not goaded him with real human rivals, and that admission leads to his own assumption of blame, which would indicate a certain moral stature. The narrator tells us a sub-story about his tomcat dad, who made the narrator cover for him "when he slipped off to see his Tuesday girl friend. Then on Wednesday he'd go bowling out of the county. Thursday he'd see a widow in town. He lived like a rabbit mostly, and you might say I had a few moms. These days I'm as loyal as bark on a tree" (82). The embedded substory points toward character rather than action. The narrator above all wants to be "two-eleven all around," scanner code "which meant that the subject was clean, with no warrants against him in the city or county" (80).

Embedded episodes are rife within "Two-Eleven All Around." The substories delay resolution, and they build a picture of the narrator's frustration. As we attend to these stories we leave behind the plot of a rival. How many men had his girlfriend been with before him, he asks her; her response is not immediate: "then it hit me that she was maybe counting up, and that number was something I did not want to hear. I wanted to shift to another channel." Finally she asks, "What year?" (83). Knowing how to milk a joke, the narrator continues. "She never gave a thing up. You could ask her if it was raining and she'd say, 'Outside?'" Instead of moving forward, we merely circle back to that locking out: "The night she locked me out, I hid in the dark, watching her in the house" (84). We have not through this episode learned much more about character. If anything, it demonstrates what habitually happens, why he is frustrated, cannot act.

We are soon sidetracked into what seems another unrelated embedded story. She is not the only one he watches: "Sometimes I watched her kid" (84). The conflict in this embedded story is between him and her boy. It is not a story impelled toward resolution, but it does create a theme that will become increasingly dominant, the stranger/enemy dichotomy. Following that aside, we again return to a retelling of the initial situation: "I stayed on the porch until I got sick of listening to the scanner's static" (84). The next sentence develops by association: "The house just sat there, dark and hard and locked. It was her house." That leads him to revealing one more embedded story, the complement of the story we have just heard about her son. He, too, has a son, and that son is being raised—"not so much raised as jerked up" by others (85). In that relationship his own son is the stranger, the ex-wife's boyfriend the enemy. The resulting sense of polarity, of balance, him watching a stranger's kid, a stranger watching his kid, is inherently paradigmatic. That theme does not yet seem to organize itself into sequence, but it is clearly competing with the plot of the rival.

Offutt manipulates frequency again by returning to the static baseline, the refrain of waiting on the porch as the narrator grows frustrated, still locked out. We move ahead slightly as he cruises to a bar. Seeing a cop leads him to the act that surprises him, throwing a rock through a window so his girlfriend will hear the "two-eleven" scanner call from the policeman, which will vindicate him as a bark-on-the-tree good guy. The story could plausibly end here, with the narrator having manipulated his rival, the scanner, to reveal himself as a two-eleven guy, but Offutt chose instead to explode and reconfigure one of his embedded stories, the story of the narrator's boy. As the narrator stands once again seemingly stalled, paradigmatically frozen, he leaps to an insight: "I stood there waiting in that streetlight's glare with broken glass at my back and garbage at my feet and the whole galaxy over my head, and suddenly I knew damn sure what would happen one day" (87). What will happen takes the shape of one more embedded story: he will have his own place, and a stranger will come banging on his door. The narrator will have been leading a considerably less than two-eleven life. He will have a beer belly and will have been living "alone in a little dump, dirty and cramped" (87–88), and the stranger will be his own son, looking for a place to flop. Momentarily the narrator wants to reveal himself as a cautionary tale, show the boy how he will "wind up" (89), but instead he opens the door to welcome his son.

Here image dominates by means of antithetical reversal. The narrator's wife may have shut him out, but he opens the door for his boy, an image that becomes a metaphor for the narrator's anticipated transformation. In opening the door he has incorporated a more realistic sense of shame and failure into a more genuine two-elevenness. We can even see the title differently at the end, a new way to be more honestly two-eleven. The story illustrates one way plot, seen in Peter Brooks's terms as the reader's reconciliation of fabula and sjuzet, can produce an all-at-once image developed as a meditation—one kind of compressed, lyrical, impressionistic story. Unlike "Out of the Woods," in which Gerald only approached an epiphany, "Two-Eleven" closes with a full epiphany. That, along with the constant circling return to the stalled time of the porch, lessens the reader's sense of temporal linearity. Manipulation of order through embedding, and the frequent return to the porch, are exploitations of inherent properties of narrative that the reader still brings to final configuration through emplotment; organized disruption (in Ricoeur's terms concordant discordance) leads from the syntagmatic to the paradigmatic. The opening of the door to his son is a reinterpretation, an overlay, of the narrator's own waiting on the porch, which itself is told as an aspect of frequency, told in its retelling rather than in linear progression—an unusual form of plotting, but a manipulation of the properties of narrative and emplotment nonetheless.

"Two-Eleven All Around" approaches the lyrical short story, ending as it does like a meditation around a central point, the fixed and returning space on the porch, while leaping to the cosmic dimension of a galaxy above. "Moscow, Idaho" is marked by an even more diminished reliance on temporality. The reader must work harder to relate the embedded substories, many of which are not analeptic but instead the product of voices that are, in Genette's analysis of voice, metadiegetic, independent stories told by one of the characters within the level of what Genette terms the first narrative.

Action seems to diffuse into a nearly postmodern series of failures to achieve any coherent narrative structure at all. The initial situation does not even promise much of a story: two ex-cons are digging up graves in a graveyard, a dead-end job if there ever was one. "They'd been hired to replace a mini backhoe that damaged the caskets, sometimes cutting them in half. A separate work crew hauled the coffins to the other side of Moscow for reburial" (60).

One of the two men, Baker, is an inveterate anecdotalist, and his anecdotes are largely pointless. He has a stock of stories he tells over and over, with the conventional stop-me-if-you've-heard-this-one-before preface. Tilden, our focal character, puts Baker's "malady," to borrow the term from "Out of the Woods," into perspective: "Baker liked to talk and needed periodic proof that someone was paying attention" (60).

Some of what Baker babbles about while he and Tilden dig graves are less stories than statements—Minnesota has "the biggest mall in the world"—but many others develop into stories proper, themes of death and birth tied into Baker's grandmother's funeral. She had "hung herself from a clothes pole in a closet" (62). For Baker the point of this story seems not to be a reflection about the grandmother or the pathos of her death, but a comment on what the administration in the nursing home did— they took away the clothes poles from everyone's closets, one way to keep grandmother's story from being reenacted by anyone else. This story immediately leads Baker to another about misuse of a staple gun, which causes art class in a place called Deer Lodge to be shut down, and then Baker tells another story about the grandmother being reburied. At times Baker's stories are virtually pointless; one involves the rumor that one guy on a firing squad is always given a blank. "To make up for it, everybody aims away from the heart. Sometimes all five guys miss and the shot man flops around awhile." His final observation undoes the story altogether: "The day before, he gets to watch any video he wants" (73). Baker's true talent is his ability to divert his miniature stories from any significant resolution.

Tilden himself would also seem to be largely outside the world of story, a man of reflection, not action. He seems more interested in compare-and-contrast thinking, in meditations on the theme of prison, about being outside, staying outside, about how prison life relates to life outside, a mode of discourse more associated with expository writing or with meditative structures in poetry. Tilden's associative thinking, these stories about various kinds of prisons opening with contrasting views that Tilden and Baker have about prisons, ultimately underlines differences between the two men: Tilden is someone who understands his relation to prison, Baker does not. Emplotment operates even during fracture, simply because the reader so doggedly awaits a story as long as the most minimal clues suggest one might take shape; the waiting itself is part of the emplotment process.

The pressure of that suspense keeps alive the possibility that conflict will emerge late, that the story will explode as "Two-Eleven" does, with its unexpected coda reassembling elements in a substantially more satisfying pattern. This possibility emerges not once but three times in "Moscow, Idaho." The first intrusion of an external element is the appearance of a runner—somebody going somewhere, which is more than we can say of Tilden and Baker. Baker "lifted his shovel like a baseball bat" (70). But Tilden restrains himself from even a warning—"it went against yard ethics." When Baker slides behind the runner to threaten him, Tilden glimpses in Baker a wild look he has seen "only in prison." That triggers an embedded story for Tilden, a story about two men coming at one another in a rec room, "slashing with weapons made from a razor blade embedded in a toothbrush handle. Each man wore magazines strapped to his torso by strips of sheet. . . . The look in their eyes had matched Baker's" (71).

But the incident remains suspended, not leading to any open conflict between Baker and Tilden. Instead, another group passes through, apparently Amish, ironically bringing another body to bury, perhaps one that Tilden and Baker will have to dig up later to rebury. The passing of this group reminds Baker of his own mother's funeral and leads him to declare, "I didn't bury my own mother and here I am digging up strangers" (75), a strong irony in itself and the first evidence that Baker can in fact interpret his situation, tell a story related to the line of first narrative. One possible ending is then delineated—Baker simply steals a car, fleeing, a very irresolute ending. Tilden knows that fleeing will not really work: Baker is "on a run, like riding a motorcycle wide open until he crashed" (77). The third and true ending to the story is Tilden's, and it is appropriately static, transcendently static, an image itself of the paradigmatic aspects of emplotment reshaping the story in a mode most identifiably lyrical:

> Tilden crossed the road and lay on his back beside the wheat. He spread his arms. Wind blew loose dirt over his body. The ground was soft, and the air was warm. In prison he had figured out that laws were made to protect the people who made the laws. He had always thought that staying out of trouble meant following those laws, but now he knew there was more. The secret was to act like the people who wanted the laws in the first place. They didn't even think about it. They just lived.
>
> Tilden wondered if he'd ever find a woman, a job he liked, or a town he wanted to stay in. Above him the Milky Way made a blizzard of stars in the sky. There was not a fence or wall in sight. (77)

Wind blows dirt over his body, symbolically burying him, but it is no burial at all—he is in fact like the people who want the laws, just beginning to live. He does not walk into a new story, finding a woman, a job, or a town. He only wonders, moves only in his head. Space itself, the surrounding world, embodies the only action—the stars are blizzards, a highly active movement for what we take to be a distant immovable object. There are no boundaries in sight, no fences, no walls. Pure mental, paradigmatic, meditative freedom, penetration of a secret of the universe, a lyrical image, is experienced by a character, not merely inferred by the reader.

Looking back on these three stories as a group, "Out of the Woods" is primarily paradigmatic only in its ending and therefore appears to be a traditional syntagmatic, linear narrative. Emplotment seems anchored in temporality. In "Two-Eleven All Around," emplotment generates a paradigmatic medley of embedded stories around the ground base of the narrator waiting outside a porch door, a condensed image of the moment of telling a story. In "Moscow, Idaho," the temporality diverts, resolves itself only tonally in the reflections, anticipations of the centrally positioned stargazer, Tilden, the man now paradoxically alive in a graveyard. He is the focus of the story, but emplotment, primarily recognizable as tensions created by apparently divergent embedded stories, is still what drives us to perceive not only the story's paradigmatic resolution but also its curiously attenuated and suspended shape, its form as a non-linear story that nevertheless coheres.

In the short story through its history, and in the range of work of one of its practitioners, Chris Offutt, we can see the power of plot to shape wholeness, a unified configuration. Narrative and lyric, different as they may initially appear, are thus part of the same process. Narrative is an impulse that leads to lyric all-at-once perception; lyrical forms of narrative are the product of fractured syntagmatic impulses. The writer's strategy of emplotment and the reader's processing of the resulting discourse are the common denominator.

Notes

1. "Chekhov and the Modern Short Story," 214.

2. I should note a distinction between how I use the term "paradigm" and the way Ricoeur uses it. Ricoeur uses "paradigm" to mean "archetype"—*Oedipus Rex*, for instance, is the paradigm of tragedy. Ricoeur's term "configuration" is closest to what I mean by paradigmatic, the vertical as opposed to the horizontal.

3. Rev. of "Out of the Woods," 602.

Works Cited

Brooks, Peter. *Reading for Plot: Design and Intention in Narrative*. New York: Knopf, 1984.

Crane, R. S. "The Concept of Plot and the Plot of *Tom Jones*." In *Critics and Criticism: Ancient and Modern*, edited by R. S. Crane, 616–47. Chicago: University of Chicago Press, 1952.

Freedman, Ralph. *The Lyrical Novel: Studies in Hermann Hesse, André Gide, and Virginia Woolf*. Princeton, N.J.: Princeton University Press, 1963.

Genette, Gérard. *Narrative Discourse: An Essay in Method*. Translated by Jane E. Lewin. Ithaca, N.Y.: Cornell University Press, 1980.

James, Henry. "The Art of Fiction." *Henry James: Selected Fiction*, edited by Leon Edel, 585–609. New York: Dutton, 1953.

May, Charles E. "Chekhov and the Modern Short Story." In *The New Short Story Theories*, edited by Charles E. May, 199–217. Athens: Ohio University Press, 1994.

―――. "Out of the Woods." In *Magill's Literary Annual 2000*, vol. 2, edited by John D. Wilson, 601–4. Englewood Cliffs, N.J.: Salem Press, 2000.

Offutt, Chris. *Out of the Woods*. New York: Scribner Paperback Fiction/Simon and Schuster, 1999.

Phelan, James. *Reading People, Reading Plots: Character, Progression, and the Interpretation of Narrative*. Chicago: University of Chicago Press, 1989.

Prince, Gerald. *A Dictionary of Narratology*. Lincoln: University of Nebraska Press, 1987.

Ricoeur, Paul. *Time and Narrative*. Vol. 1. Translated by Kathleen McLaughlin and David Pellauer. Chicago: University of Chicago Press, 1984.

Closure and Preclosure as Narrative Grid in Short Story Analysis

Some Methodological Suggestions

Per Winther

John Gerlach's 1985 study, *Toward the End: Closure and Structure in the American Short Story*, was a pioneering effort in that it was the first to develop a comprehensive system of narrative closural categories for the short story: "All short stories use at least one of five signals of closure: solution of the central problem, natural termination, completion of antithesis, manifestation of a moral, and encapsulation" (8). Gerlach recognizes that the short story shares these closural signals with poetry, the novel, and drama, but he makes the convincing point that the signals take on greater structural prominence in short fiction than in the novel/drama; because of the genre's brief format, closure in the short story "has a greater structural significance" (7). It is this greater prominence that motivated Gerlach's study, which analyzes how "anticipation of the ending [is] used to structure the whole" (3). Different approaches to closure among writers produced "direct and indirect form" in the nineteenth century and "compressed and imagist form" in the twentieth, and in his book he discusses the defining characteristics of these short story traditions. In so doing, he has demonstrated new and rewarding ways of grouping stories, groupings that usefully complement more traditional period concepts like romanticism, realism, naturalism, and modernism.

One of the strong points of Gerlach's study is precisely this contribution to genre history; his approach to closure allows him to describe developments in the genre with a keener focus on details of narrative form than any prior study in the field. In terms of *close reading* of individual stories with a view to sorting out textual difficulties and matters of interpretation, there is also considerable analytical potential in his categories, even though Gerlach himself never makes this a main objective of his study. The present essay seeks to chart some systematic ways in which to approach short story analysis and interpretation by considering the structural importance of closure. I begin by reviewing and discussing the possibilities and limitations of Gerlach's categories, before moving on to complementary categories that will enable us, hopefully, to expand the discussion of short story closure in a direction that may further serve the purposes of textual analysis and interpretation.

Gerlach's Five Signals of Closure

Solution of the central problem is the first closural signal Gerlach lists, the one most unique to the short story because more often than novels, short stories focus on one problem only. The main character is confronted with a problem or wants to reach a certain goal. When he or she solves that problem/reaches his or her goal, or if he or she and/or we as readers are convinced that the problem is unsolvable/the goal is unreachable, a sense of coherence, completeness, and stability is achieved, producing closure.[1]

Natural termination "is the completion of an action that has a predictable end" (9). Night follows day, sleep interrupts daytime activities, life ends in death. A visit normally implies a return to the point of origin; mental states like happiness and bliss suggest the end of some process.

Gerlach's third signal of closure he designates *completion of antithesis*, but, he says, "antithesis is only one (the most common) of this type." This is the most problematic of Gerlach's categories, hence a rather full rendering of his description of this signal is in order: "The concept is at its base a spatial one, though in the short story, with its emphasis on mental life, space is often metaphorical. The mental equivalent of a character setting out on an adventure is a character exploring a range of attitudes toward a subject. Antithetical markers of closure indicate that boundaries have been established, so that new territory (in its metaphorical sense) need not be explored. Circularity, a return to any aspect of the beginning, through verbal or situational echo, is one form of antithesis. More broadly defined, antithesis is any opposition, often characterized by irony, that indicates something has polarized into extremes" (10).

Manifestation of a moral is Gerlach's fourth closural signal, which he connects with the generic tradition established by the parable or the exemplum. Closure of this kind is achieved when "we are aware . . . that a story that up until the end (the end in the physical sense, the blank space that signals, if nothing else does, that the story is over) has been factual, without any obvious intent to make an abstract point, and either a character or the reader sees the more general significance, the conclusion we draw has an effect analogous to the moral in the exemplum tradition. The reader's perception that a theme has emerged can give a short story a sense of having closed" (12).

A related, and last, signal of closure in Gerlach's system is *encapsulation*, which he describes as "a coda that distances the reader from the story by altering the point of view or summarizing the passing of time" (12).

Gerlach's Closural Categories Revised

In claiming that all short stories employ at least one of these closural signals, Gerlach implies that his list is exhaustive. I would like to extend that list by adding one more category: *evaluation*.[2] Furthermore, certain questions may be raised about the way Gerlach names, and thus groups, his closural categories. I tend to apply his notion of antithesis somewhat differently and I also think a renaming of his last category, encapsulation, could serve to facilitate an easier recognition of the multiple forms that this particular closural principle may take.

Evaluations, says Teun A. van Dijk, "feature the . . . mental or emotional reaction of the narrator participant with respect to the narrated episode," and he provides the following examples: "I was glad I was not there" and "I never met such a bore in my life" (115).[3] An example of evaluation serving as a closural marker in short fiction would be the first-person narrator's exasperated final comment, which is identical with the title of Sherwood Anderson's well-known story of initiation, "I Want to Know Why."

Often evaluations will also serve as the manifestation of a moral (Gerlach's fourth closural category), as in the narrator's concluding comment in Hawthorne's "The Minister's Black Veil,"[4] but as the Anderson example makes clear, the mental or emotional reaction on the part of the protagonist may serve to bring events to a logical narrative close *without* the kind of ideational finality associated with statement of a moral. The youthful protagonist's question at the end of Anderson's text reveals that he himself is unable to make personal sense of his story, which closes with his rendering of what he takes to be conflicting actions on the part of Jerry Tilford, his number one adult role model. The reason for the narrator's identification with Jerry is the horse trainer's ability to appreciate the uncontaminated beauty of Sunstreak, the youngster's favorite racing horse. ("I guess I loved the man as much as I did the horse because he knew what I knew" [15].) However, in the course of the story the boy is thrown into confusion because of a show of vulgar carnality on the part of his adult idol; having followed the trainer and his friends to a brothel, the youngster watches through a window and discovers that Jerry Tilford looks at a prostitute with the same shine in his eyes as he had when looking at Sunstreak and the boy earlier that same day. Unable to deal with what he experiences as corruption of spiritual or emotional purity, the narrator's only possible manner of response is his big and confused, "Why?" However, this is less of an open-ended story than it seems to the narrator himself. To the mature reader the question at the end does provide a sense of narrative closure, in that the boy has to close the story when he does. There is nowhere else for him to take his narrative. At his age he is simply not equipped to deal emotionally and intellectually with the complexities of adult sexuality, and his confusion at the end therefore makes perfect narrative sense; hence the closural force of the ending for the reader.

The most problematic item on Gerlach's list of closural signals is *completion of antithesis*. In his analytical model we have completion of antithesis when the narrative moves from one pole to its opposite, thereby signaling that "boundaries have been established, so that new territory (in its metaphorical sense) need not be explored" (10). There is no denying the closural force of short fiction texts marked by antithetical narrative structure; however, it seems to me that the way Gerlach defines this term is too inclusive, which renders it too imprecise to be of great analytical use. One reason why referring to "completion of antithesis" as a separate analytical category is problematic is that on closer inspection, it seems that *all the other* closural signals that Gerlach mentions in one way or another also establish conceptual antithesis or polarization.

For instance, the sense of closure that accompanies natural termination is clearly rooted in the perception of an antithetical pattern on the part of the reader, a movement from one state to its opposite. The narrative movement of day yielding to night is a movement from day into "nonday," death in a narrative represents movement from life to "nonlife," and so on. Similarly, the solution of a problem entails that a sense of problem gives way to its opposite: a sense of nonproblem, or a problem now gone. The manifestation of a moral, that is, a character's or the reader's perception at a given point in the text that a recognizable meaning has emerged, necessarily implies that the felt absence of a moral (thesis) is replaced by a sense that a moral is now present (antithesis). Also encapsulation, the "coda that distances the reader from the story by altering the point of view or summarizing the passing of time" (12), involves a movement from one clearly defined position (thesis) to another equally clearly defined position (antithesis); for instance, as concerns time, a sudden leap from time x to time y means a movement to time non-x. Or, when the perspective shifts from person x to person y, we similarly have a movement from person x to person non-x. As for evaluation as a marker of closure, the same principle applies: mental and/or emotional response replaces absence of same. In other words, yet again a movement takes place —conceptually speaking—from thesis to its antithesis.

Gerlach mentions the following as examples of antithetical closure: "If the story passes from positive to negative or vice versa, from down to up, if a character changes from hating to loving something or someone" (10). These are indeed cases of antithetical reversal, but as I have shown, so are the narrative developments suggested by the *other* signals on his list. Hence, there is need for a term that distinguishes between the form of conceptual movement specifically identified as antithetical by Gerlach and those forms implied in the other closural signals he identifies. A suitable new name for this particular form of antithetical narrative movement would seem to be *emotional* and/or *cognitive reversal*.

Gerlach lists *circularity*—the return to an aspect of the beginning at the end of the story—as *one* of several antithetical closural markers (10).[5] It seems to me this is one closural signal that does *not* follow an antithetical pattern. Admittedly, even circularity suggests a movement away before the return, and often there will be some change in narrative circumstance so that circularity in narration seldom implies a return to status quo. As Valerie Shaw reminds us, one of the oldest principles of narrative is repetition with alteration, playing variations on initial scenes or situations (75). But circularity still describes a narrative movement notably different from those implied by the other closural markers, and it therefore ought to be given the status of a separate analytical category.

My last suggestion for a revision of Gerlach's closural categories concerns *encapsulation,* which Gerlach describes as occurring when a given point of view is suddenly altered or when a story concludes with a noticeable jump in time. A classic example would be the ending of Stephen Crane's "The Blue Hotel," in which on the last page there is a marked leap in time ("Months later . . .") as well as a change of, if not point of view in the traditional sense, then of focalization: from the perspective of the omniscient narrator in the preceding section reporting the grim circumstances of the Swede's death to the joint perspective of easterner and cowboy, when the author brings them together one last time to talk over their experiences at the Blue Hotel. *The Oxford English Dictionary* gives the following meaning for the verb "to encapsulate": "To enclose (as) in a capsule. Also *fig.,* to summarize or isolate as if in a capsule."[6] One may appreciate the metaphorical aptness of that description as used by Gerlach, but I prefer the term *perspectival shift.* Such a change of name would better accommodate a related form of closure not discussed by Gerlach, the *gradual* shift of narrative focus at the story's end, which seems to have become increasingly frequent in contemporary short stories. In these cases there is no change in point of view in that the focalizer stays the same, and time is not an essential factor. Nevertheless, a notable change of perspective marks that the narrative may now come to a halt.

An example of this type of closure occurs in Carol Shields's story "Purple Blooms." Simone Vauthier says of Shields's ending that "closure is enacted in the process of disappearance" (125). The first-person narrator is waiting in line in a park to have a copy of the book *Purple Blooms* signed by its fictional author. As she is waiting, she begins to read a different book of poetry, gradually forgetting the people around her. The last sentence of the story reads, "The bowling green fades into dimness, as do the benches and the magnolia tree and the gravel path, until all that's left is a page of print, a line of type, a word, a dot of ink, a shadow on the retina that is no bigger, I believe, than the smallest violet in the woods." The process of disappearance is rendered in terms that bring to mind a camera zooming in, "first in the (fictive) outside world, then in the fictive reader's eye, where the system of visual signs that make up the printed page shrinks to a single line, a dot, and lastly, a shadow" on the narrator's retina.[7]

A similar effect is achieved in texts wherein "the camera" moves gradually *away* from the scene, as in Bobbie Ann Mason's "Shiloh." The focalizer throughout the story is Leroy Moffitt, hence there is no change in point of view at the end as required in Gerlach's concept of encapsulation. Leroy has taken his wife, Norma Jean, to the historic site of Shiloh, Tennessee, a famous battleground during the Civil War, in response to the repeated urgings of Mable, his mother-in-law, that they ought to go where she had gone for her honeymoon. Ironically, Norma Jean chooses this site to announce her decision to ask for divorce, and then begins to physically walk away from their picnic site. Gradually she is becoming a blurred figure in Leroy's vision: "Norma Jean is far away, walking rapidly toward the bluff by the river, and he tries to hobble toward her. . . . Now she turns toward Leroy and waves her arms. Is she beckoning to him? She seems to be doing an exercise for her chest muscles. The sky is unusually pale—the color of the dust ruffle Mable made for their bed" (16). A third variant of this kind of closural marker is the enumeration at the end of Donald Barthelme's "The Indian Uprising." The narrator is brought before the Indian "Clemency Committee" and is asked to remove his belt and shoelaces, which he does: "I removed my belt and shoelaces and looked (rain shattering from a great height the prospects of silence and clear, neat rows of houses in the subdivisions) into their savage black eyes, paint, feathers, beads" (114).

The closural force of these endings is rather weak. We encounter this form of closure most frequently in stories that explore the artistic possibilities inherent in open-endedness, stories that point more resolutely than others to a future outside the text. But even open-ended stories must be brought to a narrative end point that marks that "this story ends here." Perspectival shift, then, be it sudden or gradual, marks closure in this way. However, possibly due to the weak closural impact of the latter, we will often find that it occurs in concert with other markers of closure. Embedded in the endings of both "Purple Blooms" and "Shiloh" is circularity, a return to the beginnings of the two stories. As Simone Vauthier points out, "the terminal image [of "Purple Blooms"] sends us back to the title. . . . We have slowly moved from the florid title with its off-colour suggestiveness to its attenuation in the most shrinking of flowers in the woods and the most modest flower of speech, the comparison, which nevertheless draws attention to the artificiality of storytelling" (125). The opening lines of "Shiloh" comically read: "Leroy Moffitt's wife, Norma Jean, is working on her pectorals. She lifts three-pound dumbbells to warm up, then progresses to a twenty-pound barbell. Standing with her legs apart, she reminds Leroy of Wonder Woman" (1). Comedy aside, in the context of the story, the calisthenic motif suggests that Leroy's wife has started to take charge of her own life, making it *hers* rather than his, as it were; the return to this motif at the end of the story helps to mark the completion of this process. In Barthelme's story the threat of imminent danger implied by the enumeration ("their savage black eyes, paint, feathers, beads") suggests that the Indian Uprising ends in victory for the "savages" (natural termination). However, a sense of closure is undermined in this story by the confusing information that it is the *Clemency* Committee that asks him to remove belt and shoelaces (prior to imprisonment?), as well as by the long, contextually nonsensical parenthesis about the rain "shattering from a great height the prospects of silence and clear, neat rows of houses in the subdivisions." Barthelme, antifictionist par excellence, is obviously making elaborate play here with traditional expectations concerning narrative closure.

Summing up, then, my alternative to Gerlach's list of closural narrative categories looks like this:

- solution of the central problem
- natural termination
- emotional and/or cognitive reversal
- circularity
- manifestation of a moral
- evaluation
- perspectival shift

Narrative versus Hermeneutic Closure

Gerlach's categories are first of all useful in that they sharpen our awareness of how stories progress *on the level of plot.* But as he himself is aware, *narrative* closure is not necessarily the same as *thematic* or *ideational* closure (16), even though for certain stories (frequently the less artistically sophisticated ones?) the two types of closure will seem inseparable. It is probably also the case that some of the closural markers discussed above lend themselves more readily than others to thematic as well as narrative closure; manifestation of a moral seems the most obvious candidate, with evaluation and emotional and/or cognitive reversal as potential runners-up. However, for a high number of texts—and this will apply far more frequently to twentieth-century than to nineteenth-century stories—the story line may have been brought to a logical end point, but the type of ending provided may either point beyond the text itself to further developments and/or force the reader back into the text to ponder the meaning inherent in the particular forms of closure at hand. The ultimate demise of Melville's Bartleby brings a long series of denials on this character's part to a rational close, but the circumstances of his death, lying fetuslike facing the walls of the prison garden, coupled with the narrator's "Ah, Bartleby! Ah, humanity!" force the reader back into the story to reflect once more on the reasons for his many refusals to participate in life. The nameless couple boarding the train at the end of Hemingway's "Hills Like White Elephants" brings a period of waiting to a close through natural termination, but even though the arrival of the train brings an end to their present quarrel, one realizes that this is only for the while and does not in any way resolve, or close, the emotional and ideational ramifications of the underlying conflict.

Only when we arrive at an understanding of the true import of the events and situations described in a story, the larger significance of the more or less intricate figures in the textual carpet, do we achieve a genuine sense of having brought matters to rest. Gerlach does not develop any categories for this type of closure in his study; in a forthcoming book I hope to remedy that situation somewhat by suggesting some of my own, while bearing in mind that there is no way in which one can hope to exhaust the many possibilities for closure on the deeper levels of understanding in fictional texts, be they short or long. However, as a first necessary step in an attempt to clarify the issue further, I propose to use the term *narrative* closure about the kind of closure that Gerlach concentrates on, and *hermeneutic* closure about the other kind. In her study of closure at the level of sentence in short stories, Susan Lohafer has coined a related, though not quite parallel, set of terms. In discussing the ways in which individual sentences in a story accomplish—or fail to accomplish—closure, in *Coming to Terms* she introduces the terms "physical closure" (the end of a sentence, a paragraph, a story), "immediate cognitive closure" (understanding the surface meaning of a sentence), and "deferred cognitive closure" to describe a delayed "understanding of the full significance of these words in this story" (43). These are sensible distinctions; applied to whole texts rather than at the level of sentence, one will, of course, find that hermeneutic closure will usually be deferred rather than immediate. When I adopt the term "hermeneutic closure" in lieu of Lohafer's set of coinages, I do so because it more readily connotes the kind of systematic analytical activity usually necessary to achieve closure on this level. One route to hermeneutic closure when reading short fiction will often be to trace the patterns of narrative closure in the text.

Closural Signals versus Closural Markers

I would like to propose one further refinement of Gerlach's conceptual framework. One important step in the process of recognizing closure is to respond to prior warnings that closure is imminent, or at least possible. For a reader to identify a text element as marking closure, the text must signal at some point that closure will or may follow. If this was not the case, one would not be able to perceive closure in the first place: for someone to see a textual development as the *end* of something, one must also be aware of a *beginning*. In his study Gerlach most frequently employs the term closural signal for those elements of text that bring narrative matters to a rest. On occasion he varies this phrase and uses "marker of closure" instead,[8] but he uses these terms interchangeably and does not differentiate between them conceptually. I want to suggest that it will often benefit the careful reader to distinguish between, on the one hand, closural *signals*, and, on the other, closural *markers*. In such a scheme the term "closural signal" could be used to identify a textual element that anticipates or *promises* one form of closure or another (i.e., a narrative motif that *signals* closural potential), whereas "closural marker" might be reserved for that narrative element that *delivers* on that promise. An example of a closural signal in this modified sense of the term would be the early mention in "Hills Like White Elephants" that the train is due in forty minutes; the arrival of that train is a closural marker (here, a marker of natural termination).

I have found a distinction of this kind to be of considerable help as concerns my own understanding of how closure operates in short fiction and have also discovered that examining carefully the distribution and interaction of closural signals and markers may frequently be a useful analytical tool. The procedure I follow is to tag potential closural signals as I spot them and then watch for the actual closing of that signal. The mention of the impending train in the first paragraph of "Hills" would be tagged closural *signal*$_1$ (cs$_1$), and the corresponding closural *marker* (the train's arrival) would be tagged closural *marker*$_1$ (cm$_1$). The next closural signal (in this case, the girl describing the mountains as "white elephants") would be identified as cs$_2$, while the slowly emerging identification of the girl's pregnancy as an element in the story's narrative grid (the prospect of a child *is* a white elephant in the sense of being an unwelcome gift, at least for the man) receives the tag cm$_2$, and so on. The girl's communicating her mental image of white elephants to the man is perceived as a closural signal here because it is striking, and in that sense "open," begging to be "closed." In a larger format, like a novel, a similar observation on the part of a protagonist might more easily be assumed to simply play a decorative role with low semantic content. In a brief text, however, as in the present story, readership expectations will more readily imbue images of this kind with a strong closural potential, especially since it also provides the title for the short story. Some texts will yield a high number of cs-cm combinations, and others are remarkably bare in terms of closure—which in itself often turns out to be an aesthetically and/or thematically significant fact.

Preclosure

The distinction between closural signals and closural markers necessitates the introduction of still another category with considerable analytical potential: *preclosure*. I borrow the term from Susan Lohafer's discourse analysis–inspired reader-response experiment, wherein she asked a group of students to identify those sentences before the actual ending in a short story by Kate Chopin where the author might logically have concluded her story.[9] Part of the purpose behind the experiment was to find out how differently schooled groups of students would "process" the story. In other words, Lohafer wanted to discover to what extent variations in familiarity with the workings of fictional texts would prompt readers into assessing closural possibilities differently. My concern is not reader response in any general sense; rather, my objective is to suggest a methodology whereby the individual reader may become better aware of how she or he is responding to a text in question on the level of narrative, which may in turn yield a better understanding of, and also augment confidence in, one's own interpretational work. A certain difference in analytical focus notwithstanding, Lohafer's work on preclosure suggested to me the usefulness of the following amplification of my cs-cm model of analysis: the term *pre*closural marker (pcm) could be used to refer to any sentence suggesting closure (narrative as well as hermeneutic) *prior* to the actual ending of the story. When one tags a text element as a closural signal, there is, of course, no way of knowing whether that signal will be closed at the end of the story or somewhere along the way (i.e., cs$_n$ followed by pcm$_n$ rather than cm$_n$). Frequently the latter will be the case.

When a closural signal is closed along the way rather than at the end of the story, this may give rise to a multiplicity of interpretational possibilities; one of the most prominent ones is a likely shift in thematic significance *away* from that contained in the preclosural marker, putting into sharper relief the actual ending that *is* chosen. In "Hills Like White Elephants," then, cs_2 ("white elephants") is actually followed by a preclosural marker (pcm_2) rather than a closural marker in that the connection between the girl's mental image of the mountains as white elephants and the unborn baby emerges *before* the end of the story. This does not reduce the importance of the impending abortion (presumably on arrival in Madrid, the destination of the awaited train) as an element of plot; however, it reinforces the interpretation that abortion as an ethical concern is *not* the central issue of the story.

Yet another effect of this instance of preclosure is that it helps to foreground the suitability of the setting that Hemingway chose for the story: a train station. The conversation between the couple might with equal plausibility have taken place in a hospital waiting room, with the nurse's "Next, please" serving as a suitable closural marker of natural termination, but that would have limited the author's closural options. For one thing, the setting Hemingway chose allows him to add a barroom element to the scene, yielding quite logically yet another closural signal: mindless and automatic drinking (cs_3). The girl's opening line is, "What should we drink?" In the course of the couple's brief stay in the station, they go through an ample amount, paying considerable attention along the way to brand names and the temperature of the beer. Potentially, drinking in this manner would serve to bring about an emotional reaction of some sort, be it jollity or the opposite, but as is so often the case with Hemingway, no such emotional reaction is discernible in the text. In other words, in this case closural signal is *not* followed by a narrative closural marker; cs_3 is simply *not* succeeded by an easily identifiable pcm_3 or cm_3. The anaesthetic release that the couple obviously seek in their drinking ("That's all we do, isn't it—look at things and try new drinks?") does not occur. Which ties in with yet another aspect of the train station setting. We learn that the couple's suitcase is full of tags from all the hotels where they had spent the night; the setting underscores the fact that this man and woman are spiritual drifters, between destinations, always waiting for a new train. They emerge as yet another Hemingwayian Lost Generation couple, uncertain of their values, fighting existential malaise through restless traveling and interminable drinking.

Even though the ending of the story gives us two closural markers in concert—the arrival of the train (natural termination) and the girl's final line ("I feel fine," which marks [ironic] solution of the central problem)—the narrative turn of events in no way closes the story thematically. As is so often the case with twentieth-century short stories, narrative closure fails to provide hermeneutic closure. In fact, hermeneutic closing of this story can begin only after one recognizes that narrative closure stands in ironic opposition to thematic closure. A tracking of the distribution of closural signals and the corresponding preclosural and closural markers (or absence of such) serves to bring this out. Drinking, we have seen, offers no release (cs_3 not followed by pcm_3/cm_3). Another closural signal is the couple's bickering (cs_4), creating an anticipation in the reader that cognitive and/or emotional reversal may follow. We have seen that the reference to white elephants (cs_2) is followed by a preclosural rather than a closural marker, shifting attention away from the abortion as the most central reason for their dissension. We begin to understand that their basic problem, making true human communication so hard for them to achieve, is an existential unease springing from a general failure to affirm values at large, not only those involved in a decision on whether to have an abortion. Hermeneutic closure in this story hinges on the recognition that a real cm_4 (end of bickering) *fails* to materialize. The girl apparently yields on the matter of the abortion, but this is surface cognitive reversal only. Even though the man appears to have won the battle over whether to have the "very simple" operation, the closural patterns of the story reveal this to be a Pyrrhic victory. Right before the train arrives he goes into the barroom and orders one last anis. Earlier on in the story the girl has forged a conceptual link between this drink and absinthe, a drink strongly associated with quasi-bohemian escapism and self-destruction.[10] As the man is consuming his anis, he observes that the other passengers—they, too, "were drinking"—are "waiting reasonably" for the train to come, obviously a reflection caused by the girl's failure to do precisely this. As he returns to the woman before they board the train, however, she is once again "reasonable" and smiling. But the ubiquitous pattern of ironic closures that the story has provided serves to warn us that the apparent emotional and cognitive reversal (cm_4) suggested by the girl's "I feel fine" is strongly ironic. Her newfound reasonableness is not productive: the decision to have the abortion bespeaks a willingness to embrace physical infertility, but a wider spiritual infertility is also implied in that the future life for the couple promises little else than more hotels, more train stations, and more anis-induced forgetfulness.

By way of conclusion I would like to make clear that I am not claiming for this procedure a revolutionary status in the sense of it always generating radically new knowledge about, or insight into, short fiction texts. Some of the conclusions about texts drawn on the basis of this methodology will appear rather obvious, even tautological. Also, some those points one ends up making, one also would have been able to arrive at via more traditional interpretational routes. However, I do find that a methodical tagging of closural signals and markers *can* be hermeneutically productive in that it allows one to trace connections and patterns—narrative as well as thematic—that one might otherwise have missed, or else might have been slower in spotting. And not at all infrequently, one does experience that the insights gained *do* come in the form of genuine discoveries. Thus, closural tagging in the manner suggested here provides an analytical tool that may serve as a valuable supplement to already existing analytical procedures.

Notes

1. Gerlach here adopts the central terms that Barbara H. Smith employs in her definition of closure. Gerlach, *Toward the End*, 8; Smith, *Poetic Closure*, 2.

2. I emphasize that we are talking of *narrative* closure here, which is Gerlach's main concern. Further on I shall make a distinction between narrative and hermeneutic closure; as for the latter, closural possibilities are legion and no list can hope to be exhaustive.

3. Discourse analysts list *evaluation* as one of the standard categories of narrative in everyday communication, others being *setting, complication, resolution,* and *coda* or *moral;* see van Dijk, *Macrostructures,* 112–15.

4. "The grass of many years has sprung up and withered on that grave, the burial stone is moss-grown, and good Mr. Hooper's face is dust; but awful is still the thought that it mouldered beneath the Black Veil!"

5. This closural marker is sometimes given other names. Simone Vauthier calls it "repetition" (126); Helmut Bonheim uses a term from classical rhetoric, *epanalepsis,* which he describes in the following manner: "an element which begins a clause, sentence, paragraph, or larger unit of discourse is repeated at the end. The obvious example is a repetition of the title of the work" (144).

6. http://dictionary.oed.com/cgi/entry/00074544 (accessed February 5, 2002).

7. Vauthier, *Reverberations,* 125.

8. For example, on page 10.

9. See Lohafer, "Preclosure and Story Processing."

10. The drink, which was originally produced in France by Pernod, was banned in France in 1915. The oil from wormwood, which gave the drink its bitter taste, contained a poison found to be harmful to the human nervous system. (Source: *Aschehoug og Gyldendals store norske leksikon.*) The girl in the story laments (irony again) the fact that the drink is no longer available and that one has to settle for anis as a substitute.

Works Cited

Anderson, Sherwood. "I Want to Know Why." In *The Triumph of the Egg,* 5–20. New York: B. W. Huebsch, 1921.

Barthelme, Donald. "The Indian Uprising." In *Sixty Stories,* 108–14. New York: Putnam, 1981.

Bonheim, Helmut. *The Narrative Modes: Techniques of the Short Story.* Cambridge, U.K.: D. S. Brewer, 1982.

Gerlach, John. *Toward the End: Closure and Structure in the American Short Story.* Tuscaloosa: University of Alabama Press, 1985.

Hemingway, Ernest. "Hills Like White Elephants." In *The Short Stories of Ernest Hemingway: The First Forty-nine Stories and the Play "The Fifth Column,"* 371–76. New York: Modern Library, 1938.

Lohafer, Susan. *Coming to Terms with the Short Story.* Baton Rouge: Louisiana State University Press, 1983.

———. "Preclosure and Story Processing." In *Short Story Theory at a Crossroads,* edited by Susan Lohafer and Jo Ellyn Clarey, 249–75. Baton Rouge: Louisiana State University Press, 1989.

Mason, Bobbie Ann. "Shiloh." In *Shiloh and Other Stories,* 1–16. New York: Harper and Row, 1982.

Shaw, Valerie. *The Short Story: A Critical Introduction.* London: Longman, 1983.

Smith, Barbara Herrnstein. *Poetic Closure: A Study of How Poems End.* Chicago: University of Chicago Press, 1968.

Van Dijk, Teun A. *Macrostructures: An Interdisciplinary Study of Global Structures in Discourse, Interaction, and Cognition.* Hillsdale, N.J.: Erlbaum, 1980.

Vauthier, Simone. *Reverberations: Explorations in the Canadian Short Story.* Concord, Ontario: Anansi, 1993.

The Illustrated Short Story

Toward a Typology

Stuart Sillars

Between 1891 and 1900 the first issues of a new kind of magazine were published. *The Strand Magazine,* and its less well known followers—*Cassell's,* the *Windsor,* the *English Illustrated Magazine*—appeared every month and achieved a total sale of around one and a half million copies.[1] Although they contained factual articles, interviews, and sometimes poetry and reproductions of fashionable paintings, their main content was short fiction. Rather than offering serial parts of longer fiction, as did Dickens's *Household Words* and *All the Year Round,* the magazines published single stories or self-contained episodes involving the same characters. Generally eight or ten pages in length, the stories were of a wide range—the detective stories, including those of Conan Doyle, for which the *Strand* is most remembered; stories reflecting political and social issues; stories written specifically for women; and stories for children. Like the daily papers of the so-called new journalism, they were aimed at a new readership that had been nourished by a range of social forces—the Education Act of 1870, rapid growth in printing technology, the distribution networks developed with the railways, and the need for an army of clerks, administrators, and "lady typewriters" in the burgeoning commercial centers. Sales figures, even where available, do not, of course, record total readership. Researchers into popular newspaper readership suggest a "multiplier" of four or five, so that we probably need to consider a total readership of six or seven million, at a time when the population of England and Wales was around forty million. The figure becomes more significant when it is recalled that, in November 1908, the *New Age,* the journal that began publishing Katherine Mansfield's short stories in 1910, "claimed a circulation of 21,205."[2] Even allowing a similar multiplier for this smaller journal, the readership of the new illustrated stories was clearly many times that of the now more celebrated publication. Yet despite their popularity, such magazines are almost completely ignored in serious studies of popular fiction.

    These stories interest me for a series of related reasons. The relationship between text and illustration represents a significant difference from that established in the far better known illustrated sketches and serial novels of the 1830s and 1840s, as revealed in the pioneering study by John Harvey.[3] Exploring this relationship allows us to ask significant questions about how the process of reading was actually carried on by a significant and largely overlooked group of the reading public—one, indeed, that was largely shunned by the intellectuals, if we are to believe John Carey's view of the period.[4] I would argue that this difference is related not so much to the divergence in educational background and sophistication between the two readerships as to changes in the rhetoric of the images, and the reading situation in which it was received. Instead of taking a month or a fortnight to decode the elaborate symbolism of an illustration by Phiz [Hablot Knight Browne] or George Cattermole, turn-of-the-century readers looked quickly at the image to assimilate signs of narrative, character, or setting, for a reason that is largely contextual. These short stories were read in a short time, and very often in railway trains: the reading process has become a consequence of shifts in patterns of balance between living and working.

I touched on this material in an earlier study[5] but was unable to explore there a topic that I should now like to look at: the typology of text and illustration, in particular the relation that it sets up between reader and text and the very specific temporal pattern that it establishes—something that might be termed a mystery of reading to balance the mystery of writing. I do this more in the spirit of asking questions than of trying to find answers—that word "toward" in my title allows me to retreat from suggestions as much as to make them. Yet there are ways in which, by exploring the relation between text and image, some of these questions might, at least, be a little more clearly defined and explored.

Any typology of illustration must incorporate several dimensions, and I should like to suggest a taxonomy of these. At the most practical level are the selection of the moment for illustration and the physical placement of the image within the printed text. The relation between illustration and text, in terms of how the verbal is moved across into the visual, or what the visual adds to the verbal, is fundamental to the consideration of each individual image. In a larger sequence, two other elements are as insistent as they are inseparable: the temporal dimension that is engendered during the story as a whole and the way in which the control of the story's dynamic is poised between verbal and visual elements. And finally, there is the notion of the reader's experience of the story, fundamental to which are questions of style and viewpoint within illustrations just as much as verbal discourse.

The selection of the moment for illustration is one that causes uncertainty not only here but also in any discussion of the illustrated novel. We know from the correspondence between Dickens and Cruikshank that in their case the writer selected the moment, and the two discussed the treatment in considerable detail, but little evidence survives in other cases.[6] As far as the illustrated magazines are concerned, I would suggest that two physical imperatives superseded aesthetic considerations. First, the policy of having one illustration on every page—or at least on every page opening—significantly increased the number of illustrations. As I shall later suggest, this may have had something to do with one of the most striking temporal elements of the dual text of the story. The second one is a little more arcane, relating to the size and location of plates within the large stereotype plate from which sixteen or thirty-two pages would be printed. Clearly, an excessive number of illustrations, and a large number near the edges of the plate, would weaken it and cause production difficulties. This has a dynamic effect on the relation between text and illustration. Instead of having to be printed separately, on inserted sheets often of a different weight of paper—as in the serial fictions of the 1830s—illustrations could be presented as "cuts," interspersed with the printed text at more or less any chosen point, within the constraint mentioned above, and thus the visual relationship, the *mise-en-page*, is wholly different, allowing for more interdependence between word and image and a more continuous reading process.

The typology of illustration, or the theoretical basis that may be postulated for the dual text these stories constitute, must, then, be broad enough to encompass the nature and function of the illustrations themselves, their combined function with the verbal text in producing a dual text, and the series of relationships that they engender with the reader. Here we might begin by looking at the relation between text and reader. Perhaps the simplest and most direct model of reading is that offered by Meyer Schapiro in his discussions of medieval illustrations of the Bible.[7] This erects a binary typology between those images of figures that are presented in dialogic relationship with each other, and thus present a dramatic scene to which the reader is audience, and those that look directly out toward us, looking us in the face, as it were, and in which we become more direct participants.

In the materialist short story—the story in which the physical forms and appearances of things, "the way the cushion bulged between the button," as Virginia Woolf puts it, become the primary concern[8]—one might well expect the former to predominate, and this indeed is the case. But in other instances figures look directly at us, over the heads of the characters in both verbal and visual texts. Interestingly, this happens most often in comic or satirical stories or those intended for children—for example, the images by Will Owen from stories by W. W. Jacobs or the illustrations of H. R. Millar to Edith Nesbit's *Five Children and It*. Some readers might suggest that these images produce a dual discourse in which a postmodern metafictionality is apparent, but I would prefer to see them as part of an ironic self-awareness that has been part of the discourse of the novel—both with and without illustration—in a tradition that stretches back a long way and is most immediately apparent in Laurence Sterne and Henry Fielding. However, the absence of "direct address" images in such texts implies that involvement in the fictive world of the story, not a questioning distance from it (in either aesthetic or moral terms), is basic.

So much for the individual relation with the onlooker. Any typology at this level might also, of course, be expected to include elements of style and viewpoint, and this is something to which I shall return shortly. But for the moment I would like to consider an aspect that is closely related: that of the way in which verbal and visual text work together in constructing narrative. In "The Rhetoric of the Image" (38–41), Roland Barthes offers some possibilities that may be helpful. He finds two categories of relation between text and image: anchorage and relay. Within extended narrative structures, the difference is valuable if we look at it in temporal terms. Anchorage (in which a text delimits the signification of the image, like a caption to a photograph or a strap line to an advertisement) can be said either to be static or to look backward in summarizing a situation; relay (where image and text complement each other to form part of a higher syntagmatic system) can be seen as primarily proleptic in function. This division certainly allows us to classify some illustrations in a relationship of anchorage and others in one of relay. But, that said, I am unsure what this would achieve. If, however, we combine these elements with Barthes's narrative categories of "functions" and "indices," we might arrive at something a little more valuable. "Functions" are concerned with events of plot, "nuclei" or "cardinal functions" denoting major changes of event and "catalysers" operating at a lower level in facilitating such changes. "Indices" again come in two forms, "indices proper" giving fundamental data on a character or setting and "informants" qualifying or amplifying that already given. Placing each moment of text and illustration as a "function," "nucleus," or "catalyser" would go beyond pigeonholing; it would assist in making clear the workings of the dual text.

If we add these elements together, we might arrive at a new procedure for analyzing what individual illustrations do in the course of a story. An illustration at the head of a story would most often be in a relationship of anchorage to its text—either with its short caption or, more interestingly, with the whole of the story if it was a character study or reflective image. An image depicting an event in the story would stand in the relationship of relay with the verbal text and would either record a major event (acting as a Barthesian function) or offer subtler modification by revealing new information on character or setting, or qualifying that which we already have. This may— I stress the concessive rather than the indicative—offer us a new analytical model for the dual discourse of the illustrated text.

This leads me to the most striking aspect of the use of illustration, which is fundamental to the typology that I am moving toward. Whatever the reason for the selection of moment, and whoever took the decision on this—artist, illustrator, or editor —the placement of illustrations in the great majority of stories follows a simple principle. The episodes of the story almost invariably appear significantly earlier in illustrations than they do in the verbal text. The distance of anticipation varies between half a page and about a page and a half, but most often it hovers around the length of a single page. At first sight, this may appear to be a rather arbitrary decision, based on practical needs, but it has one very important result in terms of the reading structure of the stories. Each story presented in this way is offered in a double narrative, the first a series of episodes read in the illustrations, the second in the verbal text. The reader is offered an implication of what will happen later alongside the text of the present events, and this is confirmed when the passage illustrated is read. This changes and, I would argue, enriches the reading experience. First, it makes the process of reading simpler—and this is important for those readers to whom reading is still a novelty, sometimes a difficult one—by suggesting future action. Second, it gives the reader a kind of superior knowledge, which we may equate with that of the author or omniscient narrator, in knowing to some degree what will happen in a few paragraphs' time. It may also—and I am by no means convinced about this—imbue the reading experience with something of the nature of the retelling of a folktale or traditional narrative, the shared experience that binds a culture together in a manner rarely found in a society founded on literacy. Leaving this aside, the process of what we might call "visual narrative implication" allows far greater identification in the reader with the characters and events, a sense of belonging to the fictive world, which increases as the story goes on and which is particularly appropriate to the materialist fiction of the sort that dominates in these magazines. The populist idea of losing oneself in a good book is given rather greater force by this method of enfolding the reader proleptically into the story's growth.

This process may be seen at work in a story that appeared in the first issue of the *Harmsworth Magazine* of July 1898 (pp. 11–16) and that follows clearly the typology established in the *Strand* seven years earlier: "The Golden Circlet," by Charles Kennett Burrow, with illustrations by Ralph Peacock. The first illustration appears at the top left of the first page, with the caption "He ventured to glance out."[9] This introduces a character and a setting, both familiarly metropolitan for the original reader; it also thrusts us forward, enlisting our curiosity as a dynamic to make us read further. That his glance out into the street also leads us across to the printed text of the story enhances this dynamic in a more tangible way. Among the questions that this illustration prompts are, Who is the man? And why and where is he hiding? We are given the answers by the time we reach in the text the phrase that has already been used for the caption, but we do not do this until the end of the penultimate paragraph of the page. On the next page we are offered an image showing two men and a woman seated in what, from our knowledge of the story so far, we assume to be a row of stalls in a theater, with the caption "'You are forgiven,' she said, sweetly." When we have read almost to the foot of the second column of this page, we can contextualize this: the man, known to us from the first illustration and now identified by the text as Herbert Annesley, has neglected the lady for the past six months because he has been working on a play. Already our eyes are drawn to the next illustration, at the foot of

THE GOLDEN CIRCLET.

A COMPLETE STORY BY CHARLES KENNETT BURROW.

Illustrated by Ralph Peacock.

"HE VENTURED TO
GLANCE OUT."

A NNESLEY walked past the main entrance to the Century Theatre in the curious condition of one who is able partly to regard himself from the outside. The boards were placarded with the announcement of a new play, to be produced that day week, "The Golden Circlet," by Conrad Howe. Now Annesley and Conrad Howe were the same person; but it was difficult to convince the former, who had worked so deadly hard and failed so often, that the latter was now within sight of what might prove a great success. Annesley saw people stop to look at the announcement and read his other name, with a feeling that he was almost guilty of a serious misdemeanour; he was taking them, as it were, at a disadvantage; he was almost inclined to tap one elderly gentleman on the shoulder and assure him that no harm was intended to him or any one else.

The secret of the authorship of "The Golden Circlet" had been well kept. Only three people were in the know, and not one of these was a woman. Annesley therefore felt safe. He had assumed another name because his own had brought him no luck; he imagined people shrugging shoulders and wagging wise heads; he could hear the murmur,— "What! Annesley still writing plays? If he hadn't wasted his time over that, he might have had some money left. What a fool the man is!" Annesley had therefore put down the pen and Conrad Howe had taken it up. Moreover, Conrad Howe had actually written a play which seemed to have in it the elements of popularity; hence newspaper paragraphs, discussions as to identity, and finally the fixing of the first night and the appearance of the posters.

"The Golden Circlet" represented six months' grinding work. He had practically shut himself away from the world. He had declined invitations, paid no calls, risked everything on a last throw. When the thing was finished it seemed like coming into fresh air again; he remembered people whose names he had almost forgotten, and above all a girl whom he had told himself it might be wiser to forget; and, while his passionate working fit was on, he had almost succeeded, seeing her only as a possibility at the beginning of success. It is wonderful what hard work may do for a man, for a time. But when the pause comes human nature must always have its backward glance, its old heart searchings, its reviving pains.

Annesley, then, stood watching the entrance to the Century Theatre, and, as he stood there, suddenly his heart commenced a wild stampede. He slipped into the doorway of a shop just in time to escape the eyes of a girl who was walking quickly up the Strand. He waited for a moment; she did not pass. After a time he ventured to glance out; she had left the theatre, and was disappearing in the crowd.

His first impulse was to overtake her and make a clean breast of everything, but a moment's reflection convinced him that, having restrained himself so far, it would be folly to make a doubtful step then. Connie Bolitho had probably no idea that Conrad Howe was a cloak for Herbert Annesley, and he saw an opportunity for a little comedy not to be neglected. Since his position had grown stronger he felt free to indulge his humours; a year before life had seemed all tragedy, with a diminishing banking account, and a

Charles Kennett Burrow's "The Golden Circlet" appeared in the July 1898 issue of Harmsworth Magazine. From the collection of Stuart Sillars.

sheaf of unpaid bills. He walked carelessly up to the box-office.

"Did a lady take seats a moment ago; a lady with a red hat and fur-trimmed cloak?"

"Pretty?" asked the clerk.

"Very pretty," said Annesley.

"Yes,—two stalls."

"Two!" said Annesley, with an inner question in the word. "Are the next seats engaged—the ones, I mean, on either side of those two?"

The man looked at the plan.

"No," he said.

"Book them to me, please."

"'YOU ARE FORGIVEN,' SHE SAID, SWEETLY."

The clerk smiled benignly as he handed the tickets to Annesley; the life in a box-office is dull during business hours.

Annesley walked away with his tickets, feeling that he had done a good morning's work. He had at any rate made sure of a seat near Miss Bolitho; if her companion were a man he must brace himself to eclipse that fortunate individual; if a woman, it did not matter. He would prefer the woman, for in six months a great deal might have happened. Miss Bolitho was not bound to him in any way; they had seemed to understand each other, but a struggling writer with only debts to his credit, had not dared to lay those debts and a doubtful future at his lady's feet.

During the next week Annesley's time was fully occupied, but when the great day

came and the final rehearsal was over he had a few hours in which to feel that almost unendurable excitement which precedes an ordeal the result of which is not in our own hands. His part of the work was over, but would the actors rise to theirs? He believed they would, but belief is a poor support when so much depends upon it. His excitement was also doubled by the prospect of watching the effect of his work on Miss Bolitho.

Annesley reached the theatre five minutes before the curtain rose. The house was full; the gallery seethed like a hive, people were already standing at the back of the pit. A glance showed him that Miss Bolitho was there, with a man whom he had never seen before at her side. He made his way quickly to his seat and was there before she had observed him.

"You are as interested in plays as ever?" he asked.

"Mr. Annesley!" she cried. He was sure that the hand she gave him trembled a little.

"May I ask you to forgive me for the past six months? I've been working terribly hard, almost night and day."

"At a play?"

"Yes,—at a play."

"You are forgiven," she said sweetly, "because you are brave and stick to your ideals."

"I am rewarded," he murmured. A glance at her face assured him that her beauty was not less; that, at any rate, had remained unchanged.

"Do you know who this Mr. Conrad Howe is?"

"No one seems to know; his identity has been kept secret most successfully."

"Do you suppose it is not his real name?"

"I have an idea it isn't; it sounds assumed, doesn't it?"

"I'm not sure. What do you think,

Tom? Let me introduce you to Mr. Annesley,—my cousin, Captain Bolitho, who is just home from India." They bowed severely to each other.

"We were discussing," said Connie, cheerfully, "whether Conrad Howe was a real or a pen name. What do you think?"

"I don't know anything about these writing Johnnies. I don't see why they shouldn't use their own names unless they're ashamed of them."

"Perhaps you don't quite understand, Tom," Miss Bolitho suggested.

"Perhaps I don't!" said Tom.

"The climate of India is so trying," Miss Bolitho whispered to Annesley.

"It must be," he said, smiling.

The orchestra glided into a slow movement and the curtain rose. I need not tell you the story of the play; it was simple, but intensely human, having in it the philosophy learnt in years of struggle, but always with hope and faith in the ultimate good beyond. It presented no problem of the gutter raised to drawing-room standard by meretricious gilding; it had the singular distinction of being perfectly clean and also entirely dramatic. As Annesley saw his work develop before his eyes, and felt how it was taking hold of a breathless audience, he did not grudge the experience that had gone to its making or regret that he had kept his ideals unsoiled. When the curtain fell upon the first act the clamour of applause was the true expression of genuine emotion aroused by legitimate means. Annesley felt weak and almost sick. He realised vividly what it all meant to him; he realised, above all, of what little value it would be if he failed in the greater matter of his love. Connie leaned towards him; she had tears in her eyes.

"This is the kind of thing we've been waiting for," she said. "This is quite true and human. Conrad Howe should be a happy man to-night."

"If he is in the house."

"I hope he is; there's sure to be a call." Annesley's heart thumped.

"That must be awfully trying to a man," he said.

"Why don't you write plays of this kind?"

"It's rather the sort of thing I've been aiming at."

"Go on aiming at it, then, and you'll succeed."

"With your encouragement I feel I could do anything."

"This isn't a bad play, is it?" asked Captain Bolitho.

"It's splendid," said Connie.

"The fellow knows something, too. There's not all that confounded footle that leads you nowhere. The girl's ripping."

"She is," said Annesley. As a matter of fact she was a careful study of Miss Bolitho; for that reason Miss Bolitho appeared entirely unconscious of it.

"There are only three acts, too," said the Captain; "that's sensible. Five acts, with long waits between, are killing. I call it taking your money on false pretences. You don't come to a theatre to hear the band play."

When the curtain rose again the house instantly settled into silence, a sure

"THE MANAGER WAS SIMMERING WITH JOY."

sign that things were going well. Connie leaned forward with something of the eagerness of a child; even Captain Bolitho unhinged himself, as it were, and indicated interest by a slightly curved back. Annesley began to feel master of himself again; part of the future, at least, was now safe; how much that means to a man who steps from poverty to the security of a decent income can only be realised by those who have been in a like case; the mere fact of being able to pay a debt with promptitude is capable of affording a very exquisite joy. But, now that so much was within his grasp, he longed for all; the horizon of desire, like the horizon of the actual world, always recedes as we advance; since a few months before he had travelled innumerable miles towards success; that being reached, there was still an infinite distance beyond.

In the second act there was a simple love-scene that appeared to take the audience by surprise; it was direct, touching, convincing. Annesley noticed that no one laughed, a thing almost unprecedented in a London theatre when sentiment attitudinises upon the boards. This gave him a glow of well-earned triumph; he had mentally decided beforehand that that was the crucial point of the play; when it was passed he dropped back and closed his eyes.

"You didn't see all that act," Connie said to him in the interval; "are you tired,—were you asleep?"

"I'm neither tired nor sleepy, I heard everything."

"Didn't you think the love-scene beautiful?"

"Yes," he said, blushing at his own candour.

"I didn't think much of that," said Captain Bolitho, "I suppose because I can't see myself saying pretty things to a girl. It's not in my line, you know. I feel 'em, but

BEFORE THE CURTAIN.

can't express 'em. My notion is that the girl should make love to me."

"But you must begin, surely," Connie said.

"That's just the deuce of it," said the Captain, "I can't."

Annesley rose. "I must go now," he said, "to another part of the house. When it's over will you remain here till I come? I've an idea that I can find out who this Conrad Howe is. May I bring him to see you if I'm right?"

"Do, I'll wait for you."

He went out into the Strand and lit a cigarette. The aspect of the world had changed for him; he even saw cabs and busses with different eyes. Every passenger upon the pavement seemed a friend, the roar of traffic had new music in it,—the stars above the housetops looked down with kindly eyes. The cool air put fresh courage into him, soothed his pulse, made his hope seem real. Inside the theatre it had been altogether difficult to understand substantial facts; but out there in the hurry of the street it was easy enough. There was no doubt about "The Golden Circlet," or Connie Bolitho, or about himself; they all existed, they all were of the world. The name of Conrad Howe stared at him from the placards; he even touched the letters with his fingers to make quite sure. Ten minutes later he re-entered the theatre by the stage door.

He met the manager in the wings. That gentleman was simmering with joy, his congratulations were overwhelming. Annesley bore them with resignation.

"There's sure to be a call for 'Author,'" said the manager; "you'll go to the front, won't you? It's always better; pleases them, you know. Do you feel nervous? Come to my room and have some champagne. This is a howling success, Mr. Howe—nothing like it for years. Just listen to that applause? You've fetched 'em, no doubt about it. Come along and have that champagne." Annesley went readily enough; the atmosphere of the theatre was getting on his nerves again.

When the last curtain fell the pit and gallery got upon their feet and cheered; the rest of the house was equally decisive if more discreet; "The Golden Circlet" was a success. And in the midst of the hubbub Annesley found himself before the curtain, bowing, dazzled by the footlights and straining his eyes to see one face. And, as though in obedience to his call, it rose before him, flushed, glowing, with eyes from which the delight and astonishment had hardly died, and with lips whose smile seemed tremulous with coming tears. That was the true moment of his triumph.

As soon as he could escape he found his way into the empty stalls; one figure remained. As he approached Connie raised her head. The colour had died out of her face; she was as pale as Annesley was himself. He held out his hand.

"I have brought Conrad Howe to see you," he said.

"Why didn't you tell me before? It was cruel of you."

"Perhaps it was because I thought that if I failed I could not bear that you should know it."

"That was not true friendship."

"Did I ever profess friendship for you?"

She hesitated, and played with her fan. A little wave of colour flowed back into her cheeks.

"You see," he went on, "I was pretty much alone in the world, and had to make my mark in my own way. A few months ago things were very black with me. I shut myself up and worked."

"It must have been hard for you," she said, "to cut yourself off from everything like that."

"It was hard, I'm not going to pretend it wasn't. But I had hope—not very bright, perhaps, but still it was enough to keep me from going under."

"You had faith in yourself and in your own work."

"I had more than that. Can you guess what it was?" Their voices sounded curiously hollow in the empty theatre,—the

"'I WISHED TO WIN YOUR LOVE.'"

attendants were already putting up and covering the seats.

"You hoped to get fame and money?"

"Yes, but more than either I wished to win your love. Don't kill my illusion, don't ring down the curtain on my romance, Connie, and leave me in the dark. Everything I did was for you. You inspired whatever was good in 'The Golden Circlet.' The thought of you kept my head above water. I can come to you now without feeling ashamed."

"You might have come before. You need never have been ashamed. I could have helped you, oh, so much!"

"But now that the dark days are over, you won't turn your back on me and say I don't need your help? I need it more than ever. My love, the golden circlet is yours if you will take it from me."

She gave him both her hands and lifted her face to his.

"I am your's always," she said, "but I think, perhaps, I loved you better when you were quite poor, but you never asked me then to love you. Think of what you've lost!"

Annesley took her in his arms in spite of a watchful attendant. "Never mind," he said, "everything's in the future for both of us, never mind the past. They may even damn my play now if they like."

At this point Captain Bolitho's voice was heard in loud protest.

"I tell you," he was saying, "I left a lady in your confounded theatre, and she hasn't come out. I've had a cab waiting ten minutes."

"It's Tom," Connie whispered, "I forgot all about him. Poor Tom!"

"Miss Bolitho's quite safe," said Annesley, "we've just been settling a little matter of great importance to both of us."

Captain Bolitho peered into the face of each in the uncertain light and seemed to understand.

"The devil you have!" he murmured under his breath. Then he said aloud, "Anyhow, Connie, I can't keep the cab waiting any longer. I congratulate you, Mr. Annesley Howe, on your 'Golden Circlet.' That was a deuced neat little surprise you'd hatched for us. I like your play, and I daresay I shall like you when I know more of you. Dine with me next Thursday, will you? Good-night."

A MOTHER OF TWO.

Photo by Lawlor, Ealing

the following page. Yet it is not until the foot of the succeeding page that the line of text used as caption appears in its narrative frame. By the time it does, we have worked out that "The manager was simmering with joy" as he approached Annesley because it is he who is "Conrad Howe," the playwright responsible for *The Golden Circlet*. Similarly, when we see the illustration of Annesley "Before the Curtain" on page 14, we are made aware long before the verbal text tells us that he is acknowledging the tumultuous applause of the audience. And, when we see him confronting Connie Bolitho—the young woman from the second illustration—we barely need to read the caption "I wished to win your love" to grasp the author's motives for his earlier concealment. When the verbal text ends, with Captain Bolitho—Connie's cousin, returned from India—inviting Herbert Annesley to dinner next Thursday, we are already assured of the happy ending, from the sequence presented in the illustrations.

And yes, I realize that the story is phallocentric and reinforces a patriarchal and infantilizing vision of a woman who is largely objectified. But it is worth pointing out that it appears in a magazine published by one of the most successful newspaper proprietors of the time and can thus be regarded as offering a worldview matched fairly closely to those of its intended readers. We might, in short, say that it offers a kind of love story that its readers, many of whom will be women, find attractive. And my larger point is that any narrative satisfaction that they derived from it arose in no small measure from the kind of visual anticipation that is offered by the placing of the illustrations, all of which we might categorize as Barthes's "functions."

This narrative satisfaction also derives from our sense of involvement, and this is in turn derived from the style of the illustrations, which allow us to share the events they present in a direct and immediate manner. This materialist identification is aided by one particular stylistic aspect of the illustrations. Although even by the 1890s the mechanical reproduction of photography was possible in mass circulation newspapers and was used in many of the factual articles included in the monthly illustrated magazines, all of the stories were illustrated by drawings. Indeed, it was only in the 1960s that the use of photographs to illustrate fiction was pioneered by fictional magazines, and dropped shortly thereafter. The reason is revealing: the level of physical realism detracted too much from the sense of inner involvement in the fictive world that the reader desired from such texts, and which was attainable in drawings but not photographs.

Two further elements are present to an overwhelming extent in the illustrations to these stories—exemplified in the Burrow story but in no way peculiar to it. First, the viewpoint is one that is outside that of the narrator, whether implied, omniscient, or first person, of the verbal narrative. This presents us with another element of our typology: the illustrations are presented in such a manner, stylistically, as to constitute another Bakhtinian voice in the presentation of characters and action. Even when a first-person narrator is used, as most famously in the Sherlock Holmes stories, the viewpoint is not his or hers but that of a separate, privileged spectator. The result of this, paradoxically, is to allow the reader to become more directly a part of the fictive world of the story and also to feel in control of it. One never has a sense of becoming someone else or losing control, and instead the feeling of enclosure within this world is complete.

Another stylistic aspect is important, and here the element of paradox is if anything even greater: the style of the drawings is to all practical narrative purposes irrelevant and invisible, with two significant exceptions. First, it is always naturalistic in its representationalism; second, following on from this, the use of different media—most often a shift from line to wash drawing—takes place for no easily definable reason. All that matters, it seems, is that we see what is going on; how we do this, in terms of technique and style, is of no importance.

This is, of course, another significant difference from the novels of the 1830s. Style is very important there, from the caricature figures of Phiz in *Sketches by Boz* to the inhuman, doll-like bodies of William Thackeray's own illustrations to *Vanity Fair*. Style is a visual analogue to the rhetorical timbre of the writing. Not so in these stories: pictures convey intent, and we might go so far as to say that, just as in popular fiction, the style of writing needs to be transparent to allow us to pass quickly through word to event—to pass through the glass page, as it were, into the world of the story—so the style of the illustration needs to be invisible, for exactly the same reason.

Having established the two key dimensions of typology—which we might choose to call that of temporal sequence and that of the assumed inevitability of style and viewpoint—we now need to explore the larger implications about the theoretical bases of the stories' dual dialogue of word and image and what they suggest about how the stories were originally read. If we accept the complexity of the reading process that results from the placement of the illustrations at points of anticipatory variance from the narrative episode as presented in the text, the following reading becomes persuasive. In *The Truth in Painting*, Jacques Derrida advances the idea that an image "restores in authoritarian silence an order of presence" (156). Elsewhere, in the interview titled "Spatial Arts," he expands this in a manner that is particularly helpful to my present quest because it reveals a duality in any reading of visual texts. What he calls the "absolute mutism" of a visual work is the basis on which "resistance is mounted against the authority of discourse, against discursive hegemony" (13). Yet at the same time, images are, as we read them, "full of virtual discourses" that, because of their aphoristic immediacy, give them "a discursive virtuality that is infinitely authoritarian, in a sense theologically authoritarian" (13).

Seen through this filter, the dual discourse of the illustrated short story is polarized: the temporal duality of the two discourses is revealed as containing an opposition between two forms of authority, that of the verbal and that of the visual. Within this can be seen another opposition, that between the new authority of the written word and the immediate experiential force of the illustration. These are powerful combative elements in those for whom literacy is a recent acquisition, and here Derrida's suggestion offers us another way of hypothesizing the initial reading experience: it is constituted of tensions as much as of sequential resolutions—those obtained when the expectations aroused by the illustrations are fulfilled in the completions of the verbal narrative.

If we combine Derrida's notion of the ambivalent force of the visual meaning with the idea of the dual time scheme and its effects, something very interesting is suggested about the possible reading experience. It is that, against the process of reading the story as a fictive world, the verbally unspecifiable, purely visual significations of the illustrations may be held in balance, so that the apparently very strongly materialist elements of the story may be offset by a freer and more purely visual statement or sequence. Within the larger production context of the magazines, this suggests that those readers whose reading skills were either limited or so newly achieved as to be the subject of inquiry and question—and the two may or may not occur simultaneously in the same reader—might well regard the illustrated story as a world created by purely visual means, allowing the authority of the visual to overturn or displace the authority of the verbal discourse. This allows the construction of all kinds of alternative sequences, some narrative, some situational, and returns the control over the text to the reader—or, to be Barthesian, allows the work most fully to become the text.[10] In the reading situation of many of these stories, this may imply the development of what Queenie Leavis was later to call a "corrosive habit of fantasying [that] will lead to maladjustment in actual life" (54). Alternatively, it may imply something much richer and less explicative, when the visual forms of the illustrations float free of their narrative frames to acquire totally different, and totally visual, significations, perhaps with no narrative or referential values, but only those that are purely spatial.

Taking all of this together, we might conjecture a series of different kinds of reading for these illustrated stories. At the least connotative level is the visual experience of illustrations as visual forms, running counter to the force of the verbal discourse simply by being nondiscursive and, if this is possible with images of this kind, nonreferential. The simplest form of narrative is offered by the process of reading the images as a sequence and gleaning from them as much narrative import as possible without an accompanying verbal text, much as a child might read a series of images in a comic book while not understanding the accompanying dialogue. A more complex form might be a reading of the images as prelude to a reading of the text, which would be complemented and fulfilled by a reading of the verbal text, perhaps accompanied by more thorough investigation of the images, so that anticipation is first aroused and then confirmed, or perhaps in some cases contradicted, and the involvement in the world of the story deepened by the proleptic dynamic the images offer as a result of their anticipatory placement.

All these kinds of reading, we should remind ourselves, are possible within the range of the magazine's readership, with adults of different kinds of reading sophistication as well as children reading stories addressed to them, skimming across adult narratives with images, and looking at pictures while being read to by adult companions. Within all of these, temporal sophistication generated by the placing of the images is significant, and alongside this, we should remember another significance of time. The *locus classicus* for the reading experience of these stories, lasting perhaps up to forty-five minutes of inexpert reading time, is the railway journey. The commuting experience becomes an envelope of time that, just as it demands the escape from the commercial reality that it frames in the life of the new clerkly classes, sympathetically manages the consumption of fiction by allowing a new kind of time, the double-time of the verbal-visual narrative, to make possible the escape from time in the deeper involvement of the world of the story that the dual verbal-visual fabric of text allows its reader to construct.

This constellation of significances makes the illustrated popular short story a significant textual category in its own right, and I would not wish to lessen its importance by comparison with the serious short story in terms that imply comparisons of value. Yet it is interesting and worthwhile to speculate on the relationship between writing of this sort and the more serious stories that are being produced either at this time or shortly afterward. The double use of time that is presented in popular illustrated stories, to take one point of convergence, may be seen as a kind of parallel to the sophisticated double or even multiple time schemes of Joyce, Woolf, and Mansfield. It is something quite different, but equally subtle in the way that it operates on, or is generated by, the reading consciousness. It may also, in a similar parallel, be considered as offering a series of moments outside the discursiveness of the story in a manner rather similar to the "fragments" that are discussed by Jakob Lothe elsewhere in this volume. But the most suggestive coming together lies elsewhere and may be formulated in a question: do the serious short stories of the period make direct reference to their illustrated popular equivalents in making them a precise, but absent, presence in their own texts?

This can be made clearer by a consideration of a famous moment in what is generally held as a very early modern short story, Joyce's "The Dead"—the moment when Gabriel looks up and sees his wife standing at the top of the stairs, listening to a folk song. The account is given in very specific, almost abstract, visual terms that deal in the rhythm of the panels of the skirt, to the extent that these are mentioned before the character is identified. It seems that we have here a moment of the sort identified by Derrida, where a meaning is constructed that is wholly visual, at once "theologically authoritarian" and "against discursive hegemony"—except, of course, that it is discursive, and not visual, instead using language to present what would be represented in the more immediate, because wordless, idioms of an illustration. And just as we realize this, the narrative executes a kind of double swerve, both toward this reading and away from it again: "If he were a painter he would paint her in that attitude. Her blue felt hat would show off the bronze of her hair against the darkness and the dark panels of her skirt would show off the light ones. *Distant Music* he would call the picture if he were a painter" (211). The suggestion that the scene might be better rendered visually is deftly countered by its reliance on a nineties' trick of synesthesia, in which one art is used to suggest another. Here, there is a kind of structural pun: for just after the verbal discourse has first been used to suggest the double discourse of the verbal and visual in the illustrated story, it veers away to suggest that the visual be united in its turn with the musical. Such a realization is present to some degree without the awareness that this might, in the popular magazine story, be a moment for illustration, but it is greatly enhanced by our awareness of the unseen presence of such an element. It defines itself by the absence of a visual presence, and the complexity and resonance of the moment is greatly enhanced and deepened in consequence.

One further moment might benefit from such an awareness. This is the very closing passage of a work that is not in any commonly accepted sense of the term a short story at all—except that, in many ways, it is a subtly interlinked pattern of three short stories: Virginia Woolf's *To the Lighthouse*.[11] Just as Mr. Ramsay steps ashore, Lily Briscoe paints the final stroke and lays down her brush, and the story is finished. Narrative action, the symbolic drawing together of the work of the artist, and the literary tasks of both writer and reader all complete themselves at the same moment. The presence here of an awareness of the illustrated tradition is enriching at even more levels than in the Joyce passage. For if we are aware of the silent resonance, the unseen presence of an illustration, we realize that here the completeness can work only if it is seen in complete synchronicity with the other drives of the text. It is not only the absence of the illustration that enhances this moment as something peculiarly and powerfully verbal, it is the absence of the anticipatory time scheme that the popular story has made its own. Read thus, the concluding moment of unity is all the more intense: the absent presence of the illustration allows us to see the ending's subtle complexity with no little increase of precision, and the significance of the popular illustrated short story is extended into a further plane.

Notes

1. For more information on circulation figures, see Sillars, *Visualisation in English Popular Fiction*, 72–73; and Pound, *Mirror of the Century*, 32.

2. Alpers, *Life of Katherine Mansfield*, 109n.

3. See Harvey, *Victorian Novelists*.

4. See Carey, *Intellectuals and the Masses*.

5. See Sillars, *Visualisation in English Popular Fiction*, 17–28.

6. See Storey, Tillotson, and Easson, eds. *Letters of Charles Dickens*.

7. *Words and Pictures*, 37–49.

8. "Character in Fiction," 428. I use the term "materialist" very much in the spirit of the writing discussed in Woolf's essay, and as a far less contentious term than "realist."

9. See the facsimile representation of this story immediately following page 74; prints here are made from a copy of the original 1898 volume of the *Harmsworth Magazine* in the author's private collection.

10. See "From Work to Text," in *Image, Music, Text*, 155–64.

11. While it is not my intention to suggest influence of any direct sort here, it is worth pointing out that Woolf's earliest short stories were published with covers illustrated by her sister Vanessa Bell—who paradoxically told John Lehmann that she had not read them (see Lehmann, *Thrown to the Woolfs*, 27). Woolf was clearly aware, like any well-read individual of her generation, of the tradition of the illustrated novel, and it seems unlikely that she would not have been aware of the illustrated short story of this kind. Her essay "Character in Fiction" does, after all, include a discussion of the behavior of some people on a train journey.

Works Cited

Alpers, Antony. *The Life of Katherine Mansfield.* Harmondsworth, U.K.: Penguin, 1982.

Barthes, Roland. *Image, Music, Text.* Essays selected and translated by Stephen Heath. London: Fontana, 1977.

Carey, John. *The Intellectuals and the Masses.* London: Faber and Faber, 1992.

Derrida, Jacques. *The Truth in Painting.* Translated by G. Bennington and I. Macleod. Chicago: Chicago University Press, 1987.

———. "The Spatial Arts: An Interview with Jacques Derrida." In *Deconstruction and the Visual Arts: Art, Media, Architecture,* edited by Peter Brunette and David Wills, 9–32. Cambridge: Cambridge University Press, 1994.

Harvey, John. *Victorian Novelists and Their Illustrators.* London: Sidgwick and Jackson, 1970.

Joyce, James. *Dubliners.* Edited by Terence Brown. Harmondsworth, U.K.: Penguin, 1992.

Leavis, Q. D. *Fiction and the Reading Public.* London: Chatto and Windus, 1932.

Lehmann, John. *Thrown to the Woolfs.* London: Weidenfeld and Nicholson, 1978.

Pound, Reginald. *Mirror of the Century: The Strand Magazine, 1891–1950.* New York: Barnes, 1966.

Schapiro, Meyer. *Words and Pictures: On the Literal and Symbolic in the Illustration of a Text.* The Hague and Paris: Mouton, 1973.

Sillars, Stuart. *Visualisation in English Popular Fiction, 1860–1960: Graphic Narratives, Fictional Images.* London and New York: Routledge, 1995.

Storey, Graham, Kathleen Tillotson, and Angus Easson, eds. *The Letters of Charles Dickens.* 7 vols. Oxford, U.K.: Clarendon Press, 1965–93.

Woolf, Virginia. "Character in Fiction." In *The Essays of Virginia Woolf, 1919–1924,* vol. 3, edited by Andrew McNeillie, 420–38. London: Hogarth Press, 1988.

Danish Short Shorts in the 1990s and the Jena-Romantic Fragments

Gitte Mose

Short Short Literary History

The development of Danish literature has followed that of European literary history in general—though often a little belatedly. Looking back to Romanticism, we can note two influential short story writers who—following in the footsteps of Goethe, Hoffmann, Tieck, Kleist, and so on—both begin their writing careers in the 1820s.[1] One is the world-famous Hans Christian Andersen (1805–1875) with his stories and fairy tales, and the other is the vicar Steen Steensen Blicher (1782–1848), author of more than a hundred short stories, some of them published in his own journals. Blicher was also influenced by his readings and translations of English poems and novels, including James Macpherson's Ossian poems and Oliver Goldsmith's *The Vicar of Wakefield*. His particular kind of poetic yet realistic stories, presenting, for example, an explicit and participating narrator, have given name to what is considered to be the classical Danish short story: *den Blicherske novelle* (the Blicherian short story).

During and after the so-called Modern Breakthrough, initiated by Georg Brandes (1842–1927), whose ideas and expectations of literature strongly influenced writers and dramatists like Henrik Ibsen in Norway and August Strindberg in Sweden, the short story genre was very popular. At the turn of the century even shorter and more heterogeneous forms developed, being published in the increasing number of magazines and newspapers; and designations such as "sketches," "pictures," "drafts," and "texts" began to appear as generic markers. The success of these impressionistic, hybrid forms, combining characteristics of the short story and journalistic writing, may be regarded as literary manifestations of the changes in the history of mentality. A "new" and "nervous" subject entered the stage and insisted on the privileged position of the individual in the pursuit of an adequate ontology for the new century. This subject's perceptions, emotions, and subconscious were to serve as the main instruments of intellectual and artistic exploration and analysis. Thus the center of gravity, the central point of orientation, now belonged to the observer, not to the world—in keeping with Nietzsche's dictum that "life no longer lives in totality." Writers like Jens Peter Jacobsen (1847–1885), who influenced Rainer Maria Rilke, Herman Bang (1857–1912), and a little later Johannes V. Jensen (1873–1950) continued expanding and developing the short story form, under the influence of the American tradition from Poe, Hawthorne, and Melville (both Bang and Jensen traveled in the United States). The Nobel Prize–winning author Jensen, a great fan of all new fast technology (including the steam engine, film, and photography), created his very own genre, termed *myter* (myths)—very short, momentary "snapshots" wherein the point of departure usually is a concrete sense impression being elevated to a universal level, such as Jensen's encounter with the mountain Fujiyama.

After World War I, prose fiction and the short story lost ground to poetry, and the short story, along with the subsidiary forms mentioned above, were not really en vogue until the Danish modernism of the 1950s and 1960s. During the next two decades short fiction again dropped out of focus, until a veritable revival was seen in the 1990s, now under the influence of especially Jorge Luis Borges and Raymond Carver. These new texts were frequently reduced in terms of length and most often placed under the heading *kortprosa* (short prose), understood as short *fiction*. The recent resurgence of interest in short fiction notwithstanding, one must conclude that in sum, the *novelle*, "the short story," and the short shorts in particular have had a hard time catching the attention of Danish readers as well as literary critics throughout most of the twentieth century.

One of the explanations for this is that literary critics, and some of the authors themselves, have regarded these texts as hack work, exercises or preliminary studies for works on a larger scale, using generic designations like "drafts," "reflections," and "experiments," all underlining their provisional nature. Another possible explanation is the fact that the short forms have been regarded as difficult to read. As Grace Paley puts it, "The truth is people are kind of scared by very very short stories—just as they are by long poems. A short story is closer to the poem than to the novel . . . and when it's very very short—1, 2, 2½ pages—should be read like a poem. That is slowly. People who like to skip can't skip in a 3-page story" (*Sudden Fiction*, 253). In other words, short shorts demand a rather different kind of concentration from that of "the short story" and the *novelle*—genres with which short shorts are readily compared. But reader expectations, of plot and narrativity, for example, which are carried on to these short story look-alikes, are most often frustrated when confronted with a text that in size and "plot line" is more like a flash, a frozen yet slightly expanded moment. The result is often that the text is read and understood as prose poetry, with which it shares plot elements, even if mood and illusion are found to be predominant.

Classifications and Terminology

The different generic markers mentioned above show how difficult it is to pin down these short forms. In the 1990s an additional set of collective designations and descriptions has been used by literary and newspaper criticism, calling these thin and tiny collections of texts, enclosed by a lot of empty white space on the pages, minimalistic and anorectic, diet, and light prose. By now the most popular and most widely used term is the above-mentioned *kortprosa*.

Trying to classify and determine the generic characteristics of short stories is not without problems and has not been left untried. On the contrary, the number of theory books and articles has grown considerably, not least in the Anglo-American academic community, among them Gerlach (1985), Lohafer and Clarey (1989), and May (1994 and 1995). So has the number of survey books and articles, such as the Danish professor Jørgen Dines Johansen's *Novelleteori efter 1945: En studie i litterær taxonomi* (Short Story Theory after 1945: A Study in Literary Taxonomy) and the American-based professor Leonie Marx's *Die deutsche Kurzgeschichte*. The 1985 International Association for Scandinavian Studies (IASS) Conference in Denmark was devoted to these issues—and so was the international Short Fiction Conference in Oslo in 2001, producing the present volume.

One recent Danish attempt at classification is to be found in the afterword to an anthology of short prose fiction, wherein the editors present short short prose texts as a *genrefelt* (generic field) because, as they put it, "one of the most important characteristics of short prose is that it integrates and/or contrasts stylistic features and linguistic modes from many different literary genres without ever adhering 100 per cent to one single convention."[2] Reading from the bottom up the *genrefelt* shows an increase in the "fictional" elements according to some familiar modalities:

tale

fairy tale/fable   *novelle*/"short story"

allegory   prose poem

causerie   lyrical poem

essay   sketch

report   private note

document

Moving from the almost impossible (and perhaps futile) field of "classifications," I shall now focus on some of the distinguishable traits of the poetics of Danish short shorts of the 1990s. My theoretical point of departure is Walter Höllerer's "Die kurze Form der Prosa," an article that has become a standard text in the theory of short short fiction in Denmark. Höllerer calls short fiction a *Sammelplatz* (meeting place) designated by seven characteristics. Basing his observations on analyses of short short fictional texts by Robert Musil, Günther Grass, Wolfgang Borchert, Martin Walser, and Franz Kafka, he claims that these traits are found only in the periphery of the traditional forms of short fiction. Among them we find fixations of the moment and a focus on the singular, such as a single exchange between people, a single object, a single word, a singular gesture. The nonessential is here accentuated at the expense of the essential, which *may* be present as a shadow. To the extent one can speak of an "event" at all, it is typically just hinted at and consequently rendered ambiguous. Blurred distinctions between subject and object, characters and things, may result in changes, such as in power relations. These markers allow Höllerer to delimit the short short story from what he calls "dem übrigen Kleinvieh der Prosa" (the other small cattle of prose), among them the anecdote, the joke, the fable, and the sketch.

Höllerer's investigations result in a tripartite definition of types of stories that share a suggestive narrative style, a special tone, but whose designations accentuate their characteristics. One is "die Augenblickskurzgeschichte" (the story of the moment), the second "die Arabesken-Kurzgeschichte" (the arabesque story), and the third "die Überdrehungs- und Überblendungs-geschichte" (the surprise and dissolve story).

Since Höllerer, several critics and writers have developed, modified, and attempted greater precision by focusing even more sharply on what happens when texts are compacted into short shorts. The formation of a moment that pointedly synthesizes a chain of events may result in complex temporal structures that cause the present—which is the most common temporal dimension of the short shorts—to merge with and become indistinguishable from that of the past and the future; space is expanded through one or more epiphanic moments. Characters, often two or three, including a seemingly recurring and privileged first-person narrator, are reduced in almost every respect. Matter and mood are often rooted in everyday life and everyday events, while classic rhetoric and mannerisms (e.g., paradoxes, absurd and grotesque effects, parallels and emphatic anaphoras) become part of the style. Finally, the reader seems to experience everything at the same level and at the same time as the characters and narrator, having jumped onto "the running train," one of the most frequently used observations about these short shorts, with their open beginnings and ends.

Collecting and Anthologizing

If the number of articles and theory books has grown, so has the number of anthologies. This trend usually indicates that a genre has established itself as a viable one. Two important Danish anthologies saw print toward the end of the decade. A 1998 collection by Brixvold and Jørgensen mentioned above presented texts from 1882 to 1998 to show that the short shorts had been part of twentieth-century literary history, even if their presence had not always been acknowledged. The same team edited a 1999 collection, consisting of one hundred texts totaling 247 pages and written for the occasion by ninety Danish writers belonging to both the young and the older generation. These short shorts make use of the whole spectrum of the *genrefelt*, blending and mixing, distilling and compacting the different "characteristics."

Two recent American anthologies similarly use length as a criterion for inclusion, and merit mention here, as their aesthetic credo reflects many of the same convictions that we find on the Danish short short fiction scene. One is *Sudden Fiction:*

American Short-Short Stories (1986), the other *Flash Fiction: Seventy-two Very Short Stories* (1992). In *Sudden Fiction* none of the texts exceeds 1,500 words, and in *Flash Fiction* the texts run between 250 and 750 words. Both anthologies assume that the short short finds a form of its own in the twentieth century, playing a prominent part in American journals and magazines from the 1960s onward, as in the case of Robert Coover's "Minute Stories" in *TriQuarterly*. The titles of the anthologies underline the surprising, the unforeseen, the glimpse, which the editors of *Flash Fiction* initially wished to underscore by publishing only texts that could be read without turning the pages, in other words, without an enforced break in the reader's concentration. This plan was changed, however, because it turned out to be too monotonous and because the reader actually expects and likes to turn the pages: "Turning pages, it would seem, is part of what fiction is about, part of the passing of the story" (13). The editors of *Sudden Fiction* described the artistic objective of their anthology in the following manner, which nicely echoes the aesthetic contours of the Danish short shorts discussed below: "Highly compressed, highly charged, insidious, protean, sudden, alarming, tantalizing, these short-shorts confer form on small corners of chaos, can do in a page what a novel does in two hundred. If they can stop time and make it timeless, they are here for you, above all, as living voices" (xvi).

Danish Short Shorts . . .

In 1990 a "fringe" publishing house published *&*, by Solvej Balle (b. 1962), stating on the cover that the book was part of a poetry series. The book consists of seventy-one squarelike texts printed on thirty-seven pages and divided into five parts. Due to the designation "poetry series," the book was mainly received as a collection of prose poems, seen and read as sudden flashes—frozen moments of sense perceptions. As an epigraph Balle chose a line from Sir P. F. Strawson's *Individuals: An Essay in Descriptive Metaphysics*: "Things pass through places." The line suggests that the striking short shorts such as the following be read as attempts at developing a "descriptive metaphysics":

> The seagulls have taken to the town. They hang low and only vaguely hear the sounds from the harbor, where fish is no longer unloaded. An iron ship with long chains in the water, and the containers are stacked under each other, colorful and rusty.

> We switch on all lights in the apartment, before we go. One by one we switch them on and walk away, leaving the door open to the half-darkened staircase. So that somebody can find his way back in the darkness.

> In the amphitheater the plays have ended. The glare from the spotlights still lingers on the stones around the scene, but costumes and actors have been brought in for the night. Here and there people sit on the luminous stones. Their backs are bent.

They listen or suddenly get up for no reason.

They approach the harbor from one side at the time. Alone or two by two. Speaking together or alone. Nobody leaves the town during daytime. We meet by the harbor in the dark. Cafés with open facades and tables outside. The piers being populated by slow promenades.

At the bar we order kahlua with milk, juice and grenadine, curaçao with lime. Light colorful drinks with no effect.

We draw quotation marks in the air, when we talk. Two fingers on each hand draw lines in the air, and the lines nullify the words somewhat. In this way we can speak reality and world and time, up in front of the eyes, and in this way we are left with something alive, carefully pressing down towards the ground, while we are drawing all the signs we know.

A foot and there a cobble-stone. There a cigarette stub. The old woman is hurrying among the tables. She is reaching for hands, but nobody wants their fortune told. The future is a big and moist rag, rubbing sentences and words off the thought.[3]

The reader starts reading the textual excerpts one by one, gradually beginning to combine and make relations crisscross, even if the title, &, does suggest and imply parataxis. Consisting of five parts, the collection indicates certain courses of events, maybe one or more stories about one or perhaps two couples falling in and out of love, and a story about a pending ecological disaster. However, the sense of phenomena being described in a nonhierarchical way is overwhelming, and confirmed by the author. In an interview she revealed that all the textual fragments had lain scattered around her before she wrote the book and that the composition was solely directed by the mood of the text bits themselves, not by characters or ideas about plots and events.

In 1998 & got a twin, *Eller* (Or). This collection is also made up of five parts amounting to thirty-seven pages and consisting of seventy-two texts. Unlike Balle's first book, this text was published by one of the big publishing companies, but carrying no generic marker whatsoever. Concurring with the disjunction of the title and most of the statementlike assertions, the events of the texts seem to flow more easily, embodying the central recurring perception of the river *Oder* (equals *or*), as well as epitomizing the both/and/or in text number 5, which may perhaps allude to both the composition of classical drama and the value of the number itself being "symbolic of man, health and love, and of the quintessence acting upon matter. It comprises the four limbs of the body plus the head which controls them, and likewise the four fingers plus the thumb and the four cardinal points together with the center. . . . Geometrically it is the pentagram, or the five-pointed star. It corresponds to pentagonal symmetry, a common characteristic of organic nature, to the golden section (as noted by the Pythagoreans), and to the five senses representing the five forms of matter."[4] The publication of *Eller* further underscores Balle's strong preoccupation with existential questions, a tendency found in her breakthrough work in 1994, *Ifølge loven: Fire beretninger om mennesket* (According to the Law: Four Accounts of Man) as well. This widely hailed and translated book blends natural and human sciences in four distilled short stories, consisting of compact blocks of texts and constituting a sort of "composite novel" when read.

. . . and the Jena-Romantic Fragments

From 1994 to 1997 Solvej Balle and her colleague Christina Hesselholdt (b. 1962), to whom we shall return shortly, coedited the literary journal *Den blå port* (The Blue Gate). It has often been remarked that the 1990s were preoccupied with Romanticism, and one entire issue of the journal was in fact devoted to articles on the literary fragment—translations of selected fragments by Friedrich and August Wilhelm Schlegel and Novalis, and an article on a special Scandinavian genre from the late 1960s, the *punktroman* (pointlike novel).

The fragmentary writings of the brothers Schlegel and Novalis were inspired by the French Revolution's ghostwriter Sébastien R. N. Chamfort (1740–1794) and his posthumous work *Maximes et pensées, caractères et anecdotes*. Chamfort's work consists of 1,266 fragments, which were found in three boxes and published posthumously by a friend. In addition to the members of the *Athenäum* group, the Schlegel brothers, Schelling, and Novalis, his work has inspired writers such as Schopenhauer, Nietzsche, August Strindberg, Walter Benjamin, Maurice Blanchot, and Fernando Pessoa to use the fragmentary form.

One of the accomplishments of Jena Romanticism was to give birth to a new perception of the unfinished, of the literary work as essentially open. The words the Jena Romantics mainly used about their art and thinking were "underway," "in be(com)ing," "provisional," "sketchlike," "experimenting," and so on, words explicitly denoting the idea of thinking as *movement*, onward and toward a desired unity/totality, "the Absolute":

Die romantische Poesie ist eine progressive Universalpoesie. . . . Die romantische Dichtart ist noch im Werden; ja das ist ihr eigentliches Wesen, dass sie ewig nur werden, nie vollendet sein kann.[5]

[Romantic poetry is a progressive, universal poetry. . . . The art of Romantic poetry is ever in the state of becoming; that is its true essence, eternally becoming, never reaching completion.][6]

The Absolute may manifest itself in an epiphanic moment, as in the fragment, and Schlegel's most common metaphor for this transcendental presence is the *blitz*, the sudden synthesis, creating a moment's unity in infinity. Through the flashlight of poetry, chaos is frozen into a punctual *now*, lending it a provisional form—the fragment—which

> muss gleich einem kleinen Kunstwerke von der umgebenden Welt ganz abgesondert und in sich selbst vollendet sein wie ein Igel.[7]

> [must like a miniature piece of art be entirely isolated from the world and be complete in itself like a hedgehog.]

The literary fragment, which Schlegel calls "the proper form of universal philosophy," becomes the genre par excellence of Jena Romanticism, containing the paradox of being a fragment concurring with a "hope" of becoming part of and thereby comprising a complete book, in spite of *and* because of its broken form. A famous attempt at achieving this kind of paradoxical fusion between part and whole is *Das allgemeine Brouillon* (written between 1798 and 1799), wherein Novalis tries to collect fragments about the different sciences—physics, chemistry, mathematics, philosophy, history, politics, poetics, and medicine—in order to compose an encyclopedia, a "scientific Bible."

What may come as a surprise when reading these early texts by the Jena Romantics is an enormous confidence in the reflecting consciousness. Holding poetry in high esteem does not entail a retreat into pure sentiment; it rather shows an insistence on poetry's cognitive potential, and its high-ranking position within a theory of reflection that blends poetry and thinking, literature and philosophy. In *Blüthenstaub* Novalis writes:

> Die höchste Aufgabe der Bildung ist, sich seines transzendentalen Selbst zu bemächtigen, das Ich seines Ichs zugleich zu sein.[8]

> [The highest goal of *Bildung* is to take possession of one's transcendental Self, to be the I of one's own I simultaneously.]

This process of generating a potentially infinite series of self-referring acts of thoughts, this meta-reflective level is essential to the idea of progressive, universal poetry.

Points, Lines

I have already identified a distinctly sketchlike quality and a characteristic instantaneousness as central markers of short short fiction, and I believe it is possible to view the aesthetics of Solvej Balle and her generation as a confirmation of the same kind of trust in man's cognitive potential through art that we find among the Jena Romantics. A basic sense of disarray and a lack of unity seem to find an apt outlet in Balle's squarelike forms. At the same time one senses a belief in the possibility of creating various kinds of relations between the elements. There is an urge to rebuild the world, earning these young writers the nickname "the Lego generation." This tendency is also striking in the works of Christina Hesselholdt, who published her first book in 1991, the indeterminable *Køkkenet, gravkammeret og landskabet* (The Kitchen, the Vault and the Landscape), consisting of forty tiny chapters printed on sixty-three pages (the shortest in a couple of lines, the longest in a couple of pages).[9]

Outside the Room of the Deceased

The child is trying to imagine: nothing.

Nothing appears as the contours of a man with an infinitely heavy sack over his shoulder standing in the dark on a muddy riverbank. There is only a tiny piece of bank—as much as his feet need to stand firm, and just enough darkness to surround him. He has stuffed the river that belonged to the bank into the sack, and also the remaining bank—he has placed the whole world, everything that is in it, in the sack.

He is left standing on the last piece of land. (14)

The Room Hanging Like a Drop of Water above the River

The shadow is long.

The wake from a boat down the river, farther than Audrey can see, rolls through the mosaic and pushes the tip of the shadow all the way over to the right-hand bank. The tip points to the bank where she stood and was pointed out.

When the apartment building tips over, it knocks a hole in the mosaic. It pushes the shadow down to the bottom of the river. The house covers the shadow and keeps it down with its weight.

When the house tips, the shadow disappears. (36)

The Room Hanging Like a Drop of Water above the River

Audrey looks at her hands. Pollen makes it impossible to recognize them.

A flower loses its head.

She can imagine something even stranger. (51)[10]

Twelve headlines, or titles, are repeated unsystematically, indicating rooms in a house, inviting a reading of the book as something other than a collection of poetry or a short story sequence. A development is suggested by a camera-like movement between the rooms. These could also be described as tableaux or snapshots, even though the sense of nonhierarchy between the text blocks is striking. The texts are, however, framed by the death of the main character Marlon's mother at the beginning and his father's suicide at the end—both being "immortalized" by a photographer—but shifting "the pictures" around inside this frame does not significantly alter what is perceived to be the root story.

The book turned out to be the first volume in the so-called Marlon trilogy. Volume two, *Det skjulte* (The Hidden), forty-six pages, was published in 1993. It consists of fifty-one text blocks, each beginning with capital letters in bold—mainly J, D, M (which can be read as *Jeg, Dig/Du, Mig*, meaning "I, You, Me"). Elements of story are given more room here, reaching a climax in Marlon's dissection of his girlfriend Greta in his monomaniacal search for "the unique"—which turns out to be her heart.[11]

Hesselholdt's two books have since their publication been read as so-called *punktromaner* (pointlike novels), inspired by the Norwegian author Paal-Helge Haugen's influential *Anne* (1968), a genre that has received considerable attention in the above-mentioned journal, *Den blå port*.[12] Hesselholdt translated *Anne* into Danish in 1992. Similarities in mood, the cut-up layout, and the line of prose-poetic punctual texts underline the relationship between Hesselholdt's and Haugen's books.

Seeing Hesselholdt's texts as instances of the *punktroman* invites the following digression: reading the fragments, or "points," we move along both a *metaphorical* and a *metonymic* axis. The metaphorical dimension calls for, even necessitates, a vertical cowriting of the text, amplifying the production of meaning. The recognizable elements of story, however, create a metonymic dimension and solicit a horizontal processing of the text, where the reader creates his or her own linear story. Therefore, the key significance of the text emerges from these meeting points of the metaphorical and the metonymic, which link up in ways that allow gaps on the different levels of narrative to be closed, thereby "completing" the story, such as the one about the young tubercular Anne and the psychopath Marlon.

Tiny Stories

Seen in the rearview mirror, it was mainly young female writers who took the big experimenting step into the 1990s, but in recent years young male writers have also followed suit. Among them is Peter Adolphsen (b. 1972), who has published two collections of short short stories, *Små historier* (Tiny Stories) and *Små historier 2*, consisting of thirty and thirty-eight texts (fifty-four and eighty-five pages), respectively. Some of the texts are less than a page, but their topics are none the less "big," concerning a wide variety of motifs: the bones of God, Arabic beauties, a city made of newspaper, Johann Sebastian Bach's body heat, flashes of light, and epiphanic moments. In these tiny books Adolphsen pushes against generic borders, bringing his short shorts close to the genres from which the modern short story once developed: the fairy tale, the legend, the fable, the myth, the exemplum, the chronicle, the anecdote, the aphorism, and so on. We also find a scientific article, an interactive story, a cool *roman nouveau*, and parodies, such as of a Dirty Harry film. It is indeed a *Sammelplatz*—a generic field!

Adolphsen openly acknowledges his indebtedness to several writers: in addition to a couple of Danish writers, also Franz Kafka, Heinrich von Kleist, and Jorge Luis Borges.

As an entry to *Små historier 2* he has chosen the following epigraph: "Among today's more dispassionate temperaments of sound health it has for a long time been current to view one's own work as part of a brotherly text, contributions to a constantly renewed continental conspiracy, which undismayed and until this very day has fanned its feathers through the endlessly mutating room of literature."[13] The epigraph underlines the indebtedness on the part of writers to tradition while at the same time indicating an important way in which literature renews itself. Adolphsen "fans his feathers through the room of literature" in the grandest of manners, by invoking themes like life and death, God and Satan, religion and natural sciences, destiny and existence, myths and literature. This may sound pretentious, but Adolphsen avoids falling into the trap of hyperbole because these enigmatic, paradoxical writings are topped by humor and irony. Things do happen, but the rest is "language." Here is one example:

A Japanese Rice Paper Lantern and a Haiku

One day I wrote this haiku:

> A high, high, high sun
> after a quiet drizzle.
> Hi ho, September!

I had just moved into a new apartment and had bought a rice paper lantern to cover a naked bulb. The room was high-ceilinged, and I had to stand on a chair on top of a table. The chair slipped under me, I fell down on the table and tore the lamp while falling; it was drawn out into a spiral, the top still clinging to the cord, and I was lying on the table with the bottom part.

While I was rubbing my elbows and swore under my breath, I thought about the coil being a picture of time, the naked bulb consequently death, and, being on this pseudo-metaphysical slippery slope, I thought that the electricity had to be God himself.

Afterwards I wrote the above haiku to remind myself that writing should be based on a thought firmly anchored in the real world and not strut about as a figment of the imagination donning the cloak scholarship.

And it was September, and the sun was shining after a quiet drizzle.[14]

In this compact piece of flash fiction of 185 words, plus 5 in the title, we find most of the above-mentioned characteristics of the short shorts: a story about writing, about the moment of inspiration, and the result—the quintessence of the shortest of short poems, the haiku. The combination of the demands of haiku poetics (form and themes) and the markers of the short shorts is successfully blended in this ironic meta-reflective story on the downfall of the (traditionally) assumed grandiloquent poetic process.

Provisional Forms?

I have argued that the dense short shorts by Balle, Hesselholdt, and Adolphsen mirror a world consisting of bits and pieces, but implicitly a world that may be woven into sequences of events, however "tiny." This is certainly a characteristic feature of Balle's texts and is also observable on a larger scale in the Marlon trilogy, wherein Hesselholdt moves from the stylized punctual texts to an almost old-fashioned, but still very concentrated, short novel in the third volume, *Udsigten* (The View), from 1997.

After the publication of his first book, Adolphsen said in an interview that he did not consider it to be a collection of short stories but rather a *totalroman* (total/aggregate novel). His ambition was to test and show a multiplicity of coordinated epic possibilities and "thereby in an encyclopedic way to present the non-specific about human beings, in a form where the singular text was aesthetically perfect and compact."[15] And how did the Romantics put it?

> Alle π [Poesie] soll Prosa, und alle Prosa soll π [Poesie] sein. Alle Prosa soll romantisch sein.—Alle Geisteswerke sollen romantisieren d[em] Roman s[ich] möglichst approximiren.[16]

> [All poetry must be prose, all prose must be poetry. All prose must be Romantic. All intellectual works must be romanticized and approach the novel, as closely as possible.]

By the end of the 1990s there was a growing need to create relations and networks, a move examined by, for instance, the British sociologist Anthony Giddens in his book *Modernity and Self-Identity: Self and Society in the Late Modern Age.*[17] Dissenting from postmodernism, the strategies of late modernity seek to counteract the disintegration of the central values of existence by organizing through reflection the fragmented into a temporary totality. Giddens is first and foremost preoccupied with the individual's possibilities and abilities to realize himself or herself in this provisional totality. He discusses how the individual may find "ontological security" and establish "momentary continuity," revising these states of mind continuously through reflection.

Which returns us once again to the new Romantic subject and Romanticism's enormous faith in the reflecting consciousness. In *Das allgemeine Brouillon*, Novalis writes:

> —(So fährt der Blitz aus Instinkt in der metallenen Kette nieder.) der rohe, synthetische complettirende Trieb—ein *transitorisches—Punctähnliches Ich.*[18]

> [—(So lightening intuitively strikes the metal chain.) the raw, synthetically completing drive—a *transitory—pointlike I.*]

But even before that (in a letter to his brother August in 1793), Novalis had made the following observation:

mein Wesen besteht aus Augenblicken. Will ich diese nicht ergreifen mit Männlicher Hand, so bleibt mir nichts übrig als eine unerträgliche Vegetation.[19]

[my being consists of moments. Do I not catch them with a manly hand, I am but left with unbearable vegetation.]

Catching moments and freezing them in short short forms seems to be the preoccupation of most of the avant-garde young Danish in the last decade of the twentieth century. Even though it is not really my intention to turn them into crypto-romanticists, it is hard to resist the temptation when one reads the following:

The Brightest Key

The sun-rays slope in blocks onto the dance floor. On the wall a yellow map. The pianist runs his tired eyes across the flat earth until they stop at Greenland, and he suddenly remembers something from the evening before: a drunk holds down the key on the far right in the middle of an old standard. The tone is jarring, but for a brief moment the thought glimmers that disharmony isn't the enemy of music, but its shadow. A flash of the sort in which everything is drowned by light and replaced by a thought with incalculable logical inferences which have to yield to the familiar reality immediately. The world that re-enters the pianist's field of vision is that of the drunk still holding down the key while declaring that Greenland is the world's biggest island.[20]

Through their testing and tentative art of storytelling, these writers of short shorts are able to show the world as fickle and immense, a world we cannot fathom but perhaps approach when it is captured at the "roots" of a kind of fiction that is probing and challenging the capabilities of language. Despite the possible lessons from the analyses of late modernity that all cognition must be local and temporary, they maintain that the world is full of possibilities, that it *can* be examined and told by imposing their artistic form on some small corners of chaos.

Notes

1. Danish literary criticism distinguishes between the designations *novelle* (compare with the classical German *Novelle*, after the example of Goethe), "short story" (mainly used about the American short story—Hemingway, and Carver these days; compare with the German *Kurzgeschichte*), and *fortælling* (rooted in Poe's "tale" and favored, for example, by Karen Blixen/Isak Dinesen). I place "short story" inside quotation marks when the reference is to this particular Danish genre marker; without quotation marks the reference is to the more inclusive genre concept inherent in Anglo-American use of the term.

2. Brixvold and Jørgensen, *Antologi af dansk kortprosa*, 167.

3. My translations.

4. Cirlot, *Dictionary of Symbols*, 233.

5. Schlegel, "Die Athenäums-Fragmente" no. 116, vol. 2.

6. All translations from the German are mine.

7. Schlegel, "Die Athenäums-Fragmente" no. 206, vol. 2.

8. No. 28, *W*, vol. 2.

9. The same year as Hesselholdt published this book, the poet Lene Henningsen published *Jeg siger dig* (I Am Telling You), a collection of prose poems; the reviewers had a difficult time distinguishing between the two books.

10. The translations of Hesselholdt's texts are by me, in the layout of the book.

11. The characters are named after famous actors—the mother is Elizabeth.

12. The two books have brought about a discussion of whether a more apt name for this kind of prose should be *punktprosa* (pointlike prose) in order to make its characteristics explicit, compared to those of the *novelle* / "short story," the essay, and the overall designation *kortprosa* (short prose).

13. Quoted from Højholt, *Praksis 8*, no. 5 (1989): 11. My translation from the Danish.

14. *Små historier 2*, 41; my translation.

15. Adolphsen, "Ved fiktionens rødder" [At the roots of fiction], interview in *Information*, April 11, 2000.

16. Schlegel, "Zur Theorie der Prosa" no. 606, vol. 16.

17. Interestingly, Giddens seems to argue against breaks in modernity. He talks about the late modern age coexisting with the postmodern and modern, and views all of modernity as a coherent period from industrialism until today. But the main characteristic is the *reflexivity of modernity*, with its insistence on the virtue of skepticism in epistemological matters, and where one recognizes the need to continuously revise one's foundation of knowledge. The late modern age is regarded as relational in contrast to the postmodern rejection of all relations and connections and a belief in emancipation in the fragmentation and undermining of meaning and identity.

18. No. 904, *W*, vol. 2.

19. *W*, vol. 1, p. 539.

20. Adolphsen, *Små historier*, 9; my translation.

Works Cited

Adolphsen, Peter. *Små historier*. Århus: Samleren, 1996.

———. *Små historier 2*. Viborg: Samleren, 2000.

———. "Ved fiktionens rødder." Interview in *Information*, April 11, 2000.

Balle, Solvej. &. Århus: Basilisk, 1990.

———. *Ifølge loven: Fire beretninger om mennesket*. Viborg: Lindhardt og Ringhoff, 1993.

———. *Eller*. Viborg: Lindhardt og Ringhoff, 1998.

Brixvold, Jeppe, and Hans Otto Jørgensen, eds. *Antologi af dansk kortprosa*. Haslev: Dansklærerforeningen, 1998.

———. *Kortprosa 1999*. Viborg: Arena/Lindhardt og Ringhoff, 1999.

Chamfort, Sébastien R. N. *Maximes et pensées, caractères et anecdotes*. Paris: Garnier-Flammarion, 1968.

Cirlot, J. E. *A Dictionary of Symbols*. London: Routledge and Kegan Paul, 1988.

Gerlach, John. *Toward the End: Closure and Structure in the American Short Story*. Tuscaloosa: University of Alabama Press, 1985.

Giddens, Anthony. *Modernity and Self-Identity: Self and Society in the Late Modern Age*. Cambridge, U.K.: Polity Press, 1991.

Haugen, Paal-Helge. *Anne*. Oslo: Det Norske Samlaget, 1968.

Hesselholdt, Christina. *Køkkenet, gravkammeret og landskabet, Det skjulte*. Viborg: Rosinante Paperbacks, 1996.

———. *Udsigten*. Viborg: Rosinante, 1997.

Höllerer, Walter. "Die kurze Form der Prosa." *Akzente* 9, no. 3 (1962): 226–45.

Johansen, Jørgen Dines. *Novelleteori efter 1945: En studie i litterær taksonomi*. Copenhagen: Hans Reitzel, 1970.

Lohafer, Susan, and Jo Ellyn Clarey, eds. *Short Story Theory at a Crossroads*. Baton Rouge: Louisiana State University Press, 1989.

Marx, Leonie. *Die deutsche Kurzgeschichte*. 2nd revised and expanded version. Stuttgart: Verlag J. B. Metzler, 1985.

May, Charles E., ed. *The New Short Story Theories*. Athens: Ohio University Press, 1994.

———. *The Short Story: The Reality of Artifice*. New York: Twayne, 1995.

Mose, Gitte. "Punkterede og fragmenterede tekster—og en mellemrums-læsning. Solvej Balles *& og Eller* og det romantiske fragment." *Vinduet*, Aug. 8, 2000, http://www.vinduet.no (accessed Aug. 8, 2000).

———. "Fortællinger i glimt: Dansk kort kortprosa ved århundredeskift(et)." *Norsk Litteraturvitenskapelig Tidsskrift* 1 (2001): 3–17. Appeared in English as part of the International Association for Scandinavian Studies Conference Proceedings, August 2000, University of East Anglia, Norwich, Norvik Press, 2002.

Novalis (Friedrich L. von Hardenberg). *Werke*. Vols. 1–3. Edited by H. J. Mähl. Munich: Carl Hanser Verlag, 1978.

Schlegel, Friedrich. *Kritische Friedrich-Schlegel-Ausgabe*. Vols. 2 and 16. Edited by Ernst Behler, Jean-Jacques Anstett, and Hans Eichner. Munich: F. Schoningh, 1958 and 1981.

Shapard, Robert, and James Thomas, eds. *Sudden Fiction: American Short-Short Stories*. Salt Lake City, Utah: G. M. Smith, 1986.

Thomas, James, Denise Thomas, and Tom Hazuka, eds. *Flash Fiction: Seventy-two Very Short Stories*. New York: Norton, 1992.

Aspects of the Fragment in Joyce's *Dubliners* and Kafka's *The Trial*

Jakob Lothe

According to the fourth edition of *The Penguin Dictionary of Literary Terms and Literary Theory*, written by J. A. Cuddon and revised by C. E. Preston, "the forefathers of the short story, however rude in some cases, are myth, legend, parable, fairy tale, fable, anecdote, *exemplum*, essay, character study and *Märchen*; plus the *lai*, the *fabula* and even the ballad. The term 'short story' has relatives in the shape of the French *conte* and *nouvelle*, the Spanish *novela*, the Italian *novella*, the German *Novelle* and *Kurzgeschichte* . . . the yarn, the sketch, the tale and the Russian *skaz*" (816). A term not included here yet associated with several of those mentioned by Cuddon is the fragment. Apart from the obvious point that any listing of literary terms associated with the main entry (in this case the short story) is unavoidably selective, one of Cuddon's reasons for not regarding the fragment as a forefather of the short story could be the term's affinity with "fragmentation," a concept that has become something of a cliché in descriptions of modernist and postmodernist literature. Yet, as basis for further diversification, clichés can sometimes be helpful. This essay suggests that the concepts of fragmentation and the fragment are interlinked in a manner that enhances the critical potential of both terms. Moreover, both are interestingly related to the genre of the short story in general and to the modernist short story in particular. I will focus on the fragment, yet by doing so I hope to throw some light on the label "fragmentation" as well. Although I shall begin by making some theoretical observations on genre, my discussion is text oriented, turning to two of the most interesting texts of European modernism, James Joyce's short story collection *Dubliners* (1914) and Franz Kafka's long textual fragment *Der Process* (*The Trial*), which he wrote in 1914–15 but never completed.

We tend to think of genre as a means of subdividing and ordering different forms of literature. Yet although the definition of a given genre is often typological (i.e., presenting itself as being generally valid), genre definitions are, of course, not wholly stable but are subject to change over time. For they are influenced by, and give various forms of artistic response to, historical and cultural alterations. Mikhail M. Bakhtin's classic essay "Epic and Novel" remains one of the best accounts of this problem.

Comparing and contrasting the novel with the epic—which, for Bakhtin, is characterized by national tradition and an absolute epic distance—Bakhtin puts emphasis on the novel's dynamism, flexibility, and formal and thematic range. This characteristic elasticity and generic versatility, which contribute to and yet complicate definitions of the novel, derive in part from its tendency to exploit and incorporate elements of other genres into its own. Bakhtin's main example is Dostoyevsky, but his point is just as persuasive if applied to *Ulysses* or *The Trial*.

Several of Bakhtin's points about this genre could also be made about the modern short story. If we compare the crude paraphrase of his argument just presented with my opening quotation from Cuddon, we note that the short story too is remarkable for its tendency to incorporate elements of other genres as its own. Like the modern novel, the modern short story also exploits not just one epic subgenre but aspects of several, and the manner in which it combines these elements serves cumulatively to enhance their structural and thematic significance. This point applies in large measure to Joyce's and Kafka's short fiction, which combines aspects of genres as dissimilar as the fairy tale, the legend, the parable—and the fragment.

Without in any way reducing the critical originality of Bakhtin's notions, then, I posit that several of his thoughtful observations on one particular subgenre of prose fiction, the novel, are potentially productive if applied to another epic subgenre, the short story. One justification for applying Bakhtin's thoughtful observations on the novel to the short story is the fact that they are both narratives, and the borderline between a short and a long narrative is characteristically and problematically blurred. A further reason could be that although Bakhtin does not refer to short stories by way of expounding his theory, his range of textual reference to modern novels is also curiously restricted (his main reference being Dostoyevsky's novels). For instance, many critics have noted the conspicuous absence of references to Joyce.[1] Reading Bakhtin, one sometimes gets the impression that he is discussing modern narrative as much as the modern novel.

A main asset of Bakhtin's thought is unquestionably his combined, and marvelously sustained, emphasis on genre, narrative structure, and literary history. Not only are some of his ideas about the novel applicable to the short story as well, but there is also a striking affinity between some of his main points about genre and those made by critics associated with German Romanticism, notably Johann Gottfried Herder and Friedrich Schlegel. For Herder, no genre is more inclusive than the novel because it can, and indeed tends to, incorporate "everything that in one way or another is of interest to the human mind and heart." The novel, Herder goes on to argue, "is poetry in prose" (vol. 18, p. 10; my translation). For Friedrich Schlegel, too, the art of the novel is closely related to that of poetry. For Schlegel as for Herder, the novel is a flexible and inclusive genre: a dynamic and expanding literary form capable of incorporating other genres.

I refer to Herder and Schlegel partly because I find it useful to historicize and contextualize Bakhtin's notions about the novel. Yet my main point is to emphasize the affinity, the productive interrelationship, between the genres of the fragment (as one particular variant of short fiction) and the novel, as observable in the writings of Herder, Schlegel, and also Novalis. Although the German Romantics, like the English, preferred the genre of poetry, their explorations of the genre of the fragment are thought-provoking and—as Gitte Mose shows in her contribution to the present volume—potentially very interesting for critics of the modern short story.

Before turning to Joyce and Kafka, it may be helpful to differentiate between different meanings of the word "fragment." *The Oxford English Dictionary* gives two main meanings: (1) "A part broken off or otherwise detached from a whole; a broken piece; a (comparatively) small detached portion of anything" and (2) "*transf. and fig.* A detached, isolated, or incomplete part; a (comparatively) small portion of anything; a part remaining or still preserved when the whole is lost or destroyed." As one illustrative example of the first variant, the *OED* lists a sentence from Walter Scott's novel *Waverley* (1814): "A mere precipice, with here and there a projecting fragment of granite." The *OED*'s chosen examples of the second, figurative meaning of fragment include the following one from Coleridge's *The Friend* (1809–10): "However irregular and desultory his talk, there is method in the fragments."[2]

With a view to literary analysis, the lexical definition of "fragment" given by the *OED* is usefully supplemented by the three possible meanings of the word that Gero von Wilpert identifies in his invaluable *Sachwörterbuch der Literatur*. Von Wilpert distinguishes between a *historical* fragment (a literary or nonfictional work that was presumably complete, but of which parts have been lost, such as Aristotle's *Poetics*), an *incomplete* fragment (a text left unfinished by the author), and an *intended* fragment (in which the genre of the fragment is deliberately chosen by the author, such as Schlegel's *Kritische Fragmente*) (306). Of these three main variants, the intended fragment would appear to be more closely related to the genre of narrative fiction than the former two. Borderlines are blurred here, however: is Kafka's *The Trial* an incomplete or intended fragment? As is well known, Kafka was unable to finish and publish his novel; and, as the German critical edition of *Der Process* makes clear, it has not just one but several endings. Thus, in one sense it is a fragment rather than a novel, yet it would seem impossible to decide whether the book was *intended* as a fragment by Kafka. Still, if we apply Seymour Chatman's helpful notion of "textual intention" to this text, thus drawing attention to what Umberto Eco has called "the rights of the text" rather than those of its author (Chatman, 104; Eco, 7), I suggest that *The Trial* would have been less original, and probably also less influential, had it been possessed of a conventional and more unproblematic ending. Paradoxically and characteristically, *The Trial*'s fragmentary narrative structure and the elements of the short story that it incorporates make it a more effective and powerful novel.

The fragment's affiliation with the short story and with the novel, then, contributes to its peculiarly unstable generic status. This kind of generic instability is observable in the fragments incorporated into the fiction of both Kafka and Joyce. Turning now to *Dubliners*, I choose to focus, here as in the following observations on *The Trial*, on two examples of the fragment observable in my chosen texts. Yet even though the textual segments subjected to discussion here are very different (and, indeed, some readers may dissent from my understanding of them as fragments in the first place), I would argue that all my chosen passages activate constituent elements of the definitions of the fragment listed above. To paraphrase the *OED*, they variously resemble or even exemplify parts "broken off or otherwise detached from a whole." Yet paradoxically, and in part for this very reason, all passages under consideration contribute significantly to the narratives' structural and thematic formation.

The first fragment is from the short story "Eveline," and it consists of just two words that are repeated once: "—Derevaun Seraun! Derevaun Seraun!" (40). These words are heard, not spoken, by Eveline, the short story's protagonist. What is extraordinary about them is, first, that they are spoken by a deceased person (Eveline's mother), and, second, that they are incomprehensible. As Robert Scholes and A. Walton Litz note in their edition of *Dubliners*, "although it appears to be Gaelic, this mysterious exclamation has never been satisfactorily explained. Joyce may have intended it as delirious gibberish" (472). If we relate this last point to the third meaning of the fragment identified by von Wilpert, we could rephrase it by suggesting that as "delirious gibberish" this fragment assumes, within the overall design of the short story's narrative, the form of an intended fragment radically detached from the plot. Considered as an intended fragment, however, the exclamation becomes all the more meaningful just because it is incomprehensible: although the third-person narrator reports that Eveline "stood up in a sudden impulse of terror," and although the voices of narrator and character blend in the accompanying free indirect discourse ("Escape! She must escape! Frank would save her."), it is remarkably apposite that Eveline is kept back by words she cannot understand and from which she wants to flee. For in the end, as we recall, she does not leave for South America with Frank. Unable to break away, she remains, for reasons she cannot grasp, in Dublin, kept back by the voice of the dead, whose utterance she cannot understand but whose impact on her is devastating. Jacques Derrida has written well of the compression of meaning, the virtually indefinite semantic suggestiveness, in Joyce; and Umberto Eco has shrewdly observed of *Finnegans Wake* that Joyce here "bend[s] language to express 'everything'" (83–84). As the senseless "Derevaun Seraun!" appears to represent, for Eveline, everything that constitutes her life at this decisive point when at last she has the opportunity to start a new one, Derrida's and Eco's observations could be extended to include the thematic effect of this textual segment—a fragment at once divorced from and integral to the short story's narrative discourse.

If at first reading this particular fragment seems essentially to serve the characterization of Eveline, on later readings its significance is enhanced and extended. Eveline is the protagonist of a story that is part of a collection, and the fragment is part of the short story's setting in a particular time and place: Dublin at the turn of the twentieth century. Thus the fragment accentuates and contextualizes Eveline's predicament. Overall, as Derek Attridge has observed, it "is understood as a version of a more general problem afflicting Dubliners of a certain class, and this may reduce any tendency to pass judgement on her as an individual" (9).

In order to briefly discuss a second fragment from *Dubliners*, I turn to "The Dead"—the longest and best known of the fifteen stories in the collection—and I would like to focus on this extract of text:

> O, the rain falls on my heavy locks
> And the dew wets my skin,
> My babe lies cold . . . (210)

This passage qualifies as a fragment for at least two reasons. First, it is presented as the incomplete part of a larger textual segment—compare Joyce's use of ellipses, which unambiguously indicates that the last line included in the short story's discourse is not the concluding line of the song. Mary Jane promptly identifies the singer as Bartell D'Arcy. A couple of pages later on in the narrative, D'Arcy, replying to a question asked by Gretta, says the song is called "The Lass of Aughrim." As Scholes and Litz point out in their notes to "The Dead," the three lines included in the narrative discourse are indeed part of the refrain from "The Lass of Aughrim," a ballad that exists in many versions in Scotland and Ireland. Thus, what we would appear to have here is, to repeat the first of the two definitions of the fragment given by the OED, "a part [in this case, of a poem] broken off or otherwise detached from a whole."

Second, and more interestingly, the three lines of "The Lass of Aughrim" not only qualify as a fragment in the sense just described but also *appear* as a fragment to Gabriel, whose registering consciousness is closely associated with the short story's narrative perspective at this stage of the plot. This stage, as we recall, is a crucially transitional one, marking the narrative movement from the relative harmony and gaiety of the party to the separation of Gabriel and Gretta in the hotel room. And it is the fragment, or more precisely the song of which just a fragment is presented, that precipitates this transition.

In order to substantiate this last point, let us recall a key passage just before the fragment of "The Lass of Aughrim": "Gabriel had not gone to the door with the others. He was in a dark part of the hall gazing up the staircase. A woman was standing near the top of the first flight, in the shadow also. He could not see her face but he could see the terracotta and salmonpink panels of her skirt which the shadow made appear black and white. It was his wife" (209). What is striking about this passage is the presentation of Gretta as a woman, a stranger, another, an unknown person. There is a peculiar opposition between the two words "woman" and "wife" in the quotation. Standing in the dark part of the hall and being also metaphorically in the dark, Gabriel sees as it were only a fragment of his wife: although at last he recognizes her, he does not realize that she has already become distant from him beyond the spatial distance. Ironically, the first visual impression of "a woman" is therefore more correct than the latter. The identification is illusory: as "a woman" Gretta is thinking of Michael, the boy from the west of Ireland who, as she later puts it, "died for me," and of whom she is reminded by listening to the song he used to sing, "The Lass of Aughrim." In the concluding part of "The Dead," the part of the story describing Gretta and Gabriel in the Dublin hotel with the dead Michael intervening, Gabriel comes to realize that his knowledge of his wife is incomplete, fragmentary. Thus, the two senses of fragment associated with the lines from "The Lass of Aughrim" are interlinked in an artistically productive manner.

Considered as a fragment, the lines from this poem are an intertextual installment that is generically related to other forms of narrative, such as the ballad and the legend. From a narrative perspective, this fragment at first seems to be divorced from the mechanics of the short story's plot and narrative intricacies. And yet the fragment is part of the narrative, as it serves as a kind of comment on it;[3] its meaning is greatly reduced if it is not related to the following, concluding part of "The Dead." In one sense, this fragment is both a prologue to the ending of the short story and a kind of epilogue because an adequate understanding of the lines from "The Lass of Aughrim" presupposes a response to the short story as a narrative, as fictional discourse.

As the plethora of readings of "The Dead" demonstrates, any critic of this short story becomes another in a series of interpreters, regardless of which aspects of the text he or she chooses to focus on. Joyce's narrative method is at its most effective in this long short story, whose structural and thematic range exceeds that of many novels. Throughout the text there is a productive interplay of narrative form and thematic complexity. Distancing itself from and yet curiously aligning itself with Gabriel's perspective, the third-person narrative seems to be groping for a center, a stable meaning or ground it never quite reaches. Gabriel remains, to borrow a phrase from Conrad's *Lord Jim*, "under a cloud," and so does the short story's thematic core or center. In his fragment 242, Novalis comments on the centrifugal tendency of all matter. The human mind, Novalis goes on to argue, opposes this tendency: the way in which we observe and make sense of the world at once reflects and indicates a centripetal inclination, a search for stability or ground. If the centrifugal tendency of matter makes the world appear as a series of unrelated fragments, the human mind—and Gabriel as one possible fictional personification of it—seeks to relate the fragments to each other, to explain, to create order out of a myriad of impressions. The task is a difficult one, and it is further complicated for Gabriel as he—feeling lonely in the hotel room after

Gretta has fallen asleep thinking of Michael—"was conscious of [the deads'] wayward and flickering existence" (223).

If the narrative dynamic of *Dubliners* is possessed of a tendency to relate fragments to each other to create a sense of order or direction, in Kafka's fiction this kind of inescapable challenge is all the more notable. To make this point is not to suggest that the aspects of the fragment observable in the two authors' fictional texts are unproblematically similar or identical—they are not. In Kafka as in Joyce, however, various facets of the fragment are persistently present, at once resisting and contributing to the narrative formation of larger textual entities.

That Kafka, as already indicated, found it exceedingly difficult to complete a novel is in one sense logical enough, considering that he consistently problematizes both beginning and closure. It is a nice irony of modernist fiction that one of the period's most influential novels, *The Trial*, was never completed. As short fiction elements (e.g., in the form of a short story Kafka had previously published as an independent text) are incorporated into a larger, if incomplete, whole, the linkage between short fiction and the fragment is accentuated. This feature of Kafka's novel is strikingly apparent in the new critical edition of *Der Process*, edited by Malcolm Pasley and published by Fischer Verlag in 1990. Whereas the earlier version, edited by Max Brod and published in 1925, ends with K.'s execution in the novel's last chapter, Pasley's critical edition is divided into two, "Kapitel" and "Fragmente" ("chapters" and "fragments"). There is actually an odd discrepancy between the order in which the text presents itself in the critical edition and that of its *Entstehung* (i.e., the order in which the different parts were written). If, as is usually the case, we read the novel by moving from the first to the last chapter, the "Fragmente" constitute a new beginning as they are appended to the main text. However, in the "Apparatband" that accompanies the critical edition of *Der Process* Pasley notes that Kafka wrote the chapters "Verhaftung" and "Ende" ("Beginning" and "Ending") first, both probably in August 1914. Yet the ordering and positioning of the remaining parts is far more uncertain—and the fragments ought perhaps not to be read after the ending.

In one sense, the uncertainties of order and the reader's impression of loosely related scenes in the middle of *The Trial* make the novel's beginning and ending more definite. And yet the complex nature of and/or suspension of narrative causality not only influences the reader's understanding of the text's middle but also infiltrates our reading of its beginning and ending. In an essay on the opening of *The Trial*, I have attempted to show that it begins by problematizing its own beginning. A key word here is the subjunctive verbal form "hätte" in the novel's first sentence: "Jemand musste Josef K. verleumdet haben, denn ohne dass er etwas Böses getan hätte, wurde er eines Morgens verhaftet" (7). Many translations of *The Trial*, including the English one by Douglas Scott and Chris Walker, simply state that somebody must have been telling lies about Joseph K., because one day he was arrested without having done anything wrong. But such a translation distorts and oversimplifies the meaning of this key sentence, which suggests that although K. is unaware of having done anything wrong, he perhaps still might have done something that explains, and possibly even justifies, his arrest.

If *The Trial* ends by adding fragments to its ending, it begins by drawing attention to the arbitrary and fragmentary nature of any beginning. Opening not with K.'s (possible) crime but with his arrest, *The Trial* begins in medias res. The novel's real beginning, like our sense of beginnings in general, approximates to the unknown. So does, I would argue, the beginning of "Vor dem Gesetz" ("Before the Law"), that strange short story Kafka first published in the independent Jewish weekly *Selbswehr* on September 7, 1915, and then incorporated into "Im Dom" ("In the Cathedral"), the penultimate chapter of *The Trial*.

Very briefly, "Before the Law" tells the story of a man from the country who seeks to be admitted to the Law. But before the Law stands a doorkeeper, who tells the man that he cannot grant him admission now. So the man waits—and keeps waiting not just for hours or days but for many years. The ending of this short story is deservedly famous. The old man puts all his energy into one last question he has not yet asked the doorkeeper. This is how the question is rendered in the English translation by Douglas Scott and Chris Walker: "'All men are intent on the Law,' says the man, 'but why is it that in all these many years no one other than myself has asked to enter? The door-keeper realizes that the man is nearing his end and that his hearing is fading, and in order to make himself heard he bellows at him: 'No one else could gain admission here, because this door was intended only for you. I shall now go and close it'" (240). As the complexity of this narrative is in inverse ratio to its brevity, my discussion of it is unavoidably selective. Briefly, I suggest that the beginning of "Before the Law" curiously repeats the opening of *The Trial*: beginning in medias res, it signals that the narrative recording of the story is essentially incomplete, and this characteristic feature calls the fragment strikingly to mind. I offer three points to substantiate this notion. First, although we are informed that the man from the country comes to the doorkeeper and begs for admission to the Law, his reasons for wanting to be admitted are not given. If we ask, as we are inclined to, whether the man has perhaps done something that makes admission to the Law particularly desirable or necessary for him, we draw attention to a blank or ellipsis located before the narrative's actual beginning. This kind of blank, which can be related to our limited knowledge about the reasons for K.'s arrest, resembles a fragment.

Second, although "Before the Law" first appeared as an independent story, the highly effective manner in which it is integrated into the overall narrative further strengthens the link between the predicament of the man from the country and that of K. "You are deceiving yourself about the Law," the priest tells the man, "In the writings that preface the Law this kind of deception is described thus" (239). By introducing and narrating the story, the priest brings in a new narrative level in *The Trial*, the hypodiegetic level that the parable forms. Although the priest, who communicates the parable as a first-person narrator, is the main link between the two levels, the fact that K. is "strongly drawn to the story" (240)[4] brings the shorter narrative closer to the larger one. At this point, too, beginning and ending are interrelated: once the priest's narration ends, K.'s interpretation begins.

Third, we note that the story, which the priest presumably tells K. in order to help him gain a better understanding of the Law, is not taken from the Law itself. Rather, as the story is located on the outskirts, at the beginning of the Law, it reveals just a tiny fragment of it. The function of "Before the Law" as an integral part of the novel's discourse is peculiarly indeterminate yet thematically very productive because it prompts questions that curiously repeat, and thus accentuate, those actualized by the narrative discourse of *The Trial*.

Is the story first and foremost a comment on how incomprehensible the Law is rather than a contribution to K.'s understanding of it? In his three-hundred-page study of this two-page text, Hartmut Binder argues that the widespread tendency on the part of critics to read "Before the Law" as a parable, rather than as a legend, has entailed many misreadings not just of this short text but of *The Trial* as a whole (3). I agree with Binder that the story resembles a legend, yet I doubt whether we can or should see "Before the Law" in the light of this subgenre only. Dissenting from Binder, I would suggest that the story's interpretative suggestiveness is enhanced by the manner in which it combines various subgenres of narrative fiction: folktale, legend, parable, and fragment. The way in which constituent aspects of these subgenres are interlinked furthers the complexity of this short text. For example, one meaning of parable corresponds to *mashal*, a Hebrew word meaning riddle or enigmatic narrative. But this aspect of the parable—its tendency to refer to something different or something larger than it at once illustrates and covers—resembles the fragment, which like a parable prompts the reader's interpretative activity.

As Valerie Shaw has noted, Kafka insisted that his short story "The Stoker" be subtitled "A Fragment" (241). On one level, there is an appealing modesty about this kind of insistence. But why? Is it perhaps because we tend to think of the fragment as somehow subordinate or inferior in relation to the novel? The thrust of this essay has been to suggest that it is not. Rather, like the short story (which in one sense it metonymically represents), the fragment compresses literary meaning into a short segment of text, yet by doing so it also extends meaning by drawing attention to the incomplete and fragmentary nature of verbal representation. As a variant of the short story, the fragment is semantically "loaded" in a way the novel is not. Considered from this angle, the fragment is reminiscent of the genre of poetry, and it is by no means coincidental that the German Romantics wrote both poems and fragments. Better than most literary texts, the four fragments considered here illustrate how intertwined are the temporal and spatial aspects of narrative. As Novalis writes in his fragment 492, "A penetrated space is a time space. A penetrated time [is] a space time."

Notes

1. See Kerschner, *Joyce, Bakhtin, and Popular Culture*, 17.
2. http://dictionary.oed.com/cgi/entry/ (accessed 28 March 2002).
3. Although "comment" can be understood as a form of presentation that is neither temporal nor spatial, it is also, like a descriptive pause, narrated. See my *Narrative in Fiction and Film*, 52.
4. "von der Geschichte sehr stark angezogen" (*Der Process*, 295).

Works Cited

Attridge, Derek. "Reading Joyce." In *The Cambridge Companion to Joyce*, edited by Derek Attridge, 1–30. Cambridge: Cambridge University Press, 1990.

Bakhtin, Mikhail M. "Epic and Novel." In *The Dialogic Imagination: Four Essays by M. M. Bakhtin*, edited by Michael Holquist, 3–40. Austin: University of Texas Press, 1981.

Binder, Hartmut. "*Vor dem Gesetz*": *Einführung in Kafkas Welt*. Stuttgart: Metzler, 1993.

Chatman, Seymour. *Coming to Terms: The Rhetoric of Narrative in Fiction and Film*. Ithaca, N.Y.: Cornell University Press, 1990.

Cuddon, J. A. *The Penguin Dictionary of Literary Terms and Literary Theory*. 4th ed., revised by C. E. Preston. London: Penguin, 1998.

Derrida, Jacques. "Two Words for Joyce." In *Post-Structuralist Joyce*, edited by Derek Attridge and Daniel Ferrer, 145–59. Cambridge: Cambridge University Press, 1984.

Eco, Umberto. *The Aesthetics of Chaosmos: The Middle Ages of James Joyce*. Cambridge, Mass.: Harvard University Press, 1989.

Herder, Johann Gottfried. *Sämmtliche Werke*. Edited by Bernhard Suphan. Berlin, 1877–1913.

Joyce, James. *Dubliners*. Edited by Robert Scholes and A. Walton Litz. New York: Viking Press, 1975.

Kafka, Franz. *Der Process*. Edited by Malcolm Pasley. Frankfurt am Main: Fischer, 1990.

———. *The Trial*. Translated by Douglas Scott and Chris Walker. London: Picador, 1998.

Kerschner, R. B. *Joyce, Bakhtin, and Popular Culture: Chronicles of Disorder*. Chapel Hill: University of North Carolina Press, 1981.

Lothe, Jakob. *Narrative in Fiction and Film: An Introduction*. Oxford: Oxford University Press, 2000.

———. "Das Problem des Anfangs: Kafkas *Der Process* und Orson Welles' *The Trial*." In *Franz Kafka: Zur ethischen und ästhetischen Rechtfertigung*, edited by Beatrice Sandberg and Jakob Lothe, 213–31. Freiburg: Rombach Verlag, 2002.

Novalis. *Schriften: Die Werke Friedrich von Hardenbergs*. Edited by Paul Kluckhohn and Richard Samuel. Darmstadt: Wissenschaftliche Buchgesellschaft, 1975.

Schlegel, Friedrich. *Kritische Friedrich-Schlegel-Ausgabe*. Vols. 2 and 16. Edited by Ernst Behler, Jean-Jacques Anstett, and Hans Eichner. Munich: F. Schöningh, 1958 and 1981.

Shaw, Valerie. *The Short Story: A Critical Introduction*. London: Longman, 1988.

Wilpert, Gero von. *Sachwörterbuch der Literatur*. 7th ed. Stuttgart: Alfred Kröner Verlag, 1989.

Short Notes on Tall Tales

Some Australian Examples

W. H. New

The Shape of Short Notes

My title is deliberate. I am not so much devising a single linear argument here as I am hazarding some observations about textual practices in Australian short fiction and presenting some reading strategies that seem to work and not work with them. In particular, I want to focus on a wide range of stories that can be categorized as "tall tales." I do so partly because the tall tale is so recurrent a form in Australia, and partly because I have had such problems coming to terms with it—problems connecting with the cultural sensibility it expresses (the voice of a society not my own, perhaps) and problems finding in it its narrative sophistication. I suppose I have been academically trained to think of the tall tale as a form of shaggy-dog joke, entertaining in informal exchanges but not—what terms should one use?—elegant, or realistic, or psychologically insightful, or revelatory, urban, urbane, or avant-garde. Not *artistically contemporary*, I suppose. In a way I have come to think that it *can* be *all* of these. But that has been something of a critical journey, which is what, in a very general way, these "short notes" both summarize and outline.

Why Tall Tales Are a Problem

I find that I must already distance myself from what these preliminary observations about culture and training might imply. Certainly I can blame neither my teachers nor my society for my preconceptions. There were plenty of tall tales in the conventional literary curriculum I studied as an undergraduate in Canada—though mostly they were American: Twain's crafted exaggerations of cultural mores and cultural types, Paul Bunyanesque political heroics, jokes about rural yokels. So I came to think of the tall tale as a version of the potboiler Western: braggadocio written with corn. Easy to dismiss, but still oddly appealing. Such exaggerations worked best, I thought, if they were clearly satiric. But if I am honest (and honesty is, I note as an aside, the claim of every tall-tale teller), I wonder if criticism is not itself also a set of tall tales. For using satire as a criterion of value might well be simply a justification of the pleasures of reading the Baron Munchausen stories and Chaucer's bawdy tales, exaggerations all. Perhaps that is where culture comes in. Generalizing now, it sounds as though I was conducting a joust between narrative strategy and Calvinist context, which may be true. In some cases, of course, tall tales *are* satiric, their reformative or critical function explicit. Jonathan Swift's exaggerations of Royal Society fatuousness, in book 3 of *Gulliver's Travels*, offer a rough paradigm, if not perhaps a precise example. But in other instances, the tall tale's function is primarily to entertain, through the inventiveness of its exaggerations and the dexterity of verbal wit. If it teaches or reforms or does anything else quite so functional, it does so obliquely. Which is not to say that the tall tale is without politics. Its politics, however, are embedded, I think, not in any set of events or overt message, but in its form.

As I have brought up the subject of cultural surrounds, I have, of course, to add that this obliqueness is a characteristic feature of literature in Canada as well as of numerous other literatures, which only complicates my inquiry. (It is not the story you tell, Robert Kroetsch observed about Canadian writing, it is how you tell the story.) Tall tales are, moreover, everywhere in the writing of the Canadian West—in Bob Kroetsch's own work (e.g., *The Studhorse Man*), or Bill Mitchell's (e.g., *Jake and the Kid*), or Jack Hodgins's (e.g., *The Invention of the World*) (I deliberately use their familiar names here). But for that matter tallness also punctuates the writing of the Canadian Far East, as in the baroque tales of francophone Canada or the laconic short sagas of Newfoundland. Perhaps I am just suggesting that the tall tale is one of the voices of marginal protest: it exaggerates in order to refuse the limits of a ruling convention. The Canadian Ted Stone, for example, calls his 1986 collection of prairie tales *It's Hardly Worth Talkin' If You're Goin' to Tell the Truth*. So much for tale tellers' "honesty." But as Stone's title suggests (the aural emphasis falls on the words *Talkin'* and *Truth*), the characteristic idiom of such tales is vernacular; the names are familiar, the "realities" transparent, and the *sound* of the voice is key, for it is this sound that undercuts any illusion of solemnity. The point is that such stories demand not a reader but a hearer, and by engaging the "reader" in the *act* of *hearing*, the narrative enacts a kind of *exchange*. Teller and listener have to live in a shared interpretive context for any real exchange to take place. So, if Canadians recurrently write their own many versions of tall tales (and I could appreciate *them*), and if I had been at least adequately trained to read about the American Bunyan and his blue ox, Babe, why was I not sharing readily in the ironies of the Australian tale? When I was faced with Australian fictional forms, what had gone missing? Perhaps I needed to read more widely —or listen more closely.

Looking for Stories and Finding Tall Tales

My response to this dilemma was perhaps typically academic: I looked for a book, and I started to design a postgraduate course in Australian short fiction, to be given in the fall of 2000 at the University of British Columbia in Vancouver. There were and are available numerous anthologies of Australian fiction, from standard "Oxford" and several "Best" texts to titles with the word "great" in them, titles with the word "representative" in them, and gatherings that suggest they will explain what Australian humor is all about, how women write, what it means to *be* "Australian," and so on, but some of these books were out of print, and none seemed right for the course. Unable to find what I considered an "appropriate" anthology, I decided to design the seminar in a different way, probing strategies of reading rather than focusing on single authors or a sequence of "best" stories. So the class ended up browsing the library instead, using whatever seemed appropriate at the time, wherever it was to be found. Indeterminacy-in-action. The group of eight master's students who participated in this seminar were wonderfully adventurous, willing to consider critical possibilities rather than to insist on absolutes and verities; I am indebted to them all,[1] not only for their collegiality but also for the impetus they provided to organize some of the ideas on which these "short notes on tall tales" depend.

I did find one book particularly helpful in charting a preliminary outline of Australian short fiction: Carmel Bird's anthology, *The Penguin Century of Australian Stories* (2000), a collection of one hundred stories, from Barbara Baynton's "Squeaker's Mate" in 1902 to Marele Day's "Embroidery" in 1999, not quite one per year, but not far off a century's insistently sequential time line. Neither Bird herself, as editor, nor Kerryn Goldsworthy, writing a critical introduction, claims that these are either "best" *or* "representative," though Bird hopes that the "Australian psyche" will be visited through the fiction, as will "time and meaning . . . voices now silent, [and] . . . perspectives no longer visible" (xii), and Goldsworthy, commenting on each story in turn, also accepts that cultural context shapes fiction's subjects, affirming that the early stories concern themselves with the "national" and the later ones with "the dynamic between the local and the global" (xxvii). Like any other reader, I responded more warmly to some of the stories collected here than to others, and my initial marginal notes range from ticks and stars to Xs and question marks and such annotations as "contrived," "overexplained," and the enigmatic "starts well." These "short notes" had clearly already begun.

Most recurrent was the comment "tall tale"—with an occasional variant, "light, comic, anecdotal, satiric, tall-tale-*like*, sort-of-tall-tale-in-the-long-run," and "satire of tall-tale-telling." The stories that Carmel Bird had collected were not, I emphasize, from one historical moment only, nor from only one region of the country; so I was seeing this tall-tale pattern in the work of writers both early and late in the century, among them Murray Bail, Nick Earls, Terry Lane, Henry Lawson, Peter Mathers, Barry Oakley, Steele Rudd, E. O. Schlunke, Dal Stivens, and Gerard Windsor. What becomes clear, lining them up in this way, however, is that there is at least one thing the writers have in common: they are all male. So now I had the more tangible beginnings of an inquiry into one of the modes of Australian short fiction. From reading

automatically, dismissing the tall tale as a somehow banal form, I now began to be—
I guess "metafascinated" is the word—fascinated by the fascination that this form has
exerted in Australia, especially on writers who happened also to be male. What was
there about the form that expressed a shared set of values or assumptions? What *were*
these values? How far did the "sharing" extend? How, in other words, did issues involving gender, vernacular language, and a conventional joking form come together to
reflect, undermine, reconfirm, or distill a particular version of a specific society? What
did they have to do with expressing a command over a particular knowledge? Why
did tall-tale telling become a convention? Was it ever challenged and, if so, by whom
and how? Questions, as you see, invited further questions; but answers seemed more
and more elusive, leading me back once more into "short notes," small inquiries
shaped as forays into strategies of reading.

Tall Tales Have an Australian History

It is something of a critical truism in Australia to affirm that the modern short story
developed in the 1890s with Henry Lawson and his contributions to a journal called
the *Bulletin*. Just on the edge of declaring national independence, Australian society
was seeking a distinctive national voice; the *Bulletin* claimed it would represent it;
and in critical parlance the authors who published in it, such as Lawson and Joseph
Furphy, came for critics and readers alike, over the next several decades, to epitomize
Australian idiom and Australian themes. More recent commentary has, of course, de-
constructed these claims and challenged the version of national voice that in particular the imitators of Lawson espoused. Such commentary—I would pick out Kay
Schaffer's *Women and the Bush* and Robert Dixon's *The Course of Empire* as two
influential examples of the general trends I have in mind—charges these conventional nationalist claims with bias: anti-Asian and anti-Aboriginal racism, the marginalization of women, the romanticizing of the bush and bush life, and the privileging
of a Sydney version of the national myth over any competing sets of cultural experience (those of nonconvict Adelaide and classically minded Melbourne, for example).
It is within this milieu, of consciously contrived nationalism, that the tall tale emerges
in Australia as a public medium (as distinct from whatever purchase it might have had
within oral discourse). To understand *why* this is so involves a brief glimpse at what
came before. For, of course, the nationalist "tradition" was not born in a vacuum. There
was at least a century's worth of literary production in Australia prior to the *Bulletin*,
much of it taking the form of short fiction, though very little of it is now widely read.
The primary survey of the field is still the fifty-six-page introduction that Cecil Hadgraft wrote to his 1986 anthology of twenty-one stories, *The Australian Short Story
before Lawson*. One might now disagree with some of Hadgraft's assumptions, especially those to do with evaluation. His "overriding concern," he observes, "was [within
limits] to pick the best of the period" (vii); and "it is scarcely surprising that Australia

did not excel in the field of short fiction" at this time *because* the audience was "small and scattered" and the stories were written "in the absence of good English models" (1). The concept of "best" is itself moot, and the assumption that a good Australian story required a "good English" model as a necessary prerequisite is at the very least contentious. Where, to my mind, Hadgraft's comments become most helpful is in their concern for narrative characteristics, language use, and story type.

For example, as early story types, Hadgraft lists the didactic moral tale, "stories about aborigines" (10)—which usually affirm some version of ethnic hierarchy—historical, mystery, and supernatural tales, and "lost child" stories. About these last stories, he observes that the danger of loss was a "peculiarly Australian concern" (27). Not so: children were lost in any number of wilderness landscapes, as any glance at the German fairy tale "Hansel and Gretel" or the nineteenth-century narratives of the Canadian writer Catharine Parr Traill, among others, will reveal, but be that as it may, the lost child story *was* related both to fairy tale antecedents and to the colonial settler mind-set: the seeming "threat" and the certain "fear" of the unspeakable or the unknown. Writing about nineteenth-century stories by Percy Sinnett, J. M. Conroy, Henry Kingsley, Marcus Clarke, J. F. Hogan, and others, Hadgraft extends his comments on the lost child motif, adding that though the child could be lost, he or she could also be found: "a child falls over a small cliff but is saved by tangled vines. A woman finds her, climbs down, but cannot climb up. After that, it would be a heartless author who would refuse them rescue. Or the child could be found by somebody who wanted to keep it, or who simply looked after it until the searchers arrived. Or the child could come upon a forsaken hut and remain for days. If, say, three or more children were lost, the eldest of the group would display qualities of responsible leadership and preserve the others. A child breaking from the group could be lost. An ingenious writer could have it both ways. . . . Occasionally [a] narrator would take the opportunity to expatiate upon the danger of disobedience in the child; or a moral could be extracted as a general [truism]—we are all wanderers from the truth" (27). It is clear that Hadgraft's "categories" depend on varying criteria. Subject shapes some of them, form or technical convention shapes others. His mid-to-late twentieth-century critical sensibilities also govern his assessments, many of which contemporary writers might agree with, though I think there is room in this field for closer readings of colonial Victorian conventions. "Historical" tales about the convict system are, for example, often couched as "moral" tales, likely as often to hide history than to express it, and the relation between the "lost child" tale and the incidence of puerperal fever, for example, about which Hadgraft does not comment, might well lead a contemporary critic to some interesting reflections on literary representations of trauma. For the most part, Hadgraft approves of humor but is disparaging about open didacticism (regarding Ellen August Chads, he writes that "her approved characters are always good and mostly unbearable," 9); he recurrently uses the word "grotesque"—a favorite word among nineteenth-century depictors of landscape—to comment here on events and behavior, with some degree of ambivalence; he is dismissive of complex hypotactic sentences being used to render "real" conversation, and of all forms of sentimentality.[2] Lawson, moreover, marks in Hadgraft's eyes the beginning of Australia's "notable" (1) contributions to the short story form, as in "The Loaded Dog" and "The Drover's Wife," "The Union Buries Its Dead" and "The Geological Spieler." Given the persistence of the critical criteria that Hadgraft's comments reveal, one can begin to see why the tall tale should emerge at a time of nationalist enthusiasm. If high colonial art had spent a century approving a mawkish definition of Good, in a society whose *folk* idiom celebrated the free spirit, the wrongly convicted transportee, the worthy bushranger, and the jolly swagman, then the new nationalist art was going to find a way to puncture what it saw as pretension. The ostensibly "real" voice of the vernacular tall tale provided a literary opportunity to validate the people at the same time. Only *some* people, of course. Not Asians. Not Aboriginals. Not women. And a certain kind of sentimentalism persisted even in the resistance to the conventional absolutes of the moral tales.

The Tall Tale Takes Shape

"The Loaded Dog," a 1902 story by Lawson, provides a paradigm. The narrative tells of three mates—Dave, Jim, and Andy—who are trying to find gold at a rich quartz reef that is supposed to be in the vicinity. They are less than successful, for because of the way they use blasting powder, they make potholes more than they open up a mineshaft. So they spend their time fishing, and the tale promptly goes off in a fishing direction, listing the various possibilities of relaxation; then they think of a way to use their skill at blasting to blast fish out of the water, and the blasting cartridge they design for this purpose gets bigger and bigger. As an aside we hear about their young retriever dog, named Tommy, who loves to play and loves to fetch, so when the blasting charge is set, Tommy rushes to retrieve it. Well-trained to play, he brings it back to Andy, who runs; Tommy runs after Dave, who grabs the dog, snatches the cartridge from his mouth, and flings it away. The dog, of course, chases after it again and brings it back once more. The story pauses at this point to advise the listener that there is a small pub in the vicinity, to which the three men run, slamming the front door behind them. The dog finds the back door open and rushes in with a happy grin and the blasting cartridge; all the men in the pub rush out; the dog follows them; and at this point yet another pause in the narrative introduces a vicious yellow mongrel cattle dog—adding, in case we missed the perspective we are expected to bring to this newcomer, that it is also "a sneaking, fighting, thieving canine, whom neighbours had tried for years to shoot or poison" (434–35). This "yellow dog" nips Tommy, Tommy drops the cartridge, the yellow dog picks it up; a pack of "spidery, thievish, cold-blooded kangaroo dogs, mongrel sheep and cattle-dogs, vicious black and yellow dogs"

(435) emerges from around corners and under buildings to surround the lead thief dog. And then there is another pause, to tell us how good the blasting powder is and how well-made the cartridge. After the inevitable blast—which is, pointedly, *not* described—the narrative tells how all the thievish dogs are cowed (none of them, even the yellow dog, is apparently physically damaged), how all the people in the vicinity are "trying to laugh without shrieking," how the women (the first time any are mentioned) become "hysterical," how Tommy trots up with an amiable smile to show his satisfaction at the fun he has had, and how, "for years afterward," bushmen ask Dave "in a lazy drawl and with just a hint of the nasal twang" how his "fishin'[s] getting on" (436).

The narrative features are clear: vernacular speech (in this case, gender marked and ethnically coded), anecdotal exaggeration, and elongation of simple narrative through strategies of interruption (in joke telling, this pattern is often introduced with the phrase "Have I told you yet about" or "I see I've forgotten to tell you about," both of which are designed to defer closure). Closure, when it does come, is relatively predictable, has little directly to do with the narrative climax, is understated, is intentionally comic, and reestablishes a kind of camaraderie of competition. Lawson's setting—the "bush" —and his characters—"mates"—reconfirm the illusion of egalitarian values, but the methodology of the tall tale (like its related forms: the satirical hoax and the mock insult) reveals at the same time that the myth of egalitarianism works as much to prevent presumptive claims of being Better Than (what the Australian language refers to as the "Tall Poppy" syndrome; Wilkes, 260–61) as to elevate the disenfranchised. That said, the *reality* of "egalitarianism," when it exists, is signified by friendship, which is strongest when it accepts unheroic inadequacies as well as when it praises the capacity for heroic action, and when it survives foolish human inconsistencies rather than when it presumes only in absolute human virtue.

Tall Tale Invites Theory

Many of the terms I have already raised also appear in the range of theory that addresses how to talk about the tall tale. I am thinking of terms such as *hoax, lie, joke, folly, national and regional identity, in-group, comedy, exclusion, irony, orality, narrator, folklore, exaggeration, understatement,* and the like, to which should be added further terms such as *category mistake* or *category exchange.* A Swedish commentary by Anna Birgitta Rooth, for example, argues the relation between the tall tale, intended to be disbelieved, and the tale of a sublime or idealized world, such as Paradise, which faithful tellers intended to be both believed and believed *in.* Between the two strategies lie fanciful travelers' tales (of the Land of Cockaygne, for example), tales of magic journeys and encounters with monsters and odd creatures (see also Dorson), hunting and fishing stories, mariners' tales—some of them told as fables, in which case they lean toward moral exempla, and some of them told for the sheer joy of the exaggeration, in which case they push toward acceptance in the knowledge that they simultaneously display their awareness of the ridiculousness of accepting the tale at face value. Any acceptance, in other words, invites participation in a coterie of disbelief. The techniques of such tales include reversed roles, conflicting statements, and enumerations of events or statistics—some of which are apparent in "The Loaded Dog."

Other commentators—Carolyn Brown and Henry Wonham, for example—embed their insights into the tall tale's form and function in studies of its history in the United States and its relevance to American cultural development. "[C]itizens of the New World," says Wonham, "were just as apt to parody foreign opinion by exaggerating their own depravity as they were to brag about the productivity of the native sheep. In both cases, the exaggerated response sought to deflate European criticism without actually confronting its charges. Travellers who had been exposed beforehand to baseless myths about the New World had no trouble believing in the unspeakable barbarity of its people or in the most unheard-of wonders of nature, provided that the news came from an honest-looking American or a reputable newspaper. . . . Tall humor grew up both in response to Europe's uninformed critique of life on the frontier and in response to the frontier itself" (18). "Tall humor," moreover, "was especially capable of inflating America's promises to such an extent . . . that an inevitable contrast with real conditions suggested itself in the minds of those who knew enough not to be taken in by the promise" (20). It is not exaggeration itself, in other words, that underpins the tall tale, but the kinds of "category exchange" that take place, as when a man puts an umbrella to bed and himself goes to sleep propped up in a corner,[3] and, further, the kinds of *qualified* deception that the form invokes: hyperbole alone does not constitute "tallness," in other words, nor does simple prevarication. In the tall tale, the listener is invited both to accept *and* to refute, knowing enough of the cultural environment within which the tale is told (and to which it alludes) to be in dialogue with the tenor of the tale without investing in its surface claim on factuality.

Carolyn Brown also affirms the tall tale's "special significance in American life," its role as "a tool and an emblem of national and regional identity," because from early on "the incomprehensible vastness of the continent, the extraordinary fertility of the land, and the variety of national peculiarities inspired a humor of extravagance and exaggeration . . . independent of European refinements, constraints, and mores" (2). Although she emphasizes that the tall tale was neither invented in nor is restricted to North America, there is a slippage here between country and continent of a sort that (perhaps unknown to Brown herself) is the source of much barbed, cross-border Canadian humor about American rhetorical and political assumptions. Interestingly, Brown goes on to say that the "moral atmosphere in which [a tall tale] is told" is one "in which the line between fact and fiction is hazy and the manipulation of that boundary is a source of humor" (9). But only to those who can participate, who share (28) in taking delight in the tall tale's incongruous connection between literality of narrative rendering and outrageousness of material (or, of course, those who are *helped* to share, helped by means of the teller's facial mobility, winks, gestures, raised eyebrows, aural cadences even within a deadpan delivery, and other invitations to understand the narrative duality being enacted). Given this interest in the features of oral narrative, Brown subsequently emphasizes the tall tale's oral origins and its folk-tale cognates. A tall tale is in some sense an initiation tale at least in its effect, in that it can both exclude those who do not appreciate what is going on and permit access to a narrative community to an active listener-participant. Of the critics I refer to here, only Anna Birgitta Rooth affirms that the tall tale is a Eurasian form and dominantly told by men (132–33). Her comment, however, returns these short notes to the Australian context.

The Australian Tall Tale Is Competitive

This observation suggests that criticism needs to look at the teller as well as the tale, whether this teller is deemed to be the author, an author's narrator, or a figure in the narrator's tale who tells yet another story. The point is that the story being told is told within a context of tale telling. Sometimes, moreover, in narrative context, a first teller initiates an entertainment by telling a tale that invites a second or third or nth tale teller to participate in what becomes a "capping" contest or narrative exchange. A fairly common form of nineteenth-century book-length miscellany or *Rahmenerzählung* (such as Thomas Chandler Haliburton's *The Old Judge*, 1849, or Henry Lapham's *We Four, and the Stories We Told*, 1880) brought together a range of story forms under the pretext of telling stories to endure a journey more pleasurably or to spend a limited duration of time in an exchange of wisdom and wit; it is a practice with roots in *The Canterbury Tales* and elsewhere. In a capping contest, the range of tale forms is more limited; the intent seems to be to tell as fact a series of progressively more outlandish stories. The competition comes from seeing who can get away with the greatest exaggeration—the "getting away with" being as important as the exaggeration itself, for as each new tall tale, by exaggerating further, implicitly debunks the truth of the one before it by saying it does not *really* stretch the truth, then the last tale in the series, the one that no one can finally cap, is the tacit "winner." Henry Lawson's "His Masterpiece" presents a slight variant of this pattern when a character named Green-hide Billy starts off an ostensibly true anecdote of his life in the bush, only to have the men around the campfire challenge him on details. Billy's response to these interruptions is to elaborate his story even further, repeatedly, until the men can think of no further way to challenge. At that point Billy retains his reputation as the greatest liar in the district, and the men knock their pipe ash into the fire and go to bed.

This celebration of the liar is a recurrent motif in Australian writing, with Australian slang developing a range of inventive terms for the one who manufactures stories, and the story makers happily turning the terms to their own ends. A "Tom Collins," for example, was one who started rumors; hence Joseph Furphy published his 1903 novel *Such Is Life* (about the power of rumormongering) under the pseudonym Tom Collins—only to have the name initially accepted as a real one. Ironically, however, by 1916 the word "furphy" had become a synonym for any rumor or "latrine rumor" or false report, because the water carts at the Melbourne army camps had been supplied by Joseph Furphy's brother, Furphy of Shepparton; and as the family name was imprinted in large letters on the side of the metal containers, "to furphy" came to mean to linger by the water carts telling stories. Relatedly, an "illywhacker" was, as early as 1941, a trickster or spieler at a country fair; hence when Peter Carey in 1985 titled one of his novels *Illywhacker*, the readership was presumably sufficiently warned. "Spieler," of course (from the German *spielen*, "to play"), has its own linguistic history as a word for the sideshow barker, the con man, the person with the ability to play fast and loose with speech. When Lawson calls one of his series of "Steelman" tales "The Geological Spieler," again the reader is cautioned in advance. "The Geological Spieler," however, takes a slightly different turn and reveals that the tall-tale competition can rebound on the would-be winner. In Lawson's depiction of him, Steelman is the sort of person who constantly uses his skill with words to ingratiate himself with others and win from them some sort of advantage, and in this tale he and his "pal and pupil, Smith," (149) are in New Zealand, wandering the countryside looking for whatever they can get. When they come upon a crew working on a new railway line, Steelman proposes to take advantage of the opportunity to get free board and lodging for a while. The story opens with an ostensible remark he has at one time made to Smith: "There's nothing so interesting as Geology, even to common and ignorant people, especially when you have a bank or the side of a cutting, studded with fossil fish and things and oysters that were stale when Adam was fresh to illustrate by" (149). Stepping up to a "heavy, gloomy, labouring man," Steelman opens his strategic conversation with comments on the weather, and the text—all in reported third-person, emphasizing the fact that the tale is not Steelman's but some unnamed narrator's— is studded with a deliberate Australian (*not New Zealand*) vernacular:

> The man of mullick[4] gave it as his opinion that the fine weather wouldn't last, and seemed to take a gloomy kind of pleasure in that reflection; he said there was more rain down yonder, pointing to the south-east, than the moon could swallow up— the moon was in its first quarter, during which time it is popularly believed in some parts of Maoriland that the south-easter is most likely to be out on the wallaby[5] and the weather bad. Steelman regarded that quarter of the sky with an expression of gentle remonstrance mingled as it were with a sort of fatherly indulgence, agreed mildly with the labouring man, and seemed lost for a moment in a reverie from which he roused himself to enquire cautiously after the boss. There was no boss, it was a co-operative party. That chap standing over there by the dray in the end of the

cutting was their spokesman—their representative: they called him Boss, but that
was only his nickname. (149)

The conditions, clearly, seem ripe for manipulation.

Asking if there is accommodation about (which he knows there is not), Steelman
is invited to stay over in the camp (as he has intended); asked if he is a commercial
traveler, he says no, he is a geologist (named *Stoneleigh*), and getting the sign of interest he is hoping for, he proceeds to say he suspects there is gold in the cut of the hills
above them. To sustain interest he and Smith spend the next few days chasing up and
down the hills gathering "stones and bits of rock" in a black bag and coming back to
the camp to get dinner and a bed in return for a "lecture on those minerals after tea"
(153). Then the tale pauses to change direction: "On about the fourth morning Steelman had a yarn with one of the men going to work. He was a lanky young fellow with
a sandy complexion, and seemingly harmless grin. In Australia he might have been
regarded as a 'cove' rather than a 'chap,' but there was nothing of the 'bloke' about
him" (153)—*chap* meaning "ordinary fellow," *cove* suggesting someone more like a
congenial station manager (one who would, for example, sit down to smoke with the
other men), but *bloke* implying "boss." The lanky fellow is surprised that "Stoneleigh"
has not figured out that the man they call "Boss" in the railway camp is a university
graduate whom some people once reckoned to be "'the best—what do you call it?—
the best minrologist [sic] in the country. He had a first-class billet in the Mines Department, but he lost it—you know—the booze'" (153). "Stoneleigh" figures it might be
time to be making a move—but on the way back to camp he says to another man that
he is surprised that the Boss had a university education. Then this exchange ensues;
the man says:

> "Who's been telling you that?"
> "One of your mates."
> "Oh, he's been getting at you, why: it's all the Boss can do to write his own name.
> Now that lanky sandy cove with the birth-mark grin—it's him that's had the college
> education." (153)

After this, Steelman resolves to leave right away. Quite who, if anyone, is telling the
truth is beside the point. Steelman realizes that not only has he been found out but
also that he has *long* been found out, and that his performances have been silently
received by at least one person as comedy. It is Steelman who has been excluded by
his act, not Steelman who manipulates by excluding. For the unnamed authorial narrator of the tale, however, the exaggeration has been contained within anecdote, in
which—because of the resonances of the Australian vernacular—the Australian listener will share. This is not a fable of war between belief systems or moral absolutes;
the one-upmanship neither destroys Steelman nor elevates the lanky cove above the
ordinary men he works with, and it works in this context *because* Steelman has been

exposed not by public ridicule but by the private success of an undetected "lie." He has been—with the pun intended—*taken in*. Functionally, this tale of the tall-tale teller, therefore, reaffirms a camaraderie between narrator and listener, establishing as it were the conditions for reply, an implicit invitation for a capping tale from another member of the group.

The Australian Tall Tale Is Gendered Male

Because the camaraderie is established by *not* putting oneself forward, it derives from a construction of the group rather than a construction of the individual. Paradoxically, the tall tale generally focuses on an individual's extravagant adventures or claims. The connection between these two apparently contradictory impulses draws attention back to the gendering of the tales, for the group's solidarity—like the tales themselves—usually excludes women and eschews the behavioral practices and stylistic mannerisms that criticism, like society, conventionally coded as female. Urban respectability. Domesticity. Politesse. High art. It is not that writers such as Lawson avoided sentimentalism; far from it. But they tended to admit their sentiments after the fact, as it were, and obliquely—after a friend had died, for example, rather than during the friendship itself: Lawson's "The Union Buries Its Dead" seems callous to some contemporary readers, for it tells of men who bury an unknown man but who never seek to find out his name, but the point of the story is that they provide a decent, if laconic and apparently unreflective, ritual of respect for even the unknown individual *because they recognize him* as a fellow member of their own category or class. Another tendency of such stories is to sentimentalize utility and practicality and difficulty and applicable knowledge by ennobling them as the attributes of manliness. Heroism became the heroism of concern for the group, as in the war stories of William Baylebridge and others, wherein fear is rendered as cowardice and cowardice is rendered as selfishness.[6] The sports story provides yet another variant. But the bush story provides the most recurrent paradigm within which the tall tale was told.

Given this gendered context, it seems consequently possible to argue that the tall tale's characteristic function was not merely to *represent* the actual practice of tale telling around a campfire but also, through a comprehensible system of coding, to *reaffirm* the solidarity of the group. The institution of "mateship," once so celebrated as the quintessence of Australianism[7]—affirming that the reliant friendship between men was the acme of understanding, so that if a woman were ever called a "mate" it was deemed an extraordinary tribute—is only one aspect of this solidarity. It seems to me that, while "mateship" confirms the practicality of friendship as well as the support it represents, "tall-tale telling" provides a context whereby competition can be made acceptable and given value. It becomes the ritual through which a kind of bonding between rivals can take place, as powerful as mateship, perhaps, but defused of any potential that rivalry might have for disrupting group identity, because the jocularity of the tales permits masks to *be* sustained. It seems particularly important, moreover, for the masks to be sustained. Quite why is likely a personal as well as a social question, having something to do with autobiographical psychology as well as with the link between literary conventions and public mores. In other words, as current commentary in autobiographical theory argues,[8] there is a clear distinction between the *fictive* (which makes the reader/listener aware of the strategies of a tale's own construction) and the *fictitious* (which does not). The tall tale, while it depends on surprise, nonetheless always signals its own fictive strategy; and, paradoxically, to be "perfectly" successful, it has to be effective in its deceit (and therefore unanswerable) and, at some stage, it has to be clearly apparent to the listener that he or she has been taken in by a strategy rather than by the truth.

Autobiographical theory also, of course, posits several kinds of truth—historical, narrative, personal, conditional, psychological, and so on[9]—but argues that a certain kind of authenticity of expression can result from lying. In *Telling Lies in Modern American Autobiography* (1990),[10] for example, Timothy Dow Adams quotes John Barth's *Lost in the Funhouse* (1969) to the effect that an author who abandons actuality for invention, but substitutes fabrications *patterned* on real life for the literary conventions of myth, can express truths that strict adherence to actuality would obscure (7). The importance of the tall tale to a male sense of self in Australia, at a time when nationalism demanded models of independence, is that it couched this need (essentially for heroic action) inside a form of group expression; it permitted individuality to be articulated without asserting a conventional elitism of education or wealth; it used the idiom of competition as a mode of celebrating interdependence rather than for revealing weakness; and it exaggerated—or made "fictive"—the actual lives and language of ordinary people rather than served received definitions of culture and received models of cultural power. One problem, of course, is that the tall tale could come to be accepted as the whole truth and nothing but, a convention in its own right with its own demands on the next generations of storytellers.

The Australian Tall Tale Can Subvert

Timothy Dow Adams also quotes from Flannery O'Connor's *Mystery and Manners* (1969) to the effect that people shout to those who do not hear well and draw in an exaggeratedly large fashion for those who do not see well (167–68). He does so to emphasize that lies in autobiography should not be read simply as an intent to deceive, or to falsify some abstract and unassailable truth, but as a strategy designed to invite closer attention—a strategy asking to be read for the kinds of lies it tells, for the obliqueness of the strategy itself and for what that says about the expression of personality. It is in this context that I would like to turn briefly to Frank Moorhouse's 1985 story "The Drover's Wife" (I say 1985, but there were versions of the story published before then, beginning in 1980 with an anniversary issue of the *Bulletin*; for some years Moorhouse kept adding on further sections). This story, of course—as John Thieme and others have acknowledged—is one in a series (although the series was only latterly intended as such). Henry Lawson's story called "The Drover's Wife," long regarded (largely by male critics) as the quintessential Australian story, appeared in 1893. It tells of a woman in the bush, whose ability to cope while her drover husband is away makes her practically a "mate." She has to cope with weather, Aboriginal deceit, a dangerous swagman, her several children, her "womanly" sentimentality (which in a moment of comic self-recognition she manages to suppress), and most particularly, a poisonous snake that threatens her family. In 1945 Russell Drysdale painted a picture with the same title, based on Lawson's story, in which a stocky woman with a long shadow occupies the foreground, and spindly shrubs and a horse and cart fill in the middle distance. The short story writer Murray Bail penned his own story of this title in 1975, altering the narrative point of view to that of a dentist who claims that Drysdale's portrait is not of the drover's wife but of his own, a woman named Hazel, who had a "silly streak" and who ran off with a drover after writing a *short note* to her husband telling him his tea was in the oven and not to give Trev any carrots.

Moorhouse's story sends up not only the Drover's Wife in literature and art but also, more particularly, the Drover's Wife industry in literary criticism. It purports to be the transcript of a talk given on Lawson and Company at an International Conference in Italy, sent back to the *Bulletin* by a writer who has managed to pick it up there and have it translated. The ostensible author is one Franco Casamaggiore (or "Frank Moorhouse," in case the bilingual pun is not clear), who provides us with the "real" interpretation of the fiction. In the Casamaggiore version, much depends on what is meant by the words "drover" and "wife"; he has been reliably advised, he says, by Australian travelers to Italy, that "drover" is a variant of "driver," and that on long drives to market, sheep were transported in wicker baskets to keep them in good condition, which explains why the Drysdale painting depicts no sheep at all but a poor quality cart that is sufficiently big that it could contain a thousand basketed sheep. Because this was a raw pioneering country, moreover, where women were few and men close, sometimes the sheep became attractive to the drivers; hence the term "wife" had to be understood within a context of what the folk culture of Australia now refers to as "Interspecies reciprocity" (101), and the "killing of the snake" incident had to be read in the knowledge of Freud, the Australian folk language ("much richer than its European counterpart, which is in a state of decay," Casamaggiore opines, as part of an ongoing lateral critique of capitalism), and male behavior: "'I am told that to this day [he says], Australian men are forever killing the snake'" (103). However, he adds, relations with sheep are now rarer, having been sublimated into symbolic actions that include a weekly ritual with sheep fodder called "mowing the lawn" and the act of sitting on the "artefact which remembers" (106), a sheepskin seat cover in the family car, which "gives comfort through racial memory far exceeding the need for warmth in that temperate land" (106). High Art therefore admits to "unspeakable truth" — "mate-*sheep*" — in a "coded and guilty" way (109). To which conclusion Moorhouse adds a series of "letters" to the Australian Broadcasting Corporation, the *Bulletin*, and to a distinguished academic, complaining that these comments are a vile insult to real drovers and pioneer women, that there are flaws in the interpretation, that the lady in question would be quite wise to kill any poisonous snake, and that some of the terms are obscure for a translator wishing to turn Casamaggiore into Chinese and could they please be explained further. These are followed by photo reproductions of a man and sheep on the cover of the *Bulletin* and an inaccurate and apparently straight-faced report in the National *Times* on "Franco Casa Moora's" explanation of the story; it closes with another Australian joke: "The New Zealanders, having a high sheep popu-lation themselves, received the paper in anxious silence" (114).

It seems likely that the "Drover's Wife" saga, though quiet now for over a decade, is not yet finished. Nor is the joke. For, of course, Moorhouse is adapting the tall tale form in at least four ways: telling a tall tale to criticize the canonization of Lawson *and Lawson's strategies of tale telling*; to lambaste the willingness of critics and the media to accept uncritically anything they are told, from urban legend to tourist ironies, *and* to turn it into theory; to puncture the literal-mindedness of other Aus-tralians and also their complacency about the greatness of their society and cultural accomplishments; and to revalidate the power of *fiction* to *invent* "truth" rather than simply mirror whatever had come to be accepted *as* truth, in fiction and in history. When a Moorhouse story appears in a book called *The Most Beautiful Lies*, the reader is, one would think, duly warned.

The Australian Tall Tale Can Also Be Subverted

It is clear that, however much Moorhouse subverts particular sets of reading conven-tions and assumptions about representation, other conventions are left alone, includ-ing what might be called the psychosexuality of locker-room humor: competitive in-jokes and recognizable exaggerations. The role that women are assigned in this paradigm led Barbara Jefferis to write her own version of "The Drover's Wife" in 1980, also publishing it in the *Bulletin*. For the first time in this "drover's exchange," the drover's wife is herself given a voice. Jefferis creates a character who insists that Lawson, Drysdale, Bail, and Moorhouse *all* got her story wrong: that she is neither shadow nor saint, neither silly nor sheep — *not* heroic for just doing what had to be done, not named Hazel, and not dismissible. Complaining about having been *con-structed* by men who distorted her real life, she then characterizes Mr. Lawson as a nice little bloke, says Bail's dentist was dirty and therefore deserving of being left, cannot remember Mr. Drysdale, and finds Casamaggiore to be a pitiable victim of Australian male yarning. Women, she says, have a different history — their own, free from male conventions—and someone should write it down.[11] The political intent of this story is not in doubt. But to ask if it is free from the conventions it criticizes is to raise another issue. Even in opposition, that is, Jefferis's story to some degree reinscribes the stereotypes it purports to deconstruct. Though more "realistic" in its strategies (the story is cast as an earnest documentary), it partakes in the tall tale form at least to the degree that it perpetuates the cultural centrality of the story involving the drover's wife, and however seriously and critically it does so, it extends the joke.

To subvert the politics of the tall tale *form*, other writers have adopted alternative strategies, attempting less to refuse the topics that male writers recurrently addressed than to defuse their assumptions about social consequentiality by altering the lexicon and syntax of representation. I think it significant that two of the most effective contemporary writers to challenge the dominance of the bush-tale strategy in history and its continuing presence in the literary imagination have been women, and that these women have been explicit in acknowledging their non-Anglo-Celtic immigrant heritage in Australia; I am referring to Ania Walwicz and Anna Couani. (At the same time, I also emphasize that any critical effort to *categorize* these two writers both as "immigrant" or "migrant" or "ethnic" writers pays little attention to the difference in their experience or the degree of their acceptance within mainstream Australian cultural commentary—Couani is third-generation Australian from a family with an Italian background, Walwicz an immigrant to Australia from Poland in 1963 at the age of thirteen; both are now regularly read, reviewed, and anthologized within "standard" works; see, for example, Murray; Goodwin and Lawson.) In the prose pieces Couani published in her collection *Italy and The Train* (1983),[12] to illustrate what I mean by "challenge," the author dispenses with almost all the conventions with which the term "short story" has come to be associated, instead fastening on the skeleton requirements of verbal communication. That is, she calls overt attention to the manner of telling, so that how a story is told becomes a subject, and also something of a sensory politics. A passage called "He Came, Etcetera," for example, opens with a vertically arranged series of utterances in statement form, but are they "sentences"? If so, in what sense, and if not, why?

I

he went.
he came.
he rode.
he stayed.
he thought. (40)

Each unit ends with a period; none begins with an uppercase letter. None is precisely a "sentence." But each "sentences" meaning. The passage goes on to elaborate these expressions slightly, but the units of communication establish how the language functions:

"he" is the active agent in all the transactions listed, and "he," the grammatical subject, is attributed the power of "thinking." Or, in this context, does "he thought" mean something else: does it mean "he *thinks* he has the power to do, but to anyone else it is immaterial whether he goes or stays." The apparently simple list thus turns political.

In another piece by Couani, "What a man, what a moon," the first line and a half of a sixteen-line passage read, "What a man, what a moon, what a fish, what a chip, what a block, what a mind, what a tool, what a drive" (63). Language again is at issue: what is it, how does it work, and how does it work for someone whose mother tongue is different from the one that is here being used? In "He Came, Etcetera," the basic pattern of subject-verb order constructs the bare bones of narrative; in "What a man, what a moon," the sequence of verbal units that can be substituted in the "What a [blank]" paradigm—an example of the kind of pattern drill used in English-as-a-second-language teaching—communicates in pairs. This sequencing not only makes the language seem strange to a native speaker but also demonstrates the apparent neutrality of all words (or units of sound) in any language that is totally foreign. The verbal units in this example of Couani's prose pair up words that native speakers think of as "four-letter" expletives with words with four (or more) letters that seem power-neutral to the native speaker but that for the language learner could be explosive or could be nothing.

A third example from Couani's work, "Xmas in the Bush," opens in fragment, controlled by its grammatically ambiguous opening word: "Running along far away from the road" (77). Without conventional syntax, a reader does not immediately know if "Running" is a gerundial subject or a dependent participial attribute of something else. With conventional syntax, the fragment is open to reading, but how? Interpretation becomes a critical question. In the same example—having established that "the mother, the father and the children are here. With friends" (77), each supplement modifying what has gone before—a subsequent passage reads this way: "In the morning the father throws the dog in the water. The dog paddles madly to the shore. The father talks about snags in the river. They all discuss the difference between snags as in water hazards and snags as in sausages. Sausage dogs. Smoke. Children who've drowned. Bushfires. Snakes. Carpet snakes. The long grass. The blackberry patch. The tar baby. Was there such a thing as Brere Bear. The pyjama girl. Bull-rushes. Flash floods. Flying foxes. The hazards of flying foxes. High tensile wires and electricity lines. Broken electricity lines hanging down into creeks. Fords with cars on them washed away in flash floods. River snakes. March flies. Bot flies. The difference between bot flies and sand flies. Maggots in sausages. Maggot stories. Meat safe stories. Ice chest stories. Milk delivery when milk was in pails" (78). This apparently associational list (what Sneja Gunew calls a "parodic litany" [120], in her 1994 Kristevan commentary on Couani[13]) is by no means random. The list cumulatively and punningly constructs a picture of the actions and exchanges at an Australian bush picnic (in what might be taken as an apparently realist representation: "real life" rather than "writing," say) at the same time as it rehearses the conventional subjects of the Australian bush tale (dogs, floods, snakes, flies, and lost children) and reenacts the story competition, which is the common ground of the tall tale exchange. What Couani has done *technically*, that is, is reiterate the paradigm of that tale but disrupt the syntagmatic axis of its telling. Disrupting the line of the grammar, crossing generic borderlines into what she herself called "non-narrative structure and collaging effects,"[14] she disrupts the ease with which a culturally automatic response is possible, and asks for the constructed convention to be contextualized. "Xmas in the Bush" closes with the phrase, "they remember other discussions they've had and that they always concluded with politics. The father turns down the tilly lamp" (79).[15] One could certainly read emblematically the assertion that "the father" turns down the lamp to close off further speech. For the story openly to declare that conclusions are always political, however, suggests that a reader read beyond the obvious and realize that the implicit pun in the mention of the Tilley lamp hints at a process of *dis-mantling*. Plainly, closing off speech does not close off discourse.

The Australian Tall Tale Refuses to End

It refuses to end, that is, insofar as it invites a reply. In this sense, the counterdiscourse of Couani and Walwicz can be read as part of a tale-telling dialogue in Australian cultural history. Consider a 1981 work by Walwicz called "Australia." It has been called a poem, and also a prose poem. And it appeared first in an anthology of "recent prose." It is something of a dramatic monologue, and it begins, "You big ugly. You too empty. You desert with your nothing nothing nothing." What follows is thirty lines of invective, attacking "Acres of suburbs watching the telly," the "big sea" and "Beach beach beach," the repetitive landscape ("Road road tree tree") that contrasts unflatteringly in her eyes with the landscape of her pre-immigration experience: "crowded and many." Set among these phrases of open critique, however, are several other phrases that reveal the speaker's unhappiness: she says "You're ugly" but also "You laugh at me"; "You big cow" but also "You make me a dot in the nowhere"; "You average average" but also "You never accept me. For your own" (305–6). At its most obvious, this story records the reactions of an immigrant woman who in differing ways has—and has not—been "taken in." She is berating a man both because of what he has done— at the center of the piece is a telling moment of rivalry and narrative revelation: "You engaged Doreen" (306)—and because of what he does not do. But the story accomplishes something else as well.

As the title fairly explicitly asserts, the speaker is berating the man not only because of Doreen but also as an exemplar of everything she finds alienating about Australia itself: its size, its language (which she finds both foreign and uncouth), its sameness, its middle-classness, its lack of energy and sophistication and any taste for intellectual inquiry, its unimaginativeness, its Saturday night sprees, and its Sunday morning boredom. She, by contrast, has verve. Even in using a language that is not her own, the speaker is inventive, managing to turn adjectives into evocative nouns, construct brand new resonant compounds, use repetition to evoke repetitiveness, transform fragments into metonyms of identity. But Walwicz, in addition, is taking part in yet another ongoing dialogue with Australian literary conventions. By calling her work "Australia," she enters her piece into a kind of ritual of national self-assessment; it is not exactly linear in nature, but it is sequential. It includes poems called "Australia" or "Australasia" or "Terra Australis" by (at least) W. C. Wentworth (1823; in a poem subsequently satirized by Charles Harpur in 1853), John Farrell (1886), Bernard O'Dowd (1900), Mary Gilmore (1932), A. D. Hope (1939), James McAuley (1942), Douglas Stewart (1949), and Gary Catalano (c. 1986), and it tells a kind of a story about a people who anticipated "a new Britannia in another world" (Wentworth; Goodwin, 314), who found an "unsown garden" "whose history had not begun" (Farrell; Goodwin, 251), who ironized a "Last sea-thing dredged by sailor Time from Space" (O'Dowd; Goodwin, 310), who described a "land of similes" (McAuley; Goodwin, 309), who despaired of a "Nation of trees, drab green and desolate grey / In the field uniform of modern wars," whose "five cities, like five teeming sores," house men "Whose boast is not: 'we live' but 'we survive,' / A type who will inhabit the dying earth," "second-hand Europeans" who "pullulate / Timidly on the edge of alien shores" (Hope; Goodwin, 311).

Ania Walwicz reads her "Australia" through the lens of what has gone before, disputing the closed claims on civilization that permit her character to inhabit only its margins and disrupting the language codes that enunciate these claims. In an oblique way, she might even be said to cap their exaggerated presumptions with exaggerations of her own, pushing those who—through story—think they have satisfactorily imagined the idea of community or nation to imagine it again. In her words, moreover, and through her speaker's words, she invites reply.

Notes

1. It is a pleasure to acknowledge them here: Tara Burnell, Alison Frost, Victoria Kuttainen, Charles Martell, Travis Mason, Brenda Payne, Marilee Peters, and Nicholas Travers. I wish also to thank my colleagues Mary Chapman and Susanna Egan for their suggestions.

2. Sentimental practice in fiction, and a critical resistance to sentimentalism, marked American and other national literary histories as well, and Hadgraft may well have been influenced by these trends. As Chapman and Hendler summarize critical change, in the introduction to their *Sentimental Men* (1999), American sentimentality had by the middle of the nineteenth century become almost exclusively linked with the feminine; the "domestic realm came to be considered the locus of feeling . . . the culture of sentiment less directly identified with public virtue and benevolence and more associated with women's moral, nurturing role in the private sphere of the bourgeois family. . . . The public sphere was a correspondingly masculine realm, a site of rational political discourse and economic production characterized by competition rather than sentiment. . . . That this binary was more a class, race, and national ideology than a universal social practice made it no less effective in

shaping discourse on gender, affect, and cultural space" (3). While early-twentieth-century critics solidified this position—Chapman and Hendler (4–5) refer to the way H. R. Brown, E. D. Branch, F. O. Matthiessen, and Ann Douglas respectively dismissed sentimentalism as escapist and simpleminded, as flabby and precious, as the domestic opposite of the forceful male literature of the open air (meaning Melville and Whitman), and as a debased and dishonest peddling of religion—subsequent criticism attempted to rehabilitate sentimentalism and to dismantle the binary that dismissed it. Contextualizing their own study of American male writers of sentimental fictions (5–6), Chapman and Hendler refer, for example, to Eve Kosofsky Sedgwick's reexamination of gender roles, Jane Tompkins's and others' investigations of sentimentalism as a political strategy to protest the marginalization of women and racial minorities and to engage these groups in political action, and Elizabeth Barnes's inquiry into the relation between sentimentalism and nostalgia (a subject taken up by Sneja Gunew in relation to Australian multiculturalism).

3. Wonham, *Mark Twain*, 19.

4. In Australian idiom the word "Mullick," or "mullock," refers to mine refuse, the muck at the top of a shaft, hence by extension anything perceived to be without value; to "poke mullock" or to "poke bora[c]k" means to poke fun at.

5. I.e., "out on the wallaby track," meaning out of work.

6. I am indebted to Nicholas Travers for this observation.

7. As in Moore, *Social Patterns*, 19–21. It is perhaps worth adding that Prime Minister John Howard, as reported in the *Sydney Morning Herald* (March 24, 1999), drafted (with the poet Les Murray) a preamble to a new proposed constitution, in which the following words appeared: "we value excellence as well as fairness, independence as clearly as mateship." Deborah Snow, writing next day in the same paper, was one of several people decrying the "Anglo male bonding" implicit in the word "mateship" and opposing its appearance in any constitution.

8. Adams, *Telling Lies*, 11.

9. Ibid., 8.

10. I wish to thank my colleague Susanna Egan for drawing my attention to Adams and suggesting the relevance to my topic of the critical literature on autobiography.

11. See Jones and Andrews, "Australian Humour," 62; see Thieme, "Drovers' Wives," 74, for further comment.

12. I am indebted to Alison Frost for drawing my attention to the complexity of Couani's work.

13. Gunew argues that Couani reads the familiar themes of Australian literature disruptively in order to release the "uncanny" in them, a non-Lacanian "other" that has been repressed and that is released under the eye of the writer who has not been raised in an Anglo-Celtic culture and idiom.

14. "Writing," 98.

15. A Tilley lamp is a trademark name for a camping light that (like a Coleman lamp in North America) burns a mantle.

Works Cited

Adams, Timothy Dow. *Telling Lies in Modern American Autobiography.* Chapel Hill and London: University of North Carolina Press, 1990.

Bail, Murray. "The Drover's Wife." In *Contemporary Portraits and Other Stories*, 55–61. St Lucia: University of Queensland Press, 1975.

Bird, Carmel, ed. *The Penguin Century of Australian Stories.* Introduction by Kerryn Golds-worthy. Ringwood, Victoria: Viking, 2000.

Brown, Carolyn S. *The Tall Tale in American Folklore and Literature.* Knoxville: University of Tennessee Press, 1987.

Chapman, Mary, and Glenn Hendler, eds. *Sentimental Men: Masculinity and the Politics of Affect in American Culture.* Berkeley: University of California Press, 1999.

Couani, Anna. *Italy and the Train.* Melbourne: Rigmarole Books, 1983. "Italy" was first pub-lished in 1977.

———. "Writing from a Non-Anglo Perspective." In *Striking Chords,* edited by Sneja Gunew and Kateryna O. Longley, 96–98. North Sydney: Allen and Unwin, 1992.

Dixon, Robert. *The Course of Empire: Neo-classical Culture in New South Wales, 1788–1860.* Melbourne: Oxford University Press, 1986.

Dorson, Richard M. *Man and Beast in American Comic Legend.* Bloomington: Indiana Uni-versity Press, 1982.

Goodwin, Ken, and Alan Lawson, eds. *The Macmillan Anthology of Australian Literature.* South Melbourne: Macmillan, 1990.

Gunew, Sneja. "Homeland, Nostalgia, the Uncanny: The Work of Anna Couani." In *Framing Marginality,* 111–31. Melbourne: Melbourne University Press, 1994.

Hadgraft, Cecil. "Introduction." In *The Australian Short Story before Lawson,* edited by Cecil Hadgraft, 1–56. Melbourne: Oxford University Press, 1986.

Hodgins, Jack. *The Invention of the World.* Toronto: Macmillan, 1977.

Jefferis, Barbara. "The Drover's Wife." *Bulletin* 23–30 (December 1980): 156–60.

Jones, Dorothy, and Barry Andrews. "Australian Humour." *Australian Literary Studies* 13, no. 4 (October 1988): 60–76.

Kiernan, Brian, ed. *The Most Beautiful Lies: A Collection of Five Major Contemporary Fic-tion Writers, Stories by Bail, Carey, Lawson, Lurie, Moorhouse, Wilding.* London: Angus and Robertson, 1977.

Kroetsch, Robert. *The Studhorse Man.* Toronto: Macmillan, 1969.

Lawson, Henry. "The Loaded Dog" (1902). In *Penguin Century of Australian Stories,* edited by Bird, 430–36; *Most Beautiful Lies,* edited by Kiernan, 254–58.

———. "The Geological Spieler." In *The Essential Henry Lawson: The Best Works of Aus-tralia's Greatest Writer,* selected by Brian Kiernan, 149–54. South Yarra, Victoria: Currey O'Neil, 1982.

Mitchell, W. O. *Jake and the Kid.* Toronto: Macmillan, 1961.

Moore, T. Inglis. *Social Patterns in Australian Literature.* Sydney: Angus and Robertson, 1971.

Moorhouse, Frank. "The Drover's Wife." In *Room Service,* 99–116. Ringwood: Viking, 1985.

Murray, Les, ed. *The New Oxford Book of Australian Verse.* Melbourne: Oxford University Press, 1986.

Rooth, Anna Birgitta. *Från lögnsaga till paradis* (From Tall Tale to Paradise). Uppsala: Acta Universitatis Upsaliensis, 1983. English-language summary, 127–35.

Schaffer, Kay. *Women and the Bush: Forces of Desire in the Australian Cultural Tradition.* Cambridge: Cambridge University Press, 1988.

Stone, Ted. *It's Hardly Worth Talkin' If You're Goin' to Tell the Truth.* Saskatoon: Western Producer Prairie Books, 1986.

Thieme, John. "Drovers' Wives." In *Short Fiction in the New Literatures in English*, edited by Jacqueline Bardolph, 69–75. Nice: Faculté des Lettres, Université de Nice, 1989.

Walwicz, Ania. "Australia." In *Island in the Sun: An Anthology of Recent Australian Prose*, edited by Damian White and Anna Couani, 305–6. Glebe, N.S.W.: Sea Cruise Books, 1981; reprinted Goodwin and Lawson, eds., *The Macmillan Anthology of Australian Literature* (South Melbourne: Macmillan, 1990).

Wilkes, G. A. *A Dictionary of Australian Colloquialisms*. London: Routledge and Kegan Paul, 1978.

Wonham, Henry B. *Mark Twain and the Art of the Tall Tale*. New York: Oxford University Press, 1993.

When Foreignness and Familiarity Become One

Defamiliarization in Some Canadian Short Stories

Gerd Bjørhovde

Two points should be made by way of introduction. One, for various reasons that have been interestingly explored by, for instance, W. H. New[1] —and that I shall not go into here—short stories have a very strong position in Canadian literature. Second, some interesting social and historical factors are at play in the development of the Canadian short story. Some of them are pointed out by Margaret Atwood in her introduction to *The Oxford Book of Canadian Short Stories in English*: although it is very difficult to define the Canadian short story, "a few generalizations can be made. One is the relatively large number of woman writers who have, despite adverse social conditions —women were not legally 'persons' in Canada until 1929, for instance—made contributions of a high order to the tradition" (xv). Atwood does not mention this, but she is, of course, herself one of those contributors "of a high order."

In this essay I wish to look at the way in which three Canadian women writers —Ethel Wilson, Mavis Gallant, and Margaret Atwood—use the short story format to create the effect of *defamiliarization.* They are very different writers—of different generations, for one thing—but the stories I have chosen nevertheless share some marked features. Both Wilson's "From Flores" (one of the stories in her *Mrs. Golightly and Other Stories*, 1961, but actually written in the late 1930s) and Atwood's "A Travel Piece" (published in the collection *Dancing Girls*, 1984) depict a journey—a journey that goes wrong. But whereas Wilson's story is set solidly inside a recognizably Canadian (Vancouver Island) setting, Atwood's "Travel Piece" is a more "cosmopolitan" piece of short fiction. Mavis Gallant's "The Ice Wagon Going down the Street" (*Home Truths: Selected Canadian Stories*, 1987), by contrast, is not so much about a journey as about people constantly on the move, professional travelers they may be called, and how that has affected their sense of self or identity.

Defamiliarization

My use of the concept of defamiliarization is a pragmatic adaptation of a term that in critical discourse has proved to be highly useful, in the sense that it brings into focus the problematic relationship between art or literature and so-called reality. The term *defamiliarization* (*ostranenie*: "making strange") is, of course, generally associated with Russian formalism and perhaps above all the name Viktor Shklovsky. In "Art as Technique" (1917), Shklovsky argues that "[t]he technique of art is to make objects 'unfamiliar,' to make forms difficult, to increase the difficulty and length of perception."[2] Defamiliarization in art implies a foregrounding of the act of composition and thus points ahead to postmodernist techniques of self-reflexivity, which is the aspect that interests me the most here. Bertolt Brecht's concept of the "alienation effect" (*Verfremdungseffekt*) in literature may be seen as a sort of "politicized" continuation of the concept of defamiliarization; the formalists were primarily concerned with technical matters, while Brecht was above all interested in the political aspects — and effects — of the literary text or dramatic situation. Whereas earlier formalist discussions of defamiliarization have tended to focus mostly on poetry or "long" fiction — and Brecht was primarily concerned with the workings of drama — this essay will be concerned with some of the ways in which *short fiction* uses the "making strange" technique. This could be said to add to that heightened sense of the "foreignness of the familiar" that is often claimed to be typical of Canadian identity.

The Red Danger Signal of Ethel Wilson's "From Flores"

Ethel Wilson (1888–1980), a seemingly unassuming and modest composer of short stories and novels who has not infrequently been compared to Jane Austen, is in many ways a tantalizing writer, hiding both surprises and violence in her texts.[3] "From Flores" starts out as an account of what ought to be a short and undramatic voyage through well-known waters, from Flores to Alberni on Vancouver Island in British Columbia. A small fishing boat, the *Effie Cee*, sets out with its crew of two, Captain Crabbe and his mate, Ed, to get home in time for Christmas. With them on the boat is a young man named Jason, "an anxious kid, tall, dark, and thin-faced" (41), who has talked his way into being allowed to come along although Captain Crabbe usually does not take passengers. Jason is obviously in urgent need of transportation and keeps consulting a letter from a girlfriend who seems to be in trouble.

But somehow and by chance, partly caused by the unreliability of weather and the elements, and partly by what could be called the unpredictability of life or of the human psyche, what should have been a short and uneventful voyage turns into confrontation and violence, pain, betrayal, and tragedy. The little fishing boat is called ashore by an "emergency" signal, a red shirt, and asked to take onboard a little Indian boy with a broken leg. As the weather starts worsening, tension builds up, finally causing the complete collapse of the "world order" on board the *Effie Cee*. It is Ed, the crewman, who suddenly somehow seems to go mad, refusing to take orders from his captain, instead steering the vessel straight into shipwreck and destruction. Rather than depicting this as conscious mutiny, however, the narrative seems to present Ed's behavior as some kind of natural catastrophe, parallel to the unreliability of the weather and the elements.

A quick reading of the story may leave one with the impression that it is a simple "Victorian" tale, involving characters of an almost Dickensian nature—witness such names as Captain Findlay Crabbe and his wife, Effie. The narrative voice that sets the tone of the story contributes in the same direction, with an opening that one might expect from a comfortably omniscient and old-fashioned narrator: "Up at Flores Island, Captain Findlay Crabbe readied his fishboat for the journey home and set out in good spirits while the weather was fair."

However, aspects of the text point in a different direction from the very beginning of the story: for instance, there is no introductory or expository part, such as one might expect from a "Victorian" story. Instead, the reader is plunged in media res in the very next sentence: "But even by the time he saw the red shirt flapping like mad from the rocky point just north of the Indian's place the wind had freshened." This red shirt keeps flapping in and out of sight and of the reader's attention throughout the story. It is an ordinary, everyday object, probably homemade and woman-made, but because of its color and because of what it is used to signal, it becomes the main signifier in the story and a narratological danger signal as well, indicating the direction of the drama that is to unfold. In addition it could be said to represent perfectly the process of defamiliarization or "making strange," not only lengthening the process of perception but also concentrating and intensifying the aesthetic experience of reading.

In fact, all the authorial "small talk" that is used to present the characters and the setting (for instance, all the details provided to describe the boat, the *Effie Cee*, as well as Captain Crabbe and his family) may easily lead the reader astray. The narrator's intriguingly intrusive remarks—of a kind often claimed by Wilson critics to be signs of her incompetence—actually make the sudden eruption of violence even more shocking. Consider for instance the following: "Thus they daily elevated each other in esteem and loved each other with simple mutual gratification. In bed no names were needed by Mrs Crabbe and the Captain. (*When they shall be dead, as they will be, what will avail this happy self-satisfaction. But now they are not dead, and the Captain's wife as often before awaits the Captain who is on his way down the coast from Flores Island, coming home for Christmas*)" (42; italics mine). Wilson's conspicuous insertion of the parenthetical prolepsis is experienced as a disruption by the reader. Why does the narrator, otherwise so unassuming and lighthearted in tone, deliberately break both the narratological illusion and the chronological order of the story in this manner? This is one of the ways in which Wilson's writing turns out to be far more complex than might at first appear—with such marked shifts of voice and mood, and the surprising change from what seems a comfortably monological text and an "old-fashioned" authorial voice to a "dialogical" and contradictory one.

Adding to the threatening tension in the story are other details such as the reference to "the tricky undulations of the ocean" (43), or to "a black volley of cormorants" (46). This dark line of foreboding enhances the importance of colors in the story. While the color red foregrounds danger, blood, and violence, black signals tragedy and death. When the storm breaks out, animal-like terms are used to describe the ferocity of the sea: "[T]he waves, innocent and savage as tigers, leaped at the *Effie Cee*" (48). Several references to hell also appear; for example, Ed is described as "a heller when he drank" (42), and the weather off the Pacific coast of Vancouver Island, "up in an air cauldron in the north" sometimes "roars down and attacks like hell" (43).

These are some of the constituent aspects of what W. H. New calls "the covert violence" of Wilson's work (*History of Canadian Literature*, 204). In this story, however, especially when viewed in the light of the defamiliarization technique, it is not possible to regard the violence in the Wilson text as covert. Rather, the violence is deliberately and regularly pushed into the foreground of the text. The conspicuous linking of innocence and savagery, as in the sentence describing the waves, is another characteristic element in what I would call Wilson's defamiliarizing technique.

The Foreign versus the Familiar in Mavis Gallant's "The Ice Wagon Going down the Street"

Mavis Gallant's story "The Ice Wagon Going down the Street" deals, at least on the surface, with seasoned or even "professional" travelers. In contrast to the other two stories discussed here, the Gallant story is played out against a more static backdrop (in other words, not a journey). This is actually quite paradoxical, considering that one of the story's main motifs is traveling: it depicts restless, rootless people who have made it their life's work to move around, from Canada to Paris, to Zurich, and then on to Asia, before ending up (but also starting out) in Canada once more. Peter and Sheilah Frazier and their two daughters have spent more or less a lifetime in various parts of the world, but they are at the point of narrated present time back home in Toronto for a while. In fact, the only significant movement described or made to stand out in the narrative is that which is mentioned in the title, of the ice wagon going down the street in Agnes Brusen's memory of her childhood.

Other paradoxical qualities are built into Gallant's story as well. In complete contrast to the Frazier couple stands the simple girl of Norwegian extraction from the Saskatchewan prairie, Agnes Brusen. Agnes's background is that of a large immigrant family of hardworking Protestant farmers to whom education is more important than anything. Peter Frazier, by contrast, comes from the privileged urban upper class, although by now, four generations after the family fortune was made, he has pretensions rather than money. He is the kind of Canadian who seems in some ways more

British than "New World" immigrant. In the Zurich office in which they both work, Peter becomes Agnes Brusen's subordinate. She is the office manager, he is the filing clerk. Whereas Peter and Sheilah are described as peacocks (107 and 108), tall and stunning, Agnes is a mole, "small and brown" (116). Peter, the arrogant, good-looking man used to judging people primarily on the basis of their appearance and their social connections, is at first contemptuous of this "inferior girl of poor quality" (118). It is only when the Fraziers realize that she is being patronized by the Burleighs, the local social trendsetters who have already dropped the Fraziers, that Sheilah and Peter decide they have to make an effort to get to know her.

The climax of the story occurs at a costume party given by the Burleighs and through the night following it, when Peter is asked to take Agnes, drunk for the first time in her life, home. With Agnes letting go of all her habitual defenses and open-ing up to Peter, she tells him of that most intimate and wonderful of her childhood memories, that of the ice wagon going down the street in her small hometown, and of how important it has been to her. Back in the office two days later, she explains it more fully to him, why it was and is so important to her: "In a big family, if you want to be alone, you have to get up before the rest of them. You get up early in the morn-ing in the summer, and it's you, you, once in your life alone in the universe. You think you know everything that can happen. . . . Nothing is ever like that again" (132). There is something about this complete sincerity that appeals so much to Peter that he is brought to the brink of a completely new turn in his life, some new insight about himself as well as about life, terrible but also very tempting and very powerful: "She came out of the bathroom and straight toward him. She pressed her face and rubbed her cheek on his shoulder as if hoping the contact would leave a scar. He saw her back and her profile and his own face in the mirror over the fireplace. He thought, This is how disasters happen. He saw floods of sea water moving with perfect punitive justice over reclaimed land; he saw lava covering vineyards and overtaking dogs and stragglers. A bridge over an abyss snapped in two and the long express train, suddenly V-shaped, floated like snow. He thought amiably of every kind of disaster and thought, This is how they occur" (129). A key point made in "The Ice Wagon Going down the Street" is that of the tremendous difference—and distance—that exists between Agnes and Peter. And yet the most significant development in the story is the strange com-ing together of these two people. I use the expression "coming together" tentatively but consciously in order to avoid words like "attraction" or other words that would suggest something like a conventional affair. For that is not in my view what this story is about, at least not primarily.

Although a seemingly familiar motif in a peaceful childhood setting, what does the ice wagon actually signify? As I keep reading and rereading this story, it sometimes seems to turn into more rather than less of a mystery. Obviously, the memory refers to childhood and a time of hard work with hardly any time for solitude, a solitude that seems to have been crucial to the child Agnes Brusen's sense of selfhood. However, there is surely more to the ice wagon than that. At times it even seems hard to decide whether to associate it with something pleasant or something sinister. On the one hand, the heavy blocks of ice can be associated with the promise of pleasurable relief in a hot summer world. On the other hand, ice blocks may also indicate something threatening, with their heaviness and hardness.

Gallant's story has a far less dramatic plot than the other two stories discussed here, with their focus on danger, drama, and death. Instead, its main focus is psychological, dealing with the change from childhood to adulthood, from loss of optimism and innocence to cynicism or realism. Interestingly, whereas in Ethel Wilson's story the defamiliarization process focuses primarily on the immediacy of visual impressions, the Gallant story could be said to focus more on sounds and memories. And whereas the red shirt may be seen as the primary signifier of narratological estrangement in the Wilson story, in Gallant's story defamiliarization is achieved through the simultaneous distancing and closeness of childhood memories. Still, in some ways it may be said to be the one text among the three that most skillfully demonstrates the intricacies of the defamiliarization technique. The repeated references to the memory of the sound of the ice wagon and the situation surrounding it not only make it increasingly more prominent in the narrative but also make it seem ever stranger. In this way the humble and ordinary object, a vehicle from a Canadian small-town existence, may be said to represent the perfect emblem of the Canadian "familiar becoming foreign" process.[4] But this is at the same time the effect that Agnes Brusen has on Peter Frazier. To him she becomes the trigger of defamiliarization, representing in the years following again and again the reminder of that different kind of life, a deeper, more "real" kind of life, that Agnes showed him a glimpse of during those moments when they were alone together.

Defamiliarizing the Idyllic in Margaret Atwood's "A Travel Piece"

Margaret Atwood's story "A Travel Piece" depicts a world of air travel and mass tourism, the protagonist and main focalizer being a young woman who makes her living as a travel writer and who as such is used to looking at and writing about foreign landscapes and cultures. Annette is the seemingly seasoned and somewhat world-weary travel or vacation writer: "Her job was to be pleased, and she did this well, she was evenly tanned and in trim physical shape, she had direct blue eyes and a white smile and was good at asking interested, polite questions and coping with minor emergencies" (132). Annette moves around in a world where things seem in some ways to be the opposite of what they used to be. Whereas staying home used to mean safety and traveling adventure, now to her it seems to be the reverse, with home being the dangerous place, and people going on vacation in search of some peace and quiet, "a few weeks of uneventfulness" (131). But this sense of safety is largely caused by the selective reporting of people such as her, who know that they have to keep certain things out of their writing, like the dangers that may be lurking in corners or around the next bend—unpleasantness and crime, dirt, danger, and disaster. Instead, the travel writer must work to direct the attention of the potential tourists toward the picturesque and idyllic aspects of the foreign culture.

Despite the title, "A Travel Piece" seems to be more concerned with what goes into, or on in, *writing*—about life or about traveling—than with the journey itself. The story abounds with metatextual references, for instance, to how crucial it is for a travel writer to know what to include and—even more—what to leave out in her texts ("That was the sort of thing you had to filter out" [132]).⁵ Underneath her cool and composed surface, Annette has problems. Somehow she seems unable to believe in the reality of the world. The green trees, white beaches, blue sky, and "the indecently blue ocean . . . [have] more and more come to seem like a giant screen" (132).

As the story opens, Annette is on a plane returning to Canada after a visit to the Caribbean. But suddenly things start to go wrong, and the plane has to make an emergency landing at sea. After a seemingly undramatic landing, she finds herself with a group of survivors in a lifeboat, watching the plane being sucked down. However, even this drama does not seem real to Annette, and "she's a little disappointed; she knows this is an emergency but so far everything has been so uneventful, so orderly. Surely an emergency ought to feel like one" (136). The unreal or "fictional" quality of events continues to preoccupy her. It is as if she is a character in one of the many shipwreck or castaway stories that she has read, observing and commenting on events from a distance, and not as if she is actually there and one of the group. Or she is the journalist with a constant urge to pull out her camera to record the drama. Whether heroic adventure or tragedy does not really matter; what matters is the interesting and picturesque atmosphere that can make for the good story, the journalistic scoop.

It can, in fact, be seen as a sign of Annette's growing awareness of the reality of the crash that as the drama develops, she refrains from using her camera. However, it is only toward the very end, when the passengers are running out of food and fresh water, that she finally experiences the blue ocean as real. Paradoxically, the point at which she is close to dying is also the point when she finally begins to sense that she is alive, in a real world.

All through the text runs a commentary on stories and storytelling, echoing the notion that life is nothing but story. This has become a well-rehearsed motif in contemporary literature by now and constitutes considerably less of a conceptual challenge in our contemporary media-focused world than it may have done in the mid-1970s when Atwood's story was first published. For the protagonist in "A Travel Piece," however, the notion of life as a fictionalized construct is a new discovery: "Annette goes to sleep thinking of a different story; it will have to be different now. She won't even have to write it, it will be her story As Told To, with a picture of herself, emaciated

and sunburned but smiling bravely" (141). The narrator sets the stage for such a discovery already in the first sentence: "Annette is wiped right out." As the story unfolds,
the reader begins to sense that there is more to this statement than just a colloquial
cliché. Instead, it can be seen as a marker, a signal of the terrifying collapse that is
going to take place in Annette's world or the world Annette knows and has carefully
constructed. When, toward the end, one of the survivors, Greg the student, is caught
trying to drink salt water and is found to be delirious, Annette knows that her fellow
survivors are on the point of becoming murderers: "[T]hey are going to slit his throat,
like that pig on the beach at Mexico, and for once she does not find it quaint and
unusual. . . . So this is what goes on behind her back, so this is what it means to be
alive, she's sorry she wondered" (143).

Between Familiarity and Foreignness

Atwood's story leaves the reader with a sense of profound disease and discomfort. Interestingly, some of the narrative tropes of the story bring to mind the "colorful" danger signals sent out in Ethel Wilson's story. In "From Flores" it is the red shirt of the
Indian family that above all signals distress and somehow marks the transition into a
world of chaos and violence. In "A Travel Piece" the dramatic signal is more obscure,
more indirect—but there are obvious parallels to be found in the orange life jackets
floating on the sea after the plane has made its emergency landing, and in the lipstick
markings and yellow plastic trays that the survivors protect their faces with.

There is something deeply unsettling about all the three stories, an effect to which
the defamiliarization technique contributes very strongly. And it is perhaps at this
point that we see the similarities between these three Canadian women writers the
most clearly: in their shared awareness of the disasters that await the unsuspecting just
beneath the surface of ordinary everyday events and boredom,[6] or of the beauty that
may also be there in such ordinary everyday objects as an ice wagon going down the
street of a small town in the early morning.

In "From Flores" the red shirt that is used as a distress signal by the Indian family
to call for help does not in itself signify danger or violence. Still, in narrative terms—
that is, as a marker in the story—that is how it functions. The havoc and destruction
that follow after the *Effie Cee* has made its detour to pick up the injured little boy are
as uncalled for as the violence of the storm that befalls the crew. The narrative builds
up this tension expertly by the several references (three) to the red shirt as a signpost,
and even more references (five) to the *Effie Cee*'s change of course in response to this
signal.

In "A Travel Piece" defamiliarizing textual signals are above all sent out by means
of the transformation or exotization of familiar objects such as lipsticks and plastic
sandwich trays. These are converted into useful protection against sunburn by the
resourceful Bill. Annette cannot help noticing that they are also turned into "masks

and bloody markings. What bothers her is that she can't tell any more who these people are, it could be anyone behind the white plastic faces with slit eyes. But she must look like that too" (142). This last comment, of course, reflects the supreme irony of Annette's situation. The masks, which hide the human features of her fellow survivors, are in fact also bringing out their "true" natures. Having finally made it out of her cocoon of unreality, she is now being forced to make a choice: between becoming one of them—that savage group of bloody-looking people in the lifeboat—or turning away from it all and denouncing the inhumanity of what they are about to do. In short, she now has a choice, which in existential terms is the final and ultimate proof of her existence. But at what cost, and for what sort of existence?

When exile and home become confused, when endings seem to be as much beginnings as closures, and when traveling seems more than anything to lead to a sense of being marooned, then are we perhaps beginning to get to the heart of the "Canadian condition"? This seems to be Margaret Atwood's view, as expressed, for instance, in her introduction to *The Oxford Book of Canadian Short Stories in English*: "Canada shares with all of the New World ex-colonies, and with others such as Australia and New Zealand, the historically recent experience of a collision between a landscape and a language and social history not at first indigenous to it, with each side altering the other" (xv). It is this sense of collision, as well as of dislocation and foreignness, and the ensuing alterations that take place both in human beings and their perspectives, that in my mind make contemporary Canadian writing so exciting: strange and familiar at the same time, and so eminently worth reading.

Notes

1. See *Dreams of Speech and Violence*, particularly part 1: "Story and Theory."
2. As quoted in Selden and Widdowson, *Reader's Guide*, 31.
3. See, for instance, New, *Dreams of Speech and Violence*, 83–84.
4. Compare a point made by W. H. New in *History of Canadian Literature:* "While [Gallant's] stories repeatedly recount the lives of expatriates and exiles, they do so not simply as a mimetic representation of contemporary experience; exile is more fundamentally an attitude of mind" (245).
5. Consider also the almost obsessive focus on cameras in this story: are cameras truthful or deceitful? The eye of the camera and its power over the human eye may in fact be said to be an Atwood obsession, as may be seen in *The Edible Woman, Bodily Harm*, and some of her poems.
6. See David Stouck, afterword to *Mrs. Golightly and Other Stories*, 213.

Works Cited

Atwood, Margaret. "A Travel Piece." In *Dancing Girls.* London: Virago Books, 1984. First published in *Saturday Night* in 1975.

———. Introduction to *The Oxford Book of Canadian Short Stories in English.* Edited by Margaret Atwood and Robert Weaver. Toronto: Oxford University Press, 1988.

Gallant, Mavis. "The Ice Wagon Going down the Street." In *Home Truths: Selected Canadian Stories.* Toronto: Macmillan, 1987. First published in 1981.

New, W. H. "The Genius of Place and Time: The Fiction of Ethel Wilson." In *Articulating West: Essays on Purpose and Form in Modern Canadian Literature*, 68–82. Toronto: New Press, 1972.

———. "The Irony of Order: Ethel Wilson's *The Innocent Traveller.*" In *Articulating West: Essays on Purpose and Form in Modern Canadian Literature*, 83–92. Toronto: New Press, 1972.

———. *Dreams of Speech and Violence: The Art of the Short Story in Canada and New Zealand.* Toronto: University of Toronto Press, 1987.

———. *A History of Canadian Literature.* London: Macmillan, 1989.

Selden, Raman, and Peter Widdowson. *A Reader's Guide to Contemporary Literary Theory.* 3rd ed. New York: Harvester Wheatsheaf, 1993.

Wilson, Ethel. "From Flores." In *Mrs. Golightly and Other Stories.* Toronto: McClelland and Stewart, New Canadian Library, 1990. First published in 1937.

Making the Familiar Strange

Representing the House in Sarah Orne Jewett's "The Landscape Chamber" and Linda Hogan's "Friends and Fortunes"

Laura Castor

Scarcely any other object is as commonplace in everyday life, yet so layered with human meaning, as the house. Gaston Bachelard writes in *The Poetics of Space* that it is "one of the greatest powers for integration of the thoughts, memories, and dreams of mankind" (6). As poetic image, the house thus lends itself well to the genre of the short story. The house is an image that readers easily identify as familiar, yet that just as readily can surprise, baffle, or frighten with its strangeness. In Linda Hogan's 1992 short story "Friends and Fortunes," the house is an object in the everyday world, but it is also a power that draws the narrator beneath the surface of everyday appearance. Hogan uses the image to create two kinds of knowing, an inner and an outer knowing. As image, it produces the individual moment of truth that comes when an experience jolts the reader out of his or her habitual ways of seeing the world. A moment of truth, notes Mary Louise Pratt, is one of the most common narrative structures found in the short story (99). Charles E. May has suggested that the emphasis on this kind of sudden realization produces the mythical/spiritual knowing that characterizes the nature of knowledge produced in this genre.[1] May, however, believes that the short story as such does not lend itself well to social criticism, which demands a public and social knowledge more common to the novel. I would like to take issue with his claim. In Hogan's "Friends and Fortunes," the image of the house also pulls the narrator and reader into a larger world of historically constructed gender and class relations, as well as into a web of interconnections between individuals, social worlds, and the world of nonhuman nature. Hogan's social criticism is strengthened rather than weakened by the need to defamiliarize the everyday world through moments of revelation. Her aim, expressed through her use of the image of the house, is to suggest that all knowing is relational.

Hogan's approach to writing short fiction, novels, poetry, and essays has been supported by insights developed over the past thirty years in feminist studies, Native American studies, and ecocriticism.[2] Scholarship and imaginative writing in these fields have challenged the Western dualisms on which May's separation between mythical/spiritual and social/public is based. As a Chickasaw writer, one important element Hogan identifies in her work is the dual intent to understand the Western world in history and to defamiliarize that world. For Hogan, this means exposing the illusion of separation between the social, historical world on the one hand and the world of "nature" on the other. She writes in *Dwellings*, "It has been my lifelong work to seek an understanding of the two views of the world, one as seen by native people and the other as seen by those who are new and young on this continent. It is clear that we have strayed from the treaties we once had with the land and animals. It is also clear, and heartening, that in our time there are many—Indian and non-Indian alike—who want to restore and honor those broken agreements. [This work] stretches to reflect the different histories of ways of thinking and being in the world" (11–12). Literary critic Roger Dunsmore notes that resources for thinking holistically have also been present (although often in submerged forms) in Western intellectual traditions, especially in the work of the nineteenth-century Romantics (11).[3] At the end of the nineteenth century, Sarah Orne Jewett expressed such concerns for ecological thinking in her fiction set in rural New England. Because she is a woman writer of "local color," her work has generally received less critical attention than that of her largely male contemporaries in the Romantic and realist traditions.[4] Recently, however, several of her works have been reevaluated and discussed extensively for their feminist and ecological motifs, most notably her short story composite, *The Country of the Pointed Firs*, and her story "A White Heron." These ideas are also important in her 1887 "The Landscape Chamber," a story that has been largely overlooked by critics.[5]

Like Hogan, Jewett uses a house as the focal point of her narrative in order to comment on gendered social relations and on relations between humans and landscapes. The nature of her commentary is also different from Hogan's in significant ways, because of her particular nineteenth-century Euro-American New England perspective. In my analysis, I would like to explore the various ways in which "Friends and Fortunes" and "The Landscape Chamber" focus the gendered, ecologically oriented social criticism they both make by way of the image of the house. First, how does the house in each story enter the vision of the narrator and make her familiar world strange? Second, how is it represented in relation to other elements in the landscape of the narrative? Finally, how does it draw the narrator or characters into a new awareness of the world and draw the reader into an awareness of different histories of ways of thinking and being in the world? In particular, how does it support relational ways of being in the world?

In "Friends and Fortunes" the first-person narrator is a Native American girl in a city that is likely in the American South. It is working class and ethnically diverse. As a teenager she seems at home in her world of contemporary American culture: "Where I live, people do things outdoors. Out in the open air, they do what the wealthier and more private people hide inside their homes. . . . When Mr. Wrenn across the street has his DT's, conversations continue. . . . When June Kim, the Korean woman who used to live next door, stabbed her enormous husband in his massive stomach, my father was the first to know. . . . When a Buick drove through Sylvia Smith's bedroom window, my father was the first man there, catching Mrs. Smith in her nightgown, her pale chubby hands trying to cover up the rollers in her hair" (176, 177). The urban landscape of the narrator's world is the image of a commodified tabloid newspaper where all the sensational, violent entanglements of human relationships are out in the open, ripe for public consumption. But the narrator also distances herself from the human pain underlying this portrayal, which has all the elements of slapstick comedy.

The place begins to feel strange to her, however, when Nora Penalba, a girl her age who becomes her friend, moves into the house next door. Unlike the other neighbors, the Penalbas stay inside their house most of the time, except when the daughter and mother go to church. Nora is also different because she speaks with an accent and seems older than the Native American girls in the narrator's neighborhood. It seems that both she and her house have an uncanny resemblance: "Her flesh has a gray light around it, like the grayness around the sick. Her house has the odor of burning. There is something feverish about it. The house is like the great eye of a tornado that the crows have disappeared into" (178). The picture of the elemental power of a storm is a stark contrast to the realistic view the other neighbors have of the house. What they notice is garbage in the backyard, flies all over the place, and broken windows (180). Bachelard, in his discussion of the house and universe, notes that when "faced with the hostility of the storm and the hurricane, the house's virtues of protection and resistance are transposed into human virtues. The house acquires the physical and moral energy of a human body. It braces itself to receive the downpour" (46). The Penalba house, in contrast, seems to be the storm against which the narrator tries to protect herself. At the same time, the image of the eye of the tornado suggests that she, too, might be pulled into the vision at its "eye."

The foreboding power of this eye is suggested through several seemingly unimportant incidents that accompany the narrator's account of everyday events. For instance, on her way to visit Nora one day, she notices a small earthworm, "thin and pale" in the gutter, drowning from the recent rain, and she picks it up and places it on a patch of earth (178). Later, on her way to see the local fortune-teller, she notices small lizards by Mrs. Martinez's house. She watches as she "frightens them from the sun and they go hiding beneath the foundation and under the shingles" (181). Both she and the lizards want to go into hiding to protect themselves from too much exposure to the light. In the narrator's case, Hogan suggests this is the light of new knowledge that she senses but is not yet ready to grasp. If the reader assumes that no detail in the story is extraneous, then these images of living creatures are significant in another way as well. They are not only a symbol of the narrator's psychological state, but they also have a conscious existence of their own. The narrator gives lizards and earthworms attention that suggests that these nonhuman creatures, too, are involved in their own struggles to survive in the urban landscape. The landscape in Hogan's text is therefore a space that allows for the possibility of drama throughout the living world, not only in the world of human actions. Hogan's imagery is indicative of her ecological, indigenous worldview.

One way the narrator tries to protect her predictable world of the everyday is by going to see Mrs. Martinez, the fortune-teller. Mrs. Martinez's house, with its white stucco walls and red enamel paint, would appear to be safely conventional compared with Nora's black house. The narrator imagines, ironically, that the fortune-teller's advice is a commodity whose worth can be determined in the world of market exchanges. She is therefore shrewd about what she tells: "I never give her too much information because then she will be able to figure me out and my money will be wasted with her" (181). This remark also signals to the reader that perhaps we should be skeptical of the information she has given us about how open she and her neighbors are about their personal lives. The fortune-teller surprises her, however, and asks her if she is happy. Instead of being reassured that she will have a date with the tall boy in her class, and that she will have children, and go someplace exciting (180), the narrator is propelled into an emotional crisis. Its psychological intensity is magnified in the physical spaces she describes when she gets home. For the first time in the narrative, she describes the interior of her own house, an indication that she is moving psychologically inward. Sitting in her bedroom she stares at the gray tile floor, which is, significantly, the same color she used earlier to speak of Nora's skin. She considers why she is not happy, wondering if it is because she is a Native American. Bachelard's insight that "inside and outside are both intimate—they are always ready to be reversed" (217) is useful for making sense of the psychological shift in vision experienced by the narrator at this moment; she observes that her eyes are "dark and lonely and they are mysterious in a way I have never noticed, as if Nora's presence were haunting me from the inside out" (183). For the first time, she sees that her inner world might be connected to an outer world of social inequality. She is a Native American and wonders whether that is her problem.

In the final scene of the story, Hogan condenses the images of place, bodies, and consciousness, and the boundary separating the inside of the strange Penalba house from the familiar outside world is broken. In hopes that her friend will cheer her up, the narrator meets Nora outside her house, and the two girls sit down to talk on the curb. First, Nora tells her something she says will make her friend happy, "About the rain in Nicaragua. . . . Warm rain. There are green and blue seas and rain forests of rosewood and balsa and cedar. With vines. In them live tiny, tiny monkeys and birds you call parrots with big eyebrows. It is like a paradise of the Bible, the garden called

Eden" (184). This image of original innocence seems like a cruel contrast to the everyday economic realities of which Nora suddenly reminds her: "Of course you are unhappy, being so poor for North Americans." As "Nora gestured about in a wide circle and her hand's motion opened my eyes like a camera," the images of the eye of the tornado in Nora's house and Nora's mysterious eyes are suddenly the narrator's own. What she sees are two girls sitting "like bright flowers growing out of bulbs, surrounded by the oil rags that did not run, sea-green shards of Coca-cola bottles that the boys had broken at night, and beer cans" (184). As female, nonwhite, and not of the middle class, they are surrounded by the waste rather than the rewards of American culture. Nora's image of the Edenic Nicaraguan landscape is even more ironic when she tells the narrator that her father had been a revolutionary leader who was brutally murdered for fighting against the corrupt Nicaraguan government. Just as the house in Bachelard's image does all it can to protect itself from the hurricane, so the narrator begins to scream, accusing Nora of lying even worse than her history teacher, "who scared me half to death of the Communists by telling me how they will come and cut my brother in half in front of me and will make me choose between my mother and father and then kill them both." Just as furiously, Nora stands up and insists that what she is saying is true. To protect herself from her friend's disbelief, she starts to hit the narrator, and the two fall to the ground "twisting together on the curb like flowers in a horrid wind" (185). In a final instant the narrator sees the world differently: "Time stops. I have not believed and time stops. I have been pale and American, Gringa, as she calls me now, the screaming girl breaking as the windows of her house have broken. . . . As she runs away now, she is breathing in loud gasps and then she vanishes into the house, her footsteps gone and the door slamming behind her, and the wailing breaking the solitude of that house" (186). This final compressed image of the house, Nora, and the narrator is interesting in several ways. At the level of plot, it signifies that the secret of the strange black house has been revealed. At an ideological level, it suggests that Nora has opened up the narrator's awareness to a global perspective on a world structured through economic inequality and social injustice. At a psychological level, it seems that both Nora and the narrator have until now been protecting themselves from too much knowledge of that world. After Nora had experienced terror and war in Central America, she came to North America, where she lived in isolation and silence in an American city. In her silence she has defined herself as a victim. Yet as she breaks and screams through the silence of her house, she breaks through this perception of herself. At the same time, the narrator's initially comic representation of her world as sensational tabloid drama is also breaking.

To use Charles May's terms, the mode of knowing produced in this image is mythical and spiritual. But this knowledge is meaningful in the context of social and historical relations. Hogan suggests several responses to a history of Euro-American conquest: One is the response of the tragic victim represented by Nora. A second response is the comic, ironic one that the narrator represents. But neither of these responses alone is adequate. The ironic response does not include the pain of history in its vision, whereas the victim response is unable to suggest a way of seeing beyond the historical pain. A third response is suggested when Nora's voice breaks through her house, and the narrator hears her words and their meaning. It is about gaining a voice and being heard in a relational world. This is the focal point of Hogan's feminist, ecological vision, and in the series of images she has constructed throughout her story, Hogan has shown how the possibility for this response can emerge. In terms of genre, the short story convention of leading up to a moment of revelation.supports Hogan's emphasis on the process of learning to see the world in terms of relationships. Linking the destinies of the narrator and the drowning earthworm, the frightened lizards, twisting flowers, and Nora, the author compresses an integrated view of the land in her final image, where it is as if the house itself is screaming through its broken windows.

The perspective of a three-dimensional, living landscape as enacted by Hogan in "Friends and Fortunes" is discussed by Leslie Marmon Silko in her essay on "Landscape, History, and the Pueblo Imagination." Silko says that for traditional Native peoples, nothing in the living world was perceived as separate or passive: "So long as the human consciousness remains *within* the hills, canyons, cliffs, and the plants, clouds, and sky, the term *landscape* as it has entered the English language, is misleading. 'A portion of territory the eye can comprehend in a single view' does not correctly describe the relationship between the human being and his or her surroundings. This assumes the viewer is somehow *outside* or *separate* from the territory he or she surveys" (265).

Silko's commentary is also relevant for making sense of Sarah Orne Jewett's "The Landscape Chamber." In contrast to Hogan's explicitly Native American, ecological approaches, Jewett's views were shaped within the Western conceptual framework that Silko criticizes in her essay. Silko's characterization suggests one of the reasons why English-speaking Westerners have found it so difficult to see themselves as connected to their surroundings. The vocabulary available to Westerners has the effect of limiting the conceptual categories used to critique their assumptions.[6] Yet limited attempts at such critiques have been made not only by writers in the Romantic tradition but also by writers of local color, and especially by women writers whose lived experience gave them an understanding of what Selya Benhabib more recently has called the "embodied and embedded" nature of reality.[7] An analysis of "The Landscape Chamber," informed by Bachelard's insights, can enable the reader to understand Jewett's text as a limited but significant gesture in this direction from the perspective of women's experience. This becomes apparent if we examine the interrelationship between the narrator and the various exterior and interior landscapes in the story.

In contrast to the narrator in Hogan's story, the woman narrator in "The Landscape Chamber" is older and more confident in herself and her view of the world.

She is white, comfortably middle or upper-middle class, and lives in a town designated as "my familiar neighborhood." Feeling listless and uninterested in life, she embarks on a horseback journey into the countryside, looking for adventure and equipped with, among other things, a bit of chocolate and a well-worn copy of Laurence Sterne's *A Sentimental Journey*. The image of the journey and the literary reference to Sterne's parody of eighteenth-century fashionable journeys in France signal that the narrator, like the protagonist Yorick in Sterne's narrative, will encounter the new and unexpected at the same time that she will reenact his story in some way. What happens is that her horse gets injured and she is forced to stop for the night at a decaying eighteenth-century country house.

Just as the house in Hogan's story is haunted by the strangely silent behavior of its inhabitants, so is this house. But rather than trying to protect herself from its influence, Jewett's narrator actively seeks out an explanation for the house's secret. What she discovers is that the old man who lives there with his daughter is convinced that he has been cursed by a greedy ancestor to live in miserly isolation and apparent poverty, away from the curiosity of jealous neighbors. In the end, the narrator uses her rational ability to see the contemporary world of objects realistically, and to expose the fact that the old man is trapped in his delusions about the past. Jewett closes "The Landscape Chamber" with a didactic statement that is typical of much late-nineteenth-century local color fiction. Whereas the old man believes that he and his daughter are "of those who have no hope in a world of fate," the narrator insists that "there is freedom, thank God! We can climb to our best possibilities, and outgrow our worst inheritance" (9). The narrator's moralistic assertion of the triumph of individual free will over determinism betrays an obvious attempt to make her story morally useful in a larger nineteenth-century world. I do not think this is where she makes her most interesting commentary on the world of social relations, however. If we look at how the house functions as a sensory focal point in the narrative, we see how Jewett makes a more subtle and provocative commentary on the relational nature of reality. Here, as in my discussion of Hogan, I would like to examine three issues: first, the process through which the house enters the narrator's vision. Second, how the house, especially its "landscape chamber" where the narrator sleeps, is represented in relation to other elements in the social and physical landscapes. And third, how the perspective from the landscape chamber draws the reader into a new awareness of the world.

The landscape that is represented before the narrator reaches the old house is one that is living and dynamic, perhaps more so than Silko gives Westerners credit for experiencing: "The sea was near, and the salt-marshes penetrated deep into the country, like abandoned beds of rivers winding inland among the pine woods and upland pastures. The higher land separated these marshes, like a succession of low promontories trending seaward, and the road climbed and crossed over from one low valley to another" (1). The metaphors Jewett uses to describe the land give it agency: the salt-marshes "penetrate," the land "separates" the marshes, and the road "climbed and crossed." Her relationship with the horse is based on mutual dependence, and when he twists his forward shoe so badly that she cannot continue to ride, she keeps going on foot beside him, in search of a place to rest for the night. In these opening scenes, Jewett uses a nineteenth-century realistic style to convey Romantic-era ideas about the land, both in terms of visual portrayals and in terms of the narrator's humble, but finally appreciative, attitude. The author's visual representations are reminders of a landscape painting by Frederick Church, and her words seem inspired by Henry David Thoreau, who believed that humans needed a balance between the experience of wilderness and civilization for optimum well-being.[8] When she at last comes in sight of the chimneys of a house, she decides, "I understood for the first time that the rest and change of this solitary excursion had done me much good. I was no longer listless and uninterested, but ready for adventure of any sort. It had been a most sensible thing to go wandering alone through the country" (2). The implication is that her relationship to the sea and marshes enables her to relate to whatever new elements she might find in the landscape. In effect, the surroundings seem to shape her as much as she shapes them by way of her interpretation.

When she gets closer to the house and observes its decay, her descriptions begin to reflect a double perspective of the landscape, one grounded in nineteenth-century realism, the other in an earlier eighteenth-century discourse. The notion that this older perspective is obsolete is reinforced in her reflections on the state of the property: the barn is "dreary" and "neglected," and "a straggling row of out-buildings [lean] this way and that, mossy and warped, while the blinds of the house are broken" (2). "As age creeps through the human frame, pilfering the pleasures of enthusiasm and activity one by one," reflects the narrator, "so it is with a decaying house" (3). Like Nora Penalba's house in "Friends and Fortunes," this house exhibits all the human energy of Bachelard's image. The difference is that whereas Hogan uses metaphor to merge into a unified consciousness the image of house and storm, Jewett maintains a critical distance with her use of a simile. Her consciousness is kept separate from the consciousness of her surroundings. As such, Jewett illustrates what Silko has observed as characteristic of Western, dualistic perceptions of the land. However, the narrator maintains less of a critical distance in other instances. For example, the narration slides into the consciousness of an earlier historical period, most likely influenced by her reading material. What she sees is shaped by what she has read in Sterne as well as by direct apprehension. When she describes the old man, she uses the discourse of eighteenth-century sensibility: the narrator is grateful for his "intelligent sympathy" when he admires her horse (2), and she later watches the way his "*compassionate* fingers touched and soothed [her horse's] bruised joint" (4).

In the tradition of sensibility, animals have the power to evoke deep emotional responses in humans, and the old man expresses this tendency to an extreme.[9] We might consider the extent to which this power suggests a convergence between Western and Native American histories of ways of thinking and being in the world, which in this instance would seem to share a similar awareness of the connections between human and nonhuman life. However, in Jewett's story it is ultimately closed when it becomes clear that the old man's intense interest in tending to the narrator's injured horse includes a strong need to take control of what and how much the animal is fed and to ignore the narrator's suggestions. His behavior is based on mourning for his own dead horse that had died trying to make a leap to freedom over the fence by the stable. It seems that the old man misses having the horse, not only for companionship but also, more important, for control and as a reminder of his own upper-class identity. He likewise sees the narrator's horse as a symbol of aristocratic social superiority: "I should have liked to have seen the ancestor who has stamped his likeness so unmistakably on all his descendents" (9). In the end, the relationship between the horse and the old man does not have the same potential for defamiliarizing the world that Hogan's images of living creatures have. It is, instead, based on his ideas about class privilege and the need to control. This idea of possession and control is what Silko identifies as motivating the Western notion of "landscape" as a portion of territory the eye can comprehend in a single view. It is this point of vision that perceives the land as locked into an objectified, static frame that also constructs animals and women "others" who fit into the frame.

The old man relates to his daughter in much the same controlling way he relates to the horse. He is domineering, believing that she shares his perceptions. But Jewett's portrayal of her is more ambiguous than this. Within the frame of one room in the old house called the "landscape chamber," Jewett clarifies the illusions that keep the man stuck in the past, as well as suggesting that the daughter, along with the narrator, resists this objectified vision of herself and the world. The landscape chamber is the upper bedroom where the daughter takes the narrator to sleep, against the wishes of her father.

As such it becomes an embedded space, to use Benhabib's term, for creating knowledge that emerges in the relationship between the narrator and the daughter as they talk in the room. The daughter tells the narrator that she longs for companionship, but that her father keeps visitors away, and she rarely has anything to do but keep the house clean (5). The role in which she casts herself is the nineteenth-century domestic "angel of the house"[10] who in this case is living up to a promise she made her dead mother to take care of her father. But the interaction between her and the narrator also suggests the passionate emotional bonds between women friends in the nineteenth century that Carroll Smith-Rosenberg has discussed.[11] It is in the dialogue between the two women that the new awareness in the world of the narrative occurs. It gives voice to the women and the authority of their knowledge. Because she has decided to neither internalize nor remain silent about his view of the world, the daughter is not simply a passive, suffering victim of his patriarchal tyranny, as Margaret Roman has argued in her study on Jewett in *Reconstructing Gender* (71–72). She, like Nora Penalba in Hogan's story, breaks the silence of the house with her story, just as the decaying house is unable to silence her.

The strange behavior of the father in the room confirms the authority of the women's voices in the story, both the story within the story told by the daughter, and the frame story told by the narrator to the reader. The narrator is lying in bed on the second night of her visit, "tired and dizzy with the unusual heat" when the old man sneaks into the room, peers into the curtains around her bed chamber, then goes to the closet door (7). He opens it with a key and lingers inside, then emerges and tiptoes silently out of the room. Like Nora in "Friends and Fortunes," the old man disappears into a dark, enclosed space where the reader can imagine he keeps his own awareness of the world shut, while the narrator imagines that he is checking to be sure that a family heirloom is still in its place. Unlike Nora, he remains silent, content to keep his secret locked rather than letting it out by slamming the door and screaming. In contrast to the women characters in either Jewett's or Hogan's story, the old man cannot see beyond the belief that he is the tragic victim of his greedy ancestor's curse. His inability to see this makes him seem merely pathetic to the readers, however.

Finally, it is within the space of the landscape chamber that the various relationships between women, men, time, and place converge. As such, the name signifies much more than just the old painting on the wall over its fireplace. As the narrator describes the painting, "[t]he colors were dull, the drawing quaintly conventional, and I recognized the subject, though not immediately. . . . From the costumes of the figures I saw that it must have been painted more than a hundred years before. In astonishing contrast to the present condition, it appeared like a satirical show of the house's possibilities. Servants held capering steeds for gay gentlemen to mount, and ladies walked together in fine attire down the garden alleys of the picture. . . . I wondered if the miserly old man could bear to look at this picture, and acknowledge his unlikeness to his prosperous ancestors" (6). Bachelard's insight that the boundary between inside and outside is easily reversed is useful in making sense of this room. From the perspective inside this space, the reader's awareness is pulled out into the larger world in a series of encounters in a relational, multilayered reality. First, for the narrator the painting is in once sense about an encounter with a static past. As a representation of the house's aristocratic history, she perceives it as "quaintly conventional." Its "dull, flat surface" provides a sharp contrast to her three-dimensional, multisensory experience of the room. At another level the narrator encounters a dynamic present. From her perspective in front of the fireplace she can see the present view of the garden alleys in a row of elm trees, and the actual clouds that seem to send a cloud of gloom over the painting. She also hears the sounds of lowing cows and chirping sparrows in the distance. These images sharpen Jewett's contrast between the world of two-dimensional artifice versus a three-dimensional reality, the static world of the past versus the dynamic, living world of the present. Second, for the old man the room is the site where the stagnating power of the past reasserts itself. Third, for the daughter it becomes the site of a small movement out of the past when she tells the narrator her story and separates her own views from those of her father. Fourth, for the reader it can also be thought of as an encounter with the beginning of the narrative. If the reader remembers that the narrator started out her journey with a well-worn copy of Sterne's *A Sentimental Journey* in her bag, we see that she has taken on the curiosity and sense of adventure as enacted by that eighteenth-century protagonist, and it was his model that led to the clarity of vision she now experiences, and to the chance to give hope to the lonely daughter. As such, Jewett has suggested a way of understanding the world as a web of connections between the writer and reader, inner and outer space, male and female perception, humans and the living world, and past and present time. Her narrator rejects some elements of the past as obsolete but integrates others. Considering these various levels of understanding revealed in the image of the landscape chamber, the unity of impression we as readers receive from the story is far more than the simple reinforcement of the mainstream American ideology of leaving the past behind, as the narrator's spoken words at the end of the story might imply.

In these two stories, the process of representing the house is about mediating exterior and interior landscapes and mediating various past and present moments in time. Both writers challenge the Western, dualistic oppositions between man, history, and agency on the one hand, and woman, nature, and passivity on the other. In Hogan's "Friends and Fortunes" and Jewett's "The Landscape Chamber," women and various elements in the living world have historical agency. The short story genre, with its characteristic emphasis on moments of truth that integrate the narrative elements of character, event, and image, is especially conducive to the type of feminist, ecologically aware social criticism made by Hogan and Jewett. The interrelationships between these elements of narrative, focused through the image of the house, support the idea of connectedness in the world. Both texts engage their readers in making these connections.

Notes

1. May, "Nature of Knowledge," 133.

2. Important works in each of these areas are too numerous to mention here. Several have been especially valuable for me: Barbara J. Thayer-Bacon's *Transforming Critical Thinking: Thinking Constructively* provides a succinct overview of the subfield of feminist studies known as feminist relational epistemology. For an excellent introduction to Native American holistic worldviews from the perspective of Native women, see Paula Gunn Allen's *The Sacred Hoop: Recovering the Feminine in American Indian Traditions*. A. Lavonne Brown Ruoff's *American Indian Literatures: An Introduction, Bibliographic Review, and Selected Bibliography*

is a useful introduction to the wide range of literary and critical works published by Native Americans by the early 1990s when "Friends and Fortunes" was written. *The Ecocriticism Reader: Landmarks in Literary Ecology*, edited by Cheryll Glotfelty and Harold Fromm, offers, to the best of my knowledge, the widest range of essays within the literary movement of ecocriticism published to date. The editors note that as a distinctive literary movement, ecocriticism has been growing rapidly since the early 1990s. While characterized by a broad range of approaches and disciplinary groundings, "all ecological criticism shares the fundamental premise that human culture is connected to the physical world, affecting it and affected by it" (xviii).

3. Dunsmore is among the non-Native writers and critics whom Hogan refers to as seeking ways of transforming Western attitudes toward the land. See *Earth's Mind*.

4. Webb, "Realism and Local Color Fiction."

5. I do not know of any detailed discussions of this story, although it is included as an example of entrapped daughters and paralyzed men in Margaret Roman's *Sarah Orne Jewett*. Jessica Amanda Salmonson mentions it as an example Jewett's fascination with the supernatural in "Sarah Orne Jewett and the Ghost Story."

6. In *Death of Nature*, Carolyn Merchant argues that contemporary instrumental views of the natural world are historical developments since the scientific revolution, not necessarily essential characteristics of Western thinking.

7. Quoted in Thayer-Bacon, *Transforming Critical Thinking*, 2.

8. Nash, *Wilderness and the American Mind*, 93.

9. *The Dictionary of Sensibility*. http://www.engl.virginia.edu/enec981/dictionary/intro. htm (accessed June 2002).

10. This term was originally the title of a poem by Coventry Patmore and has come to symbolize the nineteenth-century woman who keeps her husband and children morally uplifted and happy within the confines of their home (Roman, *Sarah Orne Jewett*, 1).

11. Smith-Rosenberg, "Female World of Love and Ritual."

Works Cited

Allen, Paula Gunn. *The Sacred Hoop: Recovering the Feminine in American Indian Traditions.* Boston: Beacon Press, 1986.

Bachelard, Gaston. *The Poetics of Space.* Boston: Beacon Press, 1994.

Dunsmore, Roger. *Earth's Mind: Essays in Native Literature.* Albuquerque: University of New Mexico Press, 1997.

Glotfelty, Cheryll, and Harold Fromm, eds. *The Ecocriticism Reader: Landmarks in Literary Ecology.* Athens and London: University of Georgia Press, 1996.

Hogan, Linda. "Friends and Fortunes." In *Dreamers and Desperadoes: Short Fiction of the American West*, edited by Craig Lesley and Katheryn Stavrakis, 176–86. New York: Dell Publishing, 1993. First published in *Things That Divide Us* (Seattle: Seal Press, 1992).

———. *Dwellings: A Spiritual History of the Living World.* New York: Touchstone, 1995.

Jewett, Sarah Orne. "The Landscape Chamber." In *The Sarah Orne Jewett Text Project.* May 2001. http://www.gonzaga.edu/faculty/campbell/enl311/jewett.htm (accessed June 2002). Originally published in *Atlantic Monthly* 60 (November 1887): 603–13, then as part of the collection *The King of Folly Island.*

May, Charles E. "The Nature of Knowledge in Short Fiction." In *The New Short Story Theories*, edited by Charles E. May, 131–43. Athens: Ohio University Press, 1994.

Merchant, Carolyn. *The Death of Nature: Women, Ecology, and the Scientific Revolution.* 1980. San Francisco: Harper Collins, 1983.

Nash, Roderick. *Wilderness and the American Mind.* New Haven and London: Yale University Press, 1973.

Pratt, Mary Louise. "The Short Story: The Long and the Short of It." In *New Short Story Theories*, edited by May, 91–113. Athens: Ohio University Press, 1994.

Roman, Margaret. *Sarah Orne Jewett: Reconstructing Gender.* Tuscaloosa and London: University of Alabama Press, 1992.

Ruoff, A. LaVonne Brown. *American Indian Literatures: An Introduction, Bibliographic Review, and Selected Bibliography.* New York: MLA, 1990.

Salmonson, Jessica Amanda. "Sarah Orne Jewett and the Ghost Story, with a Note on Her Influence on H. P. Lovecraft." Violet Books, May 2001. http://www.violetbooks.com/jewett.html (accessed June 2002).

Silko, Leslie Marmon. "Landscape, History, and the Pueblo Imagination." In *Ecocriticism Reader*, edited by Glotfelty and Fromm, 264–75. Athens and London: University of Georgia Press, 1996.

Smith-Rosenberg, Carroll. "The Female World of Love and Ritual: Relations between Women in Nineteenth-Century America." *Signs* 1, no. 1 (1975): 1–29.

Thayer-Bacon, Barbara J. *Transforming Critical Thinking: Thinking Constructively.* New York and London: Teachers College, Columbia University, 2000.

Webb, Dottie. "Realism and Local Color Fiction, 1865–1895." In *Particular Places: Regional Writing in the United States, 1880–1910.* Ph.D. diss., University of Michigan, May 2001. Available online at http://www.gonzaga.edu/faculty/campbell/enl311/lcolor.html (accessed June 2002).

Architexture in Short Stories by Flannery O'Connor and Eudora Welty

Jan Nordby Gretlund

Besides the basic plot text, fiction of literary merit often contains a subtext that is universally applicable. Some fiction has subtexts of a sociopolitical and perhaps propagandistic nature. In the best of short stories there may be parallel subtexts, and one of these may well be the author commenting on his or her own craft.

The supporting texts in question are *not* superimposed but thoroughly integrated in the narrative and are not necessarily noticed when first read. If they are embedded in a well-written short story, the submerged texts are invisible to the inexperienced eye. They are like bones in the body and just as necessary to keep the body of the fiction erect. With Gérard Genette we could label the subtext as a metanarrative, "one recounted within a narrative" (91); and the narrative is seen by Genette as the total product of the narrative *act* (14). It is exactly the fact that these subtexts are inextricable from the basic plot text that proves their importance, even essentiality, for what we may term "the architexture" (structure *and* texture) of the text. Yet when the subtexts are sensed (or discovered) and the fiction is allowed to flaunt its bivalence, the reading of it becomes so much more rewarding.

The sociopolitical subtexts of Flannery O'Connor's short stories are often either not recognized, just ignored, or eclipsed by the powerful, often violent, ever-present, and decidedly religious plot text. Her career can be seen as a development from the literary stereotyping of the early fiction, in the mid-1940s, to the triumphant religious allegorizing of her final years in the early 1960s. But from "A Stroke of Good Fortune" of 1949 to "The Artificial Nigger" of 1955, there *was* a creative middle period when an important subtext in her fiction was often preoccupied with the southern social order. Sally Fitzgerald once claimed that O'Connor did not write about "a current social issue" until "Everything That Rises Must Converge," which is from 1961,[1] but O'Connor's concern with southern class divisions did appear in flashes already in early stories. In "The Crop" (1946), a Miss Willerton discovers social reality when she passes a poor white couple downtown. The very sight of the poor whites makes her give up her plan of writing "arty" fiction about white sharecroppers.

In her middle period, in the early 1950s, O'Connor's relentless humor is often that of the social satirist. She felt that the social context should not be excluded from her fiction, as she said repeatedly in her talks, and it is in her account of what the class-divided society does to us that she really demonstrates her satirical powers. In the story she named after a Georgia road sign, "The Life You Save May Be Your Own" (1953), O'Connor plunges us into the life of country people, which sounds charming enough, but before we have finished the first page, we understand fully that the social situation of the lowest class of poor white country people is *not* enviable. The middle-aged Lucynell Crater Sr. does not go about without teeth because she enjoys being toothless, and she would probably not have refused help if it were offered her retarded daughter. But it is not.

The sociopolitical subtext in the long and terrifyingly Christian short story "The Displaced Person" comes to rival her religious plot text in importance; for some readers the subtext may even come to dwarf the main text. The displaced Europeans, who are unaware of the traditional social order in the region, are convinced that social mobility in America is not only possible but the inevitable reward for working hard and saving up. The social context is always present in "The Displaced Person," as O'Connor said it should be in all fiction, especially in fiction by a southern writer (*Mystery and Manners*, 198). It is, after all, the portrait of the class-divided society that makes the story about the displaced person so convincing. This should always be the case, O'Connor maintains in her advice on writing: "You can't cut characters off from their society and say much about them as individuals" (104). The Shortleys seem to have walked right off the pages of fellow-Georgian Erskine Caldwell's *Tobacco Road*, as stereotypes of poor whites from Georgia in the 1930s. The social situation of the "low-down" Shortleys is only too plain when they load their boxes and "old battered suitcases from under the bed," two iron beds with the mattresses rolled up between some rocking chairs, and a crate of chickens on top of their old car (*Complete Stories*, 212). They prepare to leave the farm in their "overfreighted leaking ark" before they are asked to leave. It is a shock to them that they are losing their "rightful place" in the social order to foreigners and not to blacks, as they had feared. The only ones worse off than poor whites are African Americans, and they will be next to go, according to Mrs. Shortley, now that nobody has mules any more (205). The only comfort for the black help is that their social position is too low for anybody to dispute with them for it. They are considered chattel rather than people, and they are below the bottom.[2]

As her language reveals, Mrs. McIntyre is of another class. Her ultimate interest is and has always been the finances of the farm. She tries to incorporate change and brings in the displaced Europeans in an attempt to maximize her profits as owner of the farm. And it is through *her* materialism that O'Connor voices her criticism of the social order. Her tenants are Mrs. McIntyre's worst worry, and the Shortleys are fully representative of their class, at least in the landowner's mind. Over the years she has had families named Ringfield, Collins, Jarrell, Perkins, Pinkin, Herrin, and now Shortley, who were all poor white help and to be kept under control. As human beings she considers her tenants completely "worthless." She behaves and sounds like Mrs. Hopewell in "Good Country People," who averaged one tenant family a year (273). To be a tenant on the McIntyre farm is not an enviable life. When the Polish refugee family, the Guizacs, arrive, they are handed things that Mrs. McIntyre does not need herself anymore. They are allowed to move in to a tenants' shack and informed that they should be grateful for anything they receive (196). For their labor the four Guizacs will receive a total of seventy dollars a month. Mrs. McIntyre claims that "people are selfish," but she herself wages a regular war on humankind (216).

The relation between the plot text and the sociopolitical subtext is that for her, "salvation" means someone who will save her *financially*, and tenants are valued only in proportion to the money they earn for the landowner. It is her place, she *owns* it, and she lets her black and white help know that they are superfluous. At one point toward the end of the story, she screams at them, "All of you are extra. Each and every one of you are extra!" (232). She never suspects her own shortcomings or questions her position at the top of the social order on the farm. The criticism leveled at Mrs. McIntyre's pride, vanity, egotism, and materialism constitutes O'Connor's violent religious denunciation of the woman, but the subtext is an equally violent attack on the social and racial systems that breed these characteristics. But what the story finally illustrates is the opposite of a revolt against the class system. Instead, it demonstrates how the system asserts itself by efficiently expelling intruders and "extras."

When Mr. Guizac threatens to upset the social and racial balance on the farm by working too hard and by planning to have Sulk, a young black hand, marry a Polish girl, Mrs. McIntyre's reaction reveals no uncertainty: "Mr. Guizac! You would bring this poor innocent child over here and try to marry her to a half-witted thieving black stinking n . . . [ellipsis mine]! What kind of monster are you!" (222). Clearly, Mrs. McIntyre feels no obligation to other human beings, but she does feel that "*her* moral obligation" is to "her own people," as she phrases it (228). She denounces the Polish farmer for "upsetting the balance." And for her this is much more important than a girl's suffering in a camp in distant Europe.

It is significant that it is Astor, an old black man, who reminds Mrs. McIntyre of the traditional social order on the farm. Their understanding reflects an ancient system that becomes decisive for what they now do. In one respect Astor's constant presence is a flaw in the story. In real life, it is hard to believe that he would not have put a quick stop to Sulk's plans, and it is difficult to imagine that Astor did not know. Given that this happens in the late 1940s or early 1950s in rural Georgia, it is also improbable that a young black man would get the notion to marry a white girl, even when encouraged by Mr. Guizac; or, perhaps especially *not* when prompted by the

Polish exile, who may be white but still remains decidedly "a furiner." O'Connor sees the weakness and indicates that Sulk is "half-witted."

It is not to play down the obvious racial contents of the story that I point out that no black man of normal intelligence, at that time and in that place, would have entertained notions of marrying a white "mail order" bride. On the contrary, I want to make it clear that provoked by national attention, the racial climate was worse than usual in the South when the story was written. Knowing this helps explain why Mrs. McIntyre reacts, and has to react, immediately and resolutely when she hears of Mr. Guizac's project. By the standards of our time she is a racist, but this is relatively unimportant, for the sad fact is that even if she had not been, Mrs. McIntyre would still have had to act—in order not to be ostracized from the norm-setting class in her area.

The difficulties between the displaced person and everybody else on the farm represent a confrontation of value systems. Everybody knows that Astor and Sulk steal, but in doing so they confirm the stereotypical image of blacks and stay within traditional group boundaries, so nobody thinks much of it. Both blacks and poor whites run stills on Mrs. McIntyre's property. It seems that everybody knows it, but it does not constitute a transgression against the expected behavior patterns for people of their classes, so nobody even considers interfering. But clearly there is a system, a social order, and this is what the Guizacs threaten to disrupt by ignoring the unimpressive work ethic in the area.

It is only at the murder of Mr. Guizac that Mrs. McIntyre begins to suspect that she may not be in full control. Although it all takes place right there on her farm, she feels that she is, with all the religious connotations of the phrase, "in some foreign country" (235). When Mr. Guizac is on his back, on the ground, repairing a tractor, the black hand Sulk, the poor white Mr. Shortley, and Mrs. McIntyre, the white landowner, watch him. They all hear the tractor slip into gear, they all see it begin to roll forward, and they all have time to cry out. But nobody does. Instead, they look at each other and then silently observe and listen to the sound of Mr. Guizac's backbone breaking under the wheel of the tractor. The irony is, of course, that the class-conscious owner of the farm would never have expected to share guilt with her "sorry" tenants, not to mention with her black help. But her attempt at profiting from change failed, and she is as guilty as the poor whites and the blacks in the killing of the foreigner —maybe even more so, as they would have taken their cue from her.

Mr. Guizac is finally sacrificed, quite unsentimentally, because the accepted traditional social order is considered more important than any moral and religious consideration or even financial gain could possibly be. The social class system proves not to be based exclusively on economic reasoning but also on unethical, albeit accepted, cultural norms. It could be argued that the Polish immigrant must die because he undermines a set class structure whose existence he does not even know about. What threatens the class system is not only a planned interracial marriage but also the potential purchase of a farm by a poor white man, who is foreign and speaks little English, and therefore is an indicator of the dissolution of all defined social and economic distinctions. The final word in the sociopolitical subtext is that the upholding of the social and racial order is considered vital for the existing economic stratification and class division.

Mrs. McIntyre is *not* rejected or punished by other landowners, for she has not upset the system. On the contrary, she has made sure that the social, racial, and economic order is maintained. Appropriately Mrs. McIntyre is punished for her shortcomings as a human being and as a Christian. The last development of the plot is that the now paralyzed, defenseless woman is punished for her abject spiritual poverty by a priest who insists on enlightening her on the subject of "the displaced person" by expounding the doctrines of the church. It is the Catholic who failed and is punished, not the southern landowner; but O'Connor's Catholic point is, of course, that a distinction between Christian and landowner is artificial and finally impossible.

An appreciation of Flannery O'Connor as a fiction writer should take into account her rendition of her time and place and the people living there and then. Her social subtexts invoke the milieu of her region and the society of which she was a product. In this sense class divisions were always her topic. Her style in "The Displaced Person" is that of the social satirist, and what is being satirized is the social order and what a blind allegiance to the accepted order can do to us. Other late short stories by O'Connor have similar sociopolitical subtexts. In "Everything That Rises Must Converge," she wrote one of the best fictional accounts of the breakdown of the old order in the late 1950s. In the story, which is often referred to in discussions of race in O'Connor's fiction, a young man named Julian finally realizes that it is not so easy to reject his southern heritage as he had thought. Heritage is not a tie, he finds out, that you can just remove whenever you want to identify with another group in the social order. The traditional stratification of southern society, and the end of it, is the subject of Mrs. Turpin's well-known vision in "Revelation," the last of her stories O'Connor saw in print. Mrs. Turpin had not expected "whole companies of white trash" and bands of blacks to precede her own tribe of middle-class respectability in the horde of souls rumbling toward heaven (508).[3]

The most vicious, and not often noted, comment on the effects of the social order is in "Parker's Back," the last story O'Connor completed. A character called Sarah Ruth has skin that is "thin and drawn as tight as the skin on an onion" (510). When she is offered an apple, she takes it quickly "as if the basket might disappear if she didn't make haste. Hungry people made Parker nervous. He had always had plenty to eat himself. He grew very uncomfortable" (515), as most of us would feel "uncomfortable" at the presence of hunger in our own backyard. But "Parker's Back" has its real strength in the presence of a powerful but easily overlooked literary subtext, which is an important part of its architexture. What Parker does is to have his body inscribed, tattooed, to celebrate God, but some fundamentalist Christians reject engraved images of the Lord and reject writers who claim to know the ways of God. André Bleikasten was the first to see that O'Connor uses O. E. Parker's tattoo with a religious motif to discuss her own creative work as she is writing her, in a religious sense, presumptuous work of art.[4] The story gains in texture as a result of O'Connor's dual agenda.

Also in Eudora Welty's fiction there is often an added dimension, in the form of a social, even political, subtext. For years Welty was criticized by New York reviewers for not having a social dimension in her fiction, but since the acid reviews of the 1940s and 1950s, many critics have pointed out obvious social subtexts in her fiction, and it is becoming clear to readers of her work that Welty's moral didacticism is often expressed in social comments. In the 1960s she gave a talk called "The Southern Writer Today: An Interior Affair." It offered advice on how a novelist can deal with *and forward* social change without becoming a mere propaganda writer. Welty suggested that a good plot may prove most disturbing to the powers that be, but insisted on art's political independence. The unpublished talk developed into her much quoted essay "Must the Novelist Crusade?" in which she in a narrow reading simply says "No!" Even though I am far from convinced that Welty wrote *The Ponder Heart* to comment in any way on the Rosenberg trial and the McCarthy hearings, or—even more far-fetched—that she was thinking of the lynching of Emmett Till when she wrote *Losing Battles*, I must admit to finding pleasure in such claims being made at all, for it is now becoming obvious that Welty's fiction is a regular treasure store of political commentary.[5] As James Baldwin argued in his essay "Everybody's Protest Novel," crusading is one thing, it is wording propaganda; social commentary, however, is another.[6] In Welty's fiction it forms an integral part of her art. And the sociopolitical subtext in Welty's fiction is not her only type of subtext; a *literary* subtext is also a frequent presence.

I had myself noted a few Welty stories with an obvious literary subtext, and many with a *social* subtext. But it was as a reader of Naoko Fuwa Thornton's refreshingly original article "The Strange Felicity: The Implicit Thought of Welty on Fiction" that I began to pay more attention to the literary subtexts.[7] Thornton writes on Welty's literary technique and her use of sociopolitical topics. In doing so she comes close to establishing the relationship between the two, but as if surprised by what she has come upon, she shies away from her discovery. The subtexts in Welty's short stories are too obviously present to be called "implicit," and the only thing that is "strange" is that nobody has realized that Welty in her short stories often comments on both social and literary issues at once. Spying a literary subtext is tempting in several Welty stories, for example, in "The Wide Net" in connection with Hazel Jamieson's suicide note, which is a lie on a piece of paper that demonstrates the power of fiction to produce "a new reality"; or in "Moon Lake," wherein Easter *names* herself, does not have *to explain* anything, and just has hopes; or in "Music from Spain," wherein the music created leads to "a lapse of all knowledge" for a solid minute or two and a "visit to a vast present-time."

At times an embedded subtext may prove thematically *more* important than the one framing it. Now and again, writers will get so caught up in the literary subtext, commenting on their own craft, that the development of the primary text and other sub- or secondary texts is sacrificed. And the framing texts, with subsidiaries, may be left abruptly as stunted growth, with basic plot promises not kept and events not completed, which may well leave the reader with a vague, often quite unspecified, sense of dissatisfaction.

In an almost postmodern way, Welty repeatedly makes it clear that we are reading fiction and invites the reader to join her in playing with fictional characters and situations. The point is that no matter how unreal, accidental, and indeterminate the fiction, it quickly becomes obvious that there is a reality under the illusion, and this reality is often brought out in subtexts. The story called "Powerhouse" is perhaps the only story with a delicate balance between two subtexts and with a surface text that does not read like fiction; it reads more like an essay reporting on a jazz concert, at which it may well have been first conceived. Powerhouse is on tour with his band, and he has many listeners in Alligator, which is between Clarksdale and Shelby in the Delta, when he announces, "I got a telegram my wife is dead" (*Collected Stories*, 33). Surprisingly, his listeners are not really concerned what the terrible message about his wife, Gypsy, will mean to the leader of the band, nor are Valentine, Little Brother, and Scoot, who are the permanent members of the band, but they lead Powerhouse on with questions and suggestions. The audience begins to question the existence of the telegram. Powerhouse only suggests, reveals a little, hints his wife had a lover, and then retracts it all. His listeners, and the readers of the story, are free to interpret his claim as they like. By suggesting and creating a story, he ignites the imagination of his audience, and in doing this he is working them like a writer. Nobody among his listeners can distinguish between fiction and reality in his story of Gypsy. During the intermission, which the musicians while away in the World Café in "Negro-town," there is a verbal jam session, and Powerhouse confesses that the truth is "something worse"—something that has not come to him yet. Back in the dance hall, Powerhouse plays furiously before his white audience and in obvious desperation shouts out "Somebody Loves Me." Welty leaves her readers with thoughts about Powerhouse's desperation and "something worse."

In the story of this dance where a "black man calls the tune," Welty "gives form to the doubts and fears" of black Americans, as Ray B. West Jr. phrased it in a seminal essay on modern fiction.[8] This is a perceptive observation, which M. Thomas Inge has accepted and brought up to date by pointing out that "Powerhouse" reveals "the unexpressed outrage of the black experience in America" (168). The original ending had Powerhouse singing "Hold Tight, I Want Some Seafood, Mama," but the *Atlantic Monthly* must have felt that the identification of Fats Waller as the real-life Powerhouse became too obvious and the sexual innuendo too powerful with the words of that song, for they insisted on the change.[9] The vagueness of the plot and the many never-confirmed suggestions, which are controlled only by references to place, allow the fiction to remain an open structure with space for growth in the reader's imagination. The vagueness allows us to keep our own existential problems in sight while we learn about the trials of Powerhouse and the mysterious nature of any human.

During the spring of 1941 Welty published three stories in the *Atlantic Monthly*: "A Worn Path," "Why I Live at The P.O.," and "Powerhouse." It was a surprise when the *Atlantic* accepted "Powerhouse,"[10] a story about blacks and whites interacting in a clearly specified local setting. The social comment on and political protest against segregation within the small town of Alligator, Mississippi, are obvious. Perhaps less obvious is the subtext on black versus white jazz musicians in the late 1930s. But Timothy Dow Adams and Richard N. Albert have shown convincingly that with the creation of the Uranus Knockwood character, the story introduces the socioeconomic subtext of white musicians' exploitation of music created by black jazz artists.[11] According to Adams, Knockwood is "intended to stand for all of the white jazzmen who have used Black jazz material for their own gain" (60). And in this way the topic is raised of the original creation of art and the stealing and copying of it by others.

We assume the narrator is white, as she is in the audience at the dance for whites, but she is also present in the all-black World Café, where the jazz musicians have to go during the intermission with their black supporters, about a "hundred dark, ragged, silent, delighted Negroes [who] have come from under the eaves of the hall, and follow wherever they go" (*Collected Stories*, 135). Just as Powerhouse, as performing artist, is able to cross the racial boundaries and ignore ideas about political correctness (also on matters sexual) for the lyrics he invents during performance, the narrator ignores the usual limits of point of view imposed on a narrator in fiction. She improvises and, like Powerhouse, takes on a new role to suit the new setting and ends up having his audience, as well as her readers, acting out their improvisations on the theme that Gypsy has been killed by, or has committed suicide because of, Uranus Knockwood. The racial subtext surfaces when Powerhouse is told that "'Tuxedo Junction'" is on the nickelodeon, but apparently only in a white rendition, possibly Glenn Miller's, and instead the leader of the band requests Bessie Smith's "Empty Bed Blues," only to find that it is not in the jukebox in the World Café.

What interests Welty is the communication, the exchanges, between artist and audience. "Powerhouse and his Tasmanians" play individually *and* as a unit, in the creative moments they become one without losing their individuality. As African Americans and artists they are traveling performers and therefore strange and outlandish people in the small Mississippi town. They speak a language to each other that is coded and not fully understood by the audience, just as the reader does not fully understand or suspect the meaning of the coded language of the story he or she is reading. When Powerhouse claims "I got a telegram my wife is dead," he may or may not be singing the truth. When he plays a requested very popular "white" song, "Pagan Love Song," he improvises, exchanging words in the call-and-response tradition with the members of his band, and he goes from the three-four waltz beat that he is mocking with great sadness to the four-four beat of the blues. The pattern of the song performed is also the structure of the narrative read, and repetitions with slightly shifting emphases move audience and readers toward an understanding of the artist's message.

The literary subtext of the story is in the relationship between the human condition and the nature of fiction. The subtext resides in the indirect comments on Powerhouse, the narrator, and Miss Welty as creative artists and storytellers. Powerhouse finally reveals that his song about his dead wife "ain't the truth" (139), but his fiction about Gypsy's fate is clearly much more powerful than truth itself (for example, the true story of how Sugar-Stick Thompson saved fourteen white people from drowning). Even though Sugar-Stick is a genuine and local hero, nobody in the audience reacts to his story or contributes to it and expands on it, except his brother. In short, it sparks no enthusiastic reaction from the audience, for there is nobody there, no artist, to perform or to re-create his story. It has to be told, and told right, to really capture the imagination, and the power of fiction surpasses that of fact. If the event is not presented by an artist, it does not become a story or a song, and it might as well never have happened, for it will not have an impact and will not be remembered.

On their way back to the white dance hall for the second session, Powerhouse tells his sidemen to spell "Uranus Knockwood," and they do, in every way possible, and "it puts them in a wonderful humor" (140). We are not told the exact spelling variations they play with, but both "Uranus" and "Knockwood," of course, offer plenty of possibilities. We are not told what the "something worse" is that Powerhouse expects, nor is it clear what the expression "come out the other side" refers to. When he starts the second part of his performance, he once again takes a favorite white song, "Somebody Loves Me, I Wonder Who!" (Gershwin), and improvises white Hollywood out of it by shouting and calling "Somebody loves me!" grotesquely piling chorus upon improvised chorus until the song belongs to him. Just as Welty took the personal experience of a Fats Waller concert and piled up line upon line about it until it belonged to *her*. Like Powerhouse's playing, her performance liberates her audience—first it entraps us in her imaginary world and then cancels the racial borders and psychological limits imposed on us. So maybe when Powerhouse answers the question in the song with "maybe it's you!" he may be right. Under the influence of the artist-performer's playing with language and racial reality, we may admit to loving somebody else, if only for a moment, and "maybe it's you," which is the last line of the story.

Even if it is not a storyteller's function to champion one cause or another, it is the hope of a writer ultimately to transcend the surface plot and its subtexts. Both Chekhov's "The Steppe" and Welty's "The Wide Net" demonstrate that one who drags the river with a wide net must expect to catch a variety of life. And one who decides to dive down into the stream and touch bottom, like Ivan Ivanovich in the river at Mironositskoe and William Wallace in the Pearl River, will find upon resurfacing that the world is more than just objectified reality. In her essay on Chekhov's realism, Welty explains a passage in "Gooseberries": "In the river, Ivan has experienced happiness of such purity that it is forgetful of self."[12] This is also what the storyteller is after; she must dive and touch bottom in her own self to attain her vision. In *The Ponder Heart* Miss Edna Earle may claim that she is only a go-between, between the Ponders and the world, and that she hardly ever gets a word in for herself, but she tells the story of the Ponders and imposes her vision on it. Implied in the vision there is a message.

It is with this determination to explore life—and *that* is the message—that Welty's young American woman leaves the frustrations of an unsuccessful marriage behind, sails on the Innisfallen, and goes ashore in Cork full of cautious curiosity. Watching girls in confirmation dresses under the blossoming trees in the streets of the Irish town, her zest for life is restored. When she takes shelter from the rain in the warm doorway of a pub, she is on the verge of breaking out of her isolation. In the last sentence of the story she is at *that* point: "Opening the door [she] walked without protection into the lovely room full of strangers" (*Collected Stories*, 518). Chekhov's last short story, "Betrothed," offers an obvious parallel to Welty's young woman in Cork. Nadya, who is the betrothed of the title, is full of high spirits and feels liberated when her husband-to-be dies. She leaves behind her native town, which is small, dusty, and provincial, and in her mind "rose the vista of a new, wide, spacious life, and that life, still obscure and full of mysteries [or "subtexts"] beckoned her and attracted her."[13]

Notes

1. Fitzgerald, introduction to *Three by Flannery O'Connor*, xxiv.

2. See Lewinson, *Race, Class, and Party*, 7.

3. It is tempting to see O'Connor's creation of this realistic southern Jacob's ladder as her reaction to the two giant murals in St. John the Baptist in Savannah. The cathedral is on the same square as O'Connor's childhood home. Whenever she was in church during the first thirteen years of her life, O'Connor was exposed to Jacob's ladders, where the individuals rising toward the light are exclusively young, well-nourished, white, and often blonde women.

4. Bleikasten, "Writing on the Flesh."

5. See Pollack and Marrs, eds., *Eudora Welty and Politics*.

6. See Baldwin, *Notes of a Native Son*, 9–17.

7. Thornton's article is as yet unpublished.

8. West, "Three Methods of Modern Fiction," 202.

9. Petty, "The Town and Writer," 35. For the identification of Powerhouse with Fats Waller, see Prenshaw, ed., *Conversations with Eudora Welty*, 85. For parallels between their lives, see Bates, "Welty's Improvisation of Powerhouse."

10. Kreyling, *Author and Agent*, 54.

11. Their articles are identified in the list of works cited.

12. *Eye of the Story*, 76.

13. *Tales of Anton Checkov*, 11:75.

Works Cited

Adams, Timothy Dow. "A Curtain of Black: White and Black Jazz Styles in 'Powerhouse.'" *Notes on Mississippi Writers* 10, no. 2 (1977): 57–61.

Albert, Richard N. "Eudora Welty's Fats Waller: 'Powerhouse.'" *Notes on Mississippi Writers* 19, no. 2 (1987): 63–71.

Baldwin, James. "Everybody's Protest Novel." In *Notes of a Native Son*, 9–17. 1949. London: Corgi Books, 1970.

Bates, Jonathan. "Welty's Improvisation of Powerhouse: Is This the Portrayal Fats Would Have Wanted?" *Notes on Mississippi Writers* 22, no. 2 (1990): 81–94.

Bleikasten, André. "Writing on the Flesh: Tattoos and Taboos in 'Parker's Back.'" *The Southern Literary Journal* 14 (Spring 1982): 8–18.

Chekhov, Anton. *The Tales of Anton Checkov*. 1917. Translated by Constance Garnett. 13 vols. New York: Ecco Press, 1984–87.

Fitzgerald, Sally. Introduction to *Three by Flannery O'Connor*. New York: New American Library, 1985.

Genette, Gérard. *Narrative Discourse Revisited*. Ithaca, N.Y.: Cornell University Press, 1988.

Hardy, John Edward. "Eudora Welty's Negroes." In *Images of the Negro in American Literature*, edited by Seymour L. Gross and John Edward Hardy, 221–32. Chicago: University of Chicago Press, 1966.

Inge, M. Thomas. "Eudora Welty's Comic Sensibility." In *Faulkner, Sut, and Other Southerners: Essays in Literary History*, 163–69. West Cornwall, Conn.: Locust Hill Press, 1992.

Kreyling, Michael. *Author and Agent: Eudora Welty and Diarmuid Russell*. New York: Farrar, Straus and Giroux, 1991.

Lewinson, Paul. *Race, Class, and Party*. New York: Oxford University Press, 1932.

O'Connor, Flannery. *Mystery and Manners*. New York: Farrar, Straus and Giroux, 1969.

———. *The Complete Stories*. New York: Farrar, Straus and Giroux, 1971.

Petty, Jane Reid. "The Town and Writer: An Interview with Eudora Welty." *Jackson Magazine*, September 1977, 29–35.

Pollack, Harriet, and Suzanne Marrs, eds. *Eudora Welty and Politics: Did the Writer Crusade?* Baton Rouge: Louisiana State University Press, 2001.

Prenshaw, Peggy, ed. *Conversations with Eudora Welty*. Jackson: University Press of Mississippi, 1984.

Thornton, Naoko Fuwa. "The Strange Felicity: The Implicit Thought of Welty on Fiction." Unpublished manuscript.

Welty, Eudora. "Must the Novelist Crusade?" In *The Eye of the Story: Selected Essays and Reviews*, 146–58. New York: Random House, 1978.

———. *The Collected Stories*. New York: Harcourt Brace Jovanovich, 1980.

West, Ray B., Jr. "Three Methods of Modern Fiction: Ernest Hemingway, Thomas Mann, Eudora Welty." *College English* 12 (January 1951): 193–202.

A Life Remembered

Store Porch Tales from Yoknapatawpha County

Hans H. Skei

Frenchman's Bend in *The Hamlet*, "hill-cradled and remote" (3), is one of the villages of William Faulkner's imaginary kingdom, Yoknapatawpha County. This, surely, is one of the most insistently backwoods areas in modern literature. Here Faulkner's characters visit Varner's crossroads store and Mrs. Littlejohn's boarding house and squat or sit on the front porch while they comment on tales of barter and trade, of limitless stupidity and fatal pride. The porch is a place admirably suited for old tales and talking, for the best of gossip, for the narratives by which people in an established society explain and understand themselves, despite an individualism that at times threatens to destabilize the order of things. Joining Faulkner's characters on that porch, we may not learn much about the short story genre as such, but we may get an impression of the flexibility of the form and learn something about the interdependency and interrelatedness of story and novel in Faulkner's work. When we struggle with descriptions and definitions of the genre, it is well worth remembering that writers may come along and smash our neat definitions. The author who once had the temerity to put the manuscript of *The Sound and the Fury* in the mail to a publisher should be expected to go beyond questions of genre and dividing lines between literary forms, even if he claimed that he wrote stories just to tell about people, with little time or patience for questions of genre, technique, narrative form, or the like. And it has, often enough, been maintained that generic concepts are of little interest in a study of Faulkner's short fiction, simply because his use of the same material in short stories and novels means that the borderlines between long and short narrative do not make sense in his case. This may well be so, yet generic concepts remain important when we analyze literature, and we should not underestimate their power in the process of naturalization, which all readings in a sense are.

One inroad to Faulkner's short fiction is to focus on the way in which the stories dramatize "existential experience" through the use of arrested motion or the frozen tableau to present epiphanic moments of revelation or insight.[1] Analyzing the epiphanic structure of Faulkner's short fiction may actually be of help in better understanding a subgroup of the modern literary short story. But all through his career, Faulkner had a strong novelistic tendency to sacrifice short story material—drafts, fragments, anecdotes —and even individual and autonomous and published short stories by subsuming them in longer narratives—in novels. So perhaps there is more to learn by looking at stories that were conceived, written, sold, and published as short stories and that, later on, nonetheless were assimilated or integrated in novels. Do we simply state that we have a short story on the one hand and a book chapter on the other and accept that the novel seems to have an unlimited capacity to include and transform any and all texts, being as it were a growing and changing genre? I think we should, but the reuse of short stories in a novel also gives us an opportunity to compare, speculate, theorize about the possible differences between the short and long narrative form.

We have to get more closely acquainted with the little lost village, the hamlet of Frenchman's Bend, and speculate on the significance of the porch before we look at the stories told there and the way they function both as magazine short stories and as episodes in a long and episodic novel.

The store porch anecdotes are oral narratives, as close to the classical oral story-telling situation with a teller and his or her listeners as you can get. They are possible only within a given structure, an established society, presupposing a sense of a real world as model behind the fictional one. The society in which these store porch tales have their roots and in which they unfold and signify attains almost mythical stature and offers a model, a structuring principle that can help hold together the loosest of narratives, link story to story to become a novel, or tell short tales that take on additional meaning because they rely on shared conventions, histories, fantasies, even to the point where a communal rhetoric is discernible. Events, information, news, and rumors are shared through this practice of storytelling, and somehow things seem to have happened only when they have been told, made into a yarn, a tall tale, or a story. Everything is shared, everybody knows his or her place. Traditions matter much in this seemingly unchanging and unchangeable world. The tales carry on the traditions and mores and values of a community of men, always told in the past tense, and even if *was* always is *is*, life itself begins to look like a life remembered, a series of store porch anecdotes lived with unflagging and almost blind energy over and over again.

Faulkner's last great novel, *The Hamlet*, is an example of this: the whole book could be seen as a store porch anecdote were it not such a markedly written and highly literary text, relying on a rich and varied metaphorical language, allusions to mythology, and stylistic excesses of various kinds. So I have chosen two short story texts, both reused in this novel, both told on the porch to a group of listeners, even if the porch and the listeners change in surprising ways from story to novel, and in different ways in the two stories. The two short stories are probably the funniest stories Faulkner ever wrote, yet there is more to them than wild exaggerations or hyperbolic humor— much more to them, at least, when revised for the novel and read in the context of the longer narrative. The stories are "Spotted Horses" and "Fool about a Horse," written in 1931 and 1935 and published in *Scribner's Magazine* in the June 1931 and August 1936 issues, respectively. The magazine versions became available in book form only with the publication of *Uncollected Stories* in 1979 (in the following referred to as *UCS*).

Faulkner lets his storytelling protagonist, V. K. Ratliff, formerly named Suratt, meet local people gathered on the porch. They remain silent and listen, chew tobacco or whittle away on a stick, add a shrewd remark to the tale, put in a question or a comment, and thus a first-person narrator is responsible for an oral transmission of a story of plain people's folly or gullibility. The stories told from the store porch by Faulkner's favorite storyteller, V. K. Ratliff, are fairly exceptional among his short stories, perhaps because an established community in which a story can unfold is needed, not a created world that can be tested through the story. A vital part in this storytelling is the scene of the telling: the porch itself.

The porch is a threshold, but also a place—with Bakhtin we could have called it a chronotope—that joins different worlds, the world of the road and the world of the house, a place for encounters of some duration, and perhaps a place of sudden revelations. More than anything else it is a place of gathering and lingering, a transitional area. The real importance of the porch becomes evident when we get to know its role as a place to transmit folklore, to tell stories. But it is also a place where people of different classes and races might meet, an intermediary zone between public and private.

On the porch of Varner's store in Frenchman's Bend, tales are told, episodes related, and the porch gets a literary function as a very potent symbol. What has happened in a community is traded down in tales on the porch, and events worth telling about quickly seem to take on the quality of a story book tale of life remembered, a part of tradition, of a community's life.

"Yes, sir." This is how both stories open. The short story "Fool about a Horse" is told as a memory of childhood to an unspecified audience, by an unnamed narrator. In manuscript versions of the story the child was named Suratt, and his story was told by a narrator who must be one of the Compson children to Grandfather. In the published version, there is no such outside or frame narrator. Here the narrator is the grownup who as a twelve-year-old boy was witness to incredible swapping of horses and mules, in a series of wildly funny, exaggerated, and improbable events in which he actively participated. What he narrates is basically the story of his father's being so much of a fool about a horse that he even traded with the legendary Pat Stamper and was "outsmarted" by him. And even if the narrator insists that it was all pure fate and could not be avoided, the driving forces behind Pap's eagerness to trade or swap horses seem to be a mixture of stupidity, pride, honor, and revenge. Also, good Yoknapatawpha money may disappear from the county since someone actually has paid Pat Stamper eight dollars for a horse. Pap is a lazy tenant farmer, living on rented land, borrowing equipment to grow corn and cotton, but more likely to be found sitting on the top rail of his fence than behind the plow in the field. He has traded some barbed wire, a sorghum mill, and other used or useless stuff that he did not own for a horse, and he is pleased because he thinks he has done well in a highly valued profession in Yoknapatawpha: horse trading. When his wife scolds him and shakes a cold skillet at him, we notice a pride that will quickly lead to his downfall, since he is not the Pat Stamper of Frenchman's Bend: "'Now Vynie; now Vynie. I always was a fool about a good horse and it ain't no use you a-scolding and jawing about it. You had better thank the Lord that when He give me a eye for horse-flesh He give me a little jedgment and gumption along with it'" (UCS, 118–19). The story elements are simple: The young boy and his father, called Pap, leave home for Jefferson to get a cream separator for Mammy, who has saved 27 dollars and 65 cents from egg sales and quilt making. They leave in a wagon with a mismatched team of a decent mule and the horse Pap had recently traded for from Beasley Kemp. When they reach Varner's store, the horse has changed color and is recognized by Jody Varner as a horse Pat Stamper had swapped for a buckboard and harness five years earlier and that Beasley Kemp had actually paid eight dollars for last summer. Pat Stamper accidentally camps alongside the road to Jefferson this day. Pap sends his son on the mule to buy saltpeter and a fish hook, creates a lively horse with shining gums, and swaps his good mule and this horse for a team of mules. The team barely lasts to Jefferson, where they buy the separator, and on their way back Pap desperately tries to trade back his team. He ends up with the mule and a new horse, but the separator is returned, and we do not know how much money changed hands. The "new" horse is impressive: "a little dark brown horse; I remember how even with it clouded up to rain and no sun, how the horse shined; a horse a little bigger than the one we traded Stamper, and hog fat. Yes, sir. That's jest exactly how it was fat: not like a horse is fat but like a hog: fat right up to its ears and looking tight as a drum" (130). In his despair and fury and raging lack of control, Pap even drinks a bottle of whiskey and then some more, and the boy drives homeward with Pap asleep in the wagon bed. Then, in the heavy rain, the horse changes color, and suddenly it more or less vanishes, and the horse they started out with in the morning appears. They even get their fish hook back! The improbabilities, not to say the impossibilities of the story, are never more visible than in this episode: "then me and Pap heard a sound like when a automobile tire picks up a nail: a sound like Whoosh! and then the rest of that shiny fat horse we had got from Pat Stamper vanished. . . . But it wasn't until we was home the next day at daylight that we found the hand pump valve behind its fore leg" (132–33). Mammy saddles the mule, rides off leading the horse along, and does not return until the next morning in a neighbor's wagon, with her separator. Having no team to pull the plows, Pap and the narrator sit on the fence, listening to the hum of the separator. Even though she has but one gallon of milk, she runs it through another time, and Pap's comment rounds off the story: "It looks like she is fixing to get a heap of pleasure and comfort outen it" (134). In the book version, Mrs. Snopes, who has replaced Mammy, has to trade in her cow to get her separator, and the son has become a young boy at the neighboring farm, the narrator V. K. Ratliff, who brings her a pail of milk so that she can use the separator! This solves some of the problematic motivation with the original story's ending and makes the whole tale more poignant.

Told with mild irony and a distance in time and place, the story is wildly improbable, its humor of the hyperbolic sort, its language a meticulous attempt at mimetic rendering of speech with personal idiosyncrasies to color a communal rhetoric in a superb version of what is, after all, a formulaic tall tale. The narration not only implies but includes a listener, an audience, presumably an audience familiar with the genre as well as the basic story elements. The narrator addresses the audience time and again, and his "Yes, sir" and "No, sir" may indicate questions or comments from the listeners, if they are not simply tricks of the tall tale trade. Repetitions abound, and the language is replete with country life metaphors, most often related to work on a dirt farm in the era of mules and horses and manpower. The structure of the story relies on a set of prolepses, in the sense that the narrator takes it for granted that the listeners know the outcome of the story, so he might as well begin by the basic facts: "It wasn't Pap that bought one horse from Pat Stamper and then sold two back to him. It was Mammy" (118). Also: "So I reckon the rest of it don't even hardly need to be told, except as a kind of sidelight" (123). The story is, of course, another tale of life remembered, told in retrospect, but with force and vitality in the historical present when the narration so requires. The narrative moves through different phases, using stronger effects as we read on. But the fact remains that the story is a childhood memory about one's parents, told by a grown-up who appears to have risen from the poverty and powerlessness of his background. Seen from this perspective, the hilariously funny story takes on new dimensions, but it remains a wildly comic tall tale, told seriously and jokingly for fun. It is not easy to see how such a story could be given other and more serious functions in a novel by being slightly rewritten. But Faulkner succeeded in doing so, even if the story we have followed here could be said to be superimposed on the text of The Hamlet and does not seem to be fully integrated in the longer narrative. Yet I think its interpretive signals are vital to this novel as a whole.

One reason why the reuse of "Fool about a Horse" is not entirely successful in the context of the novel, The Hamlet, is because it to some extent represents a digression from the story line established in the first chapter of book 1, at a point in time when the reader does not really need or want a long and winding tall tale that contributes to the understanding of only one character, Ab Snopes, who must be seen as marginal in the novel as a whole. Faulkner returns to the narrative strategy of using a named narrator, which he had abandoned in the published short story. In the novel Ratliff is the neighbor boy who sits on the fence with Ab Snopes and joins him in his outrageous horse business. The revised and expanded version in the novel retains the characterization of Pap in the story, and so Ab Snopes emerges from this episode as less of a Snopes than we as readers have been prepared for. He is at times a sympathetic character, even if he is a fool about horses and limitless in his general stupidity. The problem is also that a hilarious tall tale hardly is a text in which character traits are described realistically to create individualized fictional characters.

One function the story does have is to introduce central elements in the novel, and it also prepares the reader for the horse auction episode later on, although it takes a byway and certainly slows down the speed of the narrative considerably. Everybody listens to Ratliff, but the tale probably does not convince the listeners any more than the text does the readers in offering a simple explanation for Ab's having become a vicious barn burner: "Old man Ab aint naturally mean. He's just soured" (*The Hamlet*, 31)—and he soured because of being outsmarted in horse trading! All in all, it would not seem unfair to argue that the story remains somehow superimposed on the text and is not really assimilated into the novel's narrative.

By contrast, one may think of the novel as a more flexible and dialogic genre than the established types of short fiction and not ask for similarity of style, narrative tone, and method of characterization but rather accept different and contesting narratives within the same novelistic text. Also, we should bear in mind that the author, apparently with ease and with a heightening of the textual power of this particular section of the book, was able to integrate and completely assimilate a story such as "The Hound." Faulkner's easy and complete assimilation of all other stories into the long narrative of *The Hamlet* invites a reconsideration of the view that "Fool about a Horse" is awkward or slightly out of place and out of tune with the rest of the narrative. On closer scrutiny, there are several valid reasons for its inclusion and for its being just the kind of story it is.

First of all, it establishes Ratliff's origin among the poor tenant farmers, that is, as one of the people he trades with and lives among, but also from a background identical to that of the Snopeses. Ratliff belongs to the same class as Ab and Flem Snopes, and a simple social and historical and behaviorist explanation would make it more than likely that he would remain within this class, even to the point where we would expect his character and life to be formed decisively by this background. However, character and personality cannot be explained merely by reference to class background, obviously, and Ratliff has not only proved that social mobility—upward if not very far —is possible, but he has also shown that it is possible to turn the background of rural poverty into something very much like loyalty, love, and self-esteem. In the opening frame of a typescript prepublication version of the story, Faulkner is very explicit in his definition (not description) of his favorite storyteller, who "had escaped his birthright and into independence and even pride."[2] This element in the story serves to establish Ratliff even more as a watcher of the Snopeses and as their obvious counterpart and antagonist.

When Ratliff tells this tale, we are for the first time in the novel invited behind the scene. We are invited to listen to the best of gossip, about something in the not too distant past that is not only improbable but completely out of proportion and unrealistic, but that nevertheless shows us lives and dreams among poor tenant farmers, often called a "race of its own" by Faulkner. Pat Stamper, the horse dealer, is created through such tales, as is Ab Snopes's gullibility and foolishness, and his wife, although pleased at the end of the story, is an innocent victim of male stupidity, and she is only the first one among those we meet in the course of the novel. We are close to the origins of the mysterious backwoods people, this race of shiftless tenant farmers from whom Flem Snopes, via his father, Ab, suddenly one day emerges, and nothing will ever be the same in Frenchman's Bend. By listening to Ratliff and by witnessing his audience, we also learn something about the power of storytelling, and hence about the narrative and textual power of the text we read in which the story is contained. The impossibility of many of the "facts" of this story serves to prepare us for exaggerations and hyperbolic extravagance later on, and somehow we as readers do need to be broken in, to get ready for the use of similar rhetorical figures and nonreferential, literary language also in the more down-to-earth events and the narration of them by the unnamed, outside narrator of most of the novel's stories. The hyperbolic, tall-tale humor of this story is an antidote to the impending disaster and fear of barn burning introduced in the novel's opening pages, and we listen to a story of a childhood experience of great importance, signifying relatively little, and we get a first glimpse into a world of fun and laughter, sympathy and goodwill. This is the world of Frenchman's Bend, Yoknapatawpha County, ruled according to age-old laws of the ledger in the local store and the cycles of planting and harvest seasons, and watched over by Will Varner, a kindhearted man of goodwill and a patriarch of old, believing in what he is doing and also doing it for what he thinks is for the best of his fellow humans. A good yarn in good company on a warm and lazy day is certainly part of this world, and therefore also a necessary part of our introduction to it. Accordingly, even though I cannot help but feel that Faulkner in the case of "Fool about a Horse" remained too close to the short story version in the sense that he simply changed the protagonist's name and reinstated a narrative frame, this section of chapter 1 of book 1 nevertheless prepares us for so much of what comes later that it is difficult to think of a more effective way of doing this expository work.

I have spent some time on the short story "Fool about a Horse" and on the way it functions in *The Hamlet*, in an attempt to show that old tales and talking can be put to new and good uses in different contexts. When analyzing a short story as a text in its own right, it seems unwise to rely on its novelistic counterpart, as there are good reasons for insisting on the autonomy of the published individual story. Yet one may find it worthwhile in a study of genres or kinds of literature to undertake such comparative readings, as well as in a study of Faulkner's achievement in general. "Spotted Horses" provides another opportunity for theorizing Faulkner's reuse of short fiction material in his novels. *The Hamlet* has its origin in this story. In a much-quoted letter to Malcolm Cowley in 1945, Faulkner wrote that "THE HAMLET was incepted as a novel. When I began it, it produced Spotted Horses, went no further."³ The text in the novel is an expansion of an early version of the printed short story but leaves out the introductory material presenting Flem Snopes and his years in Frenchman's Bend until shortly after he married Eula Varner and returned from Texas with a baby too big to be his. Characters are changed in accordance with the needs of the novel, and even if Ratliff is central in the novel and the only opponent to Flem's new usurpation of the village, he is no longer the narrator. He carries some of the narrative burden in his dialogue, but the narration is omniscient and, one might say, free from the restraints of Ratliff's dialect. Despite these changes, it is possible to maintain that the spotted horses material—the prepublication versions are many and bewildering—is perfectly and totally integrated in the novel. Everything in the book leads up to it, and then away from it toward the conclusion of this first volume of the Snopes trilogy.

In the present context, space allows only for a very brief account of those magic moments on Mrs. Littlejohn's porch and in and around her barn, where Flem Snopes and a Texan bring in a bunch of wild cattymounts from Texas, to auction off to the poor farmers of Frenchman's Bend.⁴ Even if the main event—the auction—belongs to the immediate past, it is quickly turned into myth. The story describes crucial moments of exploitation and small-scale tragedy, but also a rare moment of dream and poetry and virility and male stupidity. The narrative situation is in a sense doubled in this tale: Suratt tells the story now, to a captive audience in Jefferson, and the story he tells is basically how and what he told (including responses from central characters on the porch of Varner's store) at an earlier point in Frenchman's Bend. "Spotted Horses" is straightforward oral storytelling by a first-person narrator who addresses his audience now and then, invites them into his tale, suggests that they know people he mentions, and quickly establishes the immediate reason for telling the story of the spotted horses: one of them "flew right over my team, big as a billboard and flying through the air like a hawk" (*UCS*, 165).

The opening words of the story set the tone of the narrative; this introduction defines the speech acts to be used and establishes as truth something that the story as a whole will confirm but for which there is never any proof: "Yes, sir. Flem Snopes filled that whole country full of spotted horses" (165). Flem arrives with horses but so also does a Texan with "one of these two-gallon hats and an ivory-handled pistol and a box of gingersnaps sticking out of his hind pocket." The horses, however, dominate the scene: "They was colored like parrots and they was quiet as doves, and ere a one of them would kill you quick as a rattlesnake. Nere a one of them had two eyes the same color, and nere a one of them had ever seen a bridle, I reckon; and when that Texas man got down offen the wagon and walked up to them to show how gentle they was, one of them cut his vest clean offen him, same as with a razor" (167).

We never know for certain, yet we are as readers never in doubt that Flem owns the horses. He is away most of the time but present at crucial points during and after

the auction. After a slow start, all the horses are auctioned off, but when Henry Armstid, with five dollars his wife has earned weaving at night, enters the lot to fetch his
horse, he is almost trampled to death, and the other horses scatter all over the countryside, almost killing Vernon Tull and his womenfolks at the wooden bridge nearby.
The Texan gives Henry's money back to him, but Henry persists in trying to buy the
horse and it eventually ends up in Flem's hands. After all the accidents, with Henry
lying half-dead in Mrs. Littljohn's house, his wife asks Flem for the money, but he
flatly says that the Texan took it with him when he left. But Faulkner's favorite storyteller knows how to balance comedy and tragedy and bring about the right reaction.
A small, innocent episode passes between Flem and Mrs. Armstid. Flem asks her to
wait, enters the store, and returns with a nickel's worth of candy, saying, "A little
sweetening for the chaps," to which poor Mrs. Armstid says, "You're right kind" (182).
At this point we do not know which way to look or whether to cry or to cry out. The
narrator knows that only Flem can get away with what he has done and ends his story
the way he began it: "Yes, sir" (183), confirming that you cannot beat Flem.

"Spotted Horses" is an almost tragic study in poverty, suffering, and human frailty
exploited to the utmost by a shrewd and inhuman businessman whose only interest
is profit. "Spotted Horses" is certainly also one of the funniest stories Faulkner ever
wrote, a classic in American humor, one of the funniest American stories since Mark
Twain. But the farce of this "frontier trickster tale"[5] is carefully qualified with pathos,
its humor tempered by the consequences that the shrewd deals and the funny events
have on pitiable individuals. The tone is kept unchanged and at the same pitch all
through the story, so that comic and grotesque elements are juxtaposed with elements
of suffering and tragedy.

Two short stories, turned into chapters in the same novel, with a narrator who
turns up everywhere in Faulkner's late work, located in well-known fictional places
with characters we know from other stories and novels. Clearly, questions of genre
and generic conventions must be asked with other questions about kinds of literature
in mind. I am not saying that genre studies do not help, but that Faulkner's reuse of
short story material at least may be a cautionary lesson in the sense that clear-cut definitions of what a short story is or can be do not work so well here. We see how texts
can belong to different genres. What we thought was a short story suddenly turns up
as a chapter of a novel, or as a central scene in a long, epic work.

One cannot read Faulkner for entertainment alone, nor for identification, nor for
the uplifting of the heart, because there is always a sense of a pervasive darkness in
his texts. But there is also a magic force, and an almost inaudible voice above and
beyond the texts, a voice still in good faith. If I have communicated some of this faith,
and some of the magic of a born storyteller's oral performance on the southern porch,
that is exactly what I wanted to do.

Notes

1. See Skei, "Beyond Genre?" and *Reading Faulkner's Best Short Stories.*

2. Creighton, *William Faulkner's Craft of Revision,* 26.

3. Blotner, ed., *Selected Letters,* 197.

4. I deem "Spotted Horses" to be among the twelve most successful stories in the Faulkner canon; for a full discussion, see Skei, *Reading Faulkner's Best Short Stories,* 165–77.

5. Carothers, *William Faulkner's Short Stories,* 116.

Works Cited

Blotner, Joseph, ed. *The Selected Letters of William Faulkner.* New York: Random House, 1977.

Carothers, James B. *William Faulkner's Short Stories.* Ann Arbor, Mich.: UMI Research Press, 1985.

Creighton, Joanna V. *William Faulkner's Craft of Revision: The Snopes Trilogy, "The Unvanquished," and "Go Down, Moses."* Detroit: Wayne State University Press, 1977.

Faulkner, William. *The Hamlet.* New York: Random House, 1940.

———. *The Uncollected Stories.* New York: Random House, 1979.

Skei, Hans H. "Beyond Genre? Existential Experience in Faulkner's Short Fiction." In *Faulkner and the Short Story,* edited by Evans Harrington and Ann J. Abadie, 62–77. Jackson: University of Mississippi Press, 1992.

———. *Reading Faulkner's Best Short Stories.* Columbia: University of South Carolina Press, 1999.

Faulkner, Welty, and the Short Story Composite

Sandra Lee Kleppe

William Faulkner's *Go Down, Moses* (1942) has been called a short story collection, a novel, a composite novel, a short story composite, a short story cycle, a short story compound, a blend, and a hybrid. Eudora Welty's *The Golden Apples* (1949) has been described in similar terms: as a short story collection, a novel, a short story composite, a collection of interlocking stories, a short story cycle, and a *Bildungsroman*. "Anything that comes out of the South," as O'Connor has notoriously noted, "is going to be called grotesque by the Northern reader" (40). The critical grappling with what to call such works that come out of the South has a long and tangled history. In this essay I will take into consideration one genre, which I choose to call the short story composite, following the terminology of one of its leading theorists, Rolf Lundén. The first section examines this term and how it has been applied to these two works by Faulkner and Welty. In the middle section, by considering how Welty and Faulkner conceived of their own works, I turn to a discussion of how authorial intention plays a role in how we determine genre. The final section is an attempt to resolve the genre controversy of the books under scrutiny by examining some traits specific to southern literature.

The Disunited Stories of America

Since *Go Down, Moses* and *The Golden Apples* have been considered by several scholars as representative examples of a genre that is in between the short story collection and the novel, these two works provide a good starting point for an examination of this hybrid form. Both of these books are discussed at length in Rolf Lundén's *The United Stories of America: Studies in the Short Story Composite* (1999), a work that deserves attention from anyone interested in the study of genre in general and the study of the composite in particular. Lundén not only manages to gather and comment on virtually all existing critical work on this literary phenomenon, but he also presents us with a comprehensive theory of what he believes to be an unacknowledged ancient genre, a genre, moreover, that has had a renaissance in twentieth-century American fiction.

A more appropriate title for Lundén's book might be "The *Dis*united Stories of America." This is because Lundén makes such a strong case for the ways in which previous critical works attempt to highlight the short story composite as an organic whole and tone down the key generic feature of disjuncture. "[U]nity, coherence and closure," Lundén writes, "have been privileged at the expense of discontinuity, fragmentation and openness" (8). Lundén underlines that it is the *tension* between the centripetal unifying strategies and the centrifugal forces of disjuncture that characterizes the short story composite and that the tendency to emphasize unity is an unfortunate critical impulse. He suggests that the wish to give this genre the status of novel inevitably leads to a blind spot in critical inquiry. The distinctiveness of the composite is overlooked or ignored when critics set out to broaden the category of novel in order to accommodate complex hybrid works such as the composite.

Theorists of the short story composite such as Lundén, Forrest Ingram, and Susan Mann have documented that it is a legitimate literary genre with its own specific traits, ones that have been overshadowed on the one hand by the novel and on the other by the short story collection. The short story composite can be defined as a book consisting of several stories that function simultaneously as autonomous units and as parts of an interrelated whole. It is, in Lundén's words, "an open work consisting of closed stories" (60). Formally, both *Go Down, Moses* and *The Golden Apples* are indeed prime examples of the short story composite. Lundén documents how they contain several of the key criteria of the composite, such as separate individual story titles, a repetition of characters and setting, a structure consisting of kernel or core stories and satellite or more loosely integrated stories, and a balance between the closural strategies of the individual stories and the openness of the volume as a whole. In addition, both Faulkner and Welty have included what Lundén defines as a "fringe story" — "Pantaloon in Black" and "Music from Spain," respectively. The function of the fringe story is to ensure the disjuncture of the composite rather than the unifying organicism of the novel.[1]

We have much information on the genesis and composition of *The Golden Apples* and *Go Down, Moses* that can supplement a study of the formal generic features of the published work. Welty has explained on several occasions that she started out writing separate stories and discovered connections between them as she continued writing. In Forrest Ingram's analysis, Welty's book would fall under the category he terms "completed cycle," a collection in which the author becomes aware of unifying strands between the stories during the process of writing and hence completes the "unifying task" (18).

In Joanne Creighton's thorough study of the manuscripts that went into the making of *Go Down, Moses*, she reconstructs the stages ten Faulkner stories went through in order to become the seven sections of the finished version, and makes a good case for reading the book as a composite rather than a novel. Creighton documents how

Faulkner went about the task of creating the volume with scrupulous care to the double commitment of the stories as separate units and as parts of an integrated whole. Creighton writes: "Having closely studied Faulkner's process of revision and composition in *Go Down, Moses,* I am convinced that he was attempting to create a new synthetic form, the short story composite, in which the stories are autonomous units governed by their own principles while they are at the same time integral parts of a larger whole. I do not think that Faulkner was self-consciously establishing a new genre, but that he was attempting to find a form flexible enough to accommodate both the expansive panoramic across-the-generations look at a host of characters and . . . an intensive examination of the moral consciousness of one individual, Isaac McCaslin. Those critics who have proclaimed its 'novelistic' unity have underestimated the unusual development of *Go Down, Moses*" (86). Thomas McHaney points to some similar issues involved in reading *The Golden Apples* when he states that there is "a sincere desire to canonize an admirable piece of work within an accepted form. Welty students want to endow *The Golden Apples* with the prestige, the presumption of higher seriousness, and the opportunity to win the wider audience that novels, as opposed to story collections, enjoy" (173). McHaney terms Welty's book a short story cycle, which in Lundén's terminology corresponds to a subgroup of short story composites.

The illuminating work done on the short story composite in the past few decades has done much to repair its status and prestige by attempting to give this genre the acceptance it deserves. Lundén's *The United Stories of America* is noteworthy in this context, and his readings of *Go Down, Moses* and *The Golden Apples* as short story composites are thorough and convincing. In what follows, by suggesting that the issue of authorial intention complicates how we read genre, I do not wish to prove that previous critical work has misread the genre of *Go Down, Moses,* only that our theoretical considerations would benefit from a more consistent treatment of this polemical issue.[2]

Authorial Intention and Race

Welty has explicitly stated that her book is not a novel and was never intended as such, even though readers at the time of its publication in 1949 and even some today tend to view it as a novel. In an interview with Welty, Jan Gretlund posed the question "Why is *The Golden Apples* not a novel?" to which Welty replied the following: "Well, for the reason, I guess, that they were conceived as stories. Also, I didn't want the responsibilities of trying to connect them, as they would have to be in a novel. Because it would mean tearing down everything I had. What I wanted to do with those characters is what I did, and that means stories" (385). Obviously, Welty does not want her book to be given the burden of a novel when she consciously strove to work within the formal and aesthetic realm of another genre. The fact that Welty composed *The Golden Apples* as a series of stories more closely related than a conventional collection, yet not as unified as a novel, supports the claim that the book is indeed a composite. This claim does not necessarily conflict with Welty's intention of writing a collection, since she herself has admitted that the stories evolved into linked clusters as she wrote them. In such a case, authorial intention does not warrant elaboration unless the reader insists on terming the book a novel, since the issue of intention can be balanced against the information about the genesis of the book and a close study of the formal features.

Faulkner, however, has stated explicitly that his book *was* intended as a novel.[3] We also know that the first publication of *Go Down, Moses* with the subtitle *"and Other Stories"* was an editorial decision made without Faulkner's consent. In his article "Structure and Theme in Faulkner's *Go Down, Moses*" (1975), Weldon Thornton makes the observation that Faulkner dedicated "thought and energy to the question of what a novel is, what holds it together, and upon what basis its unity and progression rest" (73). I would like to reconsider this old genre debate in light of some disturbing issues that I believe also belong to a consideration of *Go Down, Moses*.

During the years following its publication, *Go Down, Moses* was termed a failure on the basis of the story/chapter "Pantaloon in Black," which did not seem to fit with the rest. As it turns out, this story is the only sustained narrative in Faulkner's career with an African American as focalizer. Since the issue of race is so central to Faulkner's book, the negative critical attention given to this one story seems to have some political implications.[4] While critics are quick to praise "The Bear," a story with a self-centered white protagonist who agonizes about the history of the South and his place in it, they seem just as hasty to dismiss "Pantaloon in Black" as an inappropriate anomaly.

Lundén points out that some critical considerations of "Pantaloon in Black" attempt to repair the earlier tendency toward dismissal through an opposite strategy of affirmative action by considering it what he calls an "emblematic" story (140). It would seem that our critical interpretation of this story is caught up in the stereotyping strategies of the twentieth century, which confine the character Rider to the emblematic status of either "bad Negro" or "good Negro," a character who either makes the work disintegrate or cohere, depending on one's reading. One way out of this critical impasse is to consider the role of genre in light of authorial intention.

While Lundén gives an admirable reading of the challenging genre issues of *Go Down, Moses*, he nevertheless fails to provide sufficient reason to overlook Faulkner's own intention of writing a novel. Early on in *The United Stories of America*, he writes in his discussion of *Go Down, Moses* that what "the authorial or editorial intention once harbored" is irrelevant (35). Yet in other places he implies that authorial intention is, in fact, an important trait in determining genre: "Since Faulkner paid so much attention to revising the stories, it seems quite clear that he *intended* these two—particularly 'Pantaloon [in Black]' which displays even fewer connective devices than 'Go Down, Moses'—to remain marginally integrated" (139; italics mine). An author's choice of genre, I believe, involves a type of *formal* intention[5] in addition to the personal, cultural, and historical aspects of intention. Even if we regard the personal reasons for Faulkner's choice as irrelevant to our understanding of the work, the other issues should arrest our attention.

From a comparative literary vantage point, Faulkner's work is at the very heart of the major changes in novelistic form and technique that we associate with the transition from realism to modernism in Western literature. From a cultural point of view, Faulkner's work is inextricably linked to transitions in social and racial relations in the twentieth-century South. In this context it is significant that Faulkner's only book with a focalizer not of his own race is the center of a critical debate about genre. I find it therefore relevant to suggest that the author's choice of genre should be scrutinized with particular care in this case. This I have done at length elsewhere,[6] finding that the book is indeed a novel. Among the reasons for incorporating "Pantaloon in Black" as well as the title story "Go Down, Moses" into the novel form is that they are both about the status of African American male and female narratives in the twentieth-century South and that both of these stories have their ultimate sources in music. The idea for "Pantaloon in Black" came from the blues song "I Know You, Rider,"[7] and "Go Down, Moses" is a well-known southern spiritual that links the Old Testament story of the liberation of slaves to the plight of the slaves and ex-slaves of the South. There is thus a *structural* intention in the book that provides a framework of point and counterpoint within an orchestrated whole, allowing the African American voices to signify in a culturally different way (musically) than the white, land-owning, loquacious McCaslins.

The significance of this information, in my view, is striking. By incorporating cultural elements not entirely his own into the title and two contrapuntal sections of his book, Faulkner is making a subtle but important concession to other voices of the South: he is, in short, changing his conception of the novel and changing his novel form *from within* by allowing other discourses to signify in a way different from the traditional Eurocentric Western novel. Faulkner's contemporary Zora Neale Hurston achieved in one stroke in *Their Eyes Were Watching God* (1937) what Faulkner was only moving toward in *Go Down, Moses*: an incorporation of southern folk culture, including African American music, dialect, and point of view as structuring principles of the novel. While it is true that Faulkner frequently portrayed African Americans and made use of their dialect in many of his works, Rider in "Pantaloon in Black" is the only instance of a sustained narrative from a black point of view. Characters such as Ringo in *The Unvanquished* and Nancy in "That Evening Sun" are seen through the eyes of white protagonists. Dilsey in *The Sound and the Fury* (1929) is perhaps Faulkner's most important attempt at incorporating a black perspective prior to *Go Down, Moses*, but her point of view is nevertheless subordinated to that of the omniscient narrator.

In "Pantaloon in Black," Faulkner employs a third-person limited point of view that allows Rider a larger measure of independent perception, as the description is not filtered through the thoughts of another character or narrator. Consider, for example, the scene in which Rider encounters the ghost of his cherished wife: "She was standing in the kitchen door, looking at him. He didn't move. He didn't breathe nor speak until he knew his voice would be all right, his face fixed too not to alarm her. 'Mannie,' he said. 'Hit's awright. Ah aint afraid.' Then he took a step toward her, slow, not even raising his hand yet, and stopped. Then he took another step. But this time as soon as he moved she began to fade. . . . 'Wait,' he said, talking as sweet as he had ever heard his voice speak to a woman: 'Den lemme go wid you, honey'" (136). The blues theme, the ghost story, and the perspective of an insider who is a participant-observer rather than of a white outsider are all elements that this work shares with, for example, Toni Morrison's novel *Beloved* (1987). It is important that Faulkner, as a representative of a literary culture with deep roots in the West, made this attempt at incorporating an oral and folk culture with deep roots in the South and Africa.

Had Faulkner consciously chosen to view his book as a composite or a collection of stories, as Welty had viewed hers, this point might be lost. If we consider that the short story composite is an open structure with closed stories, then it is clear that the two stories "Pantaloon in Black" and "Go Down, Moses" must remain fringe or marginal stories, separate and closed off from the core stories about the McCaslin dynasty. In such a reading their formal importance is that they contribute to the disjuncture of the whole but are not essential to it.[8] If we consider that readers conceive of the chapters of a novel as more open structures checked by the unifying tendency of the whole, then these two chapters contribute to the musical quality of the composition as a whole; they function as counterpoint to the main theme of the disinheritance of Isaac McCaslin but are also inextricably linked to it.

In Welty's *The Golden Apples*, the fringe story "Music from Spain" is about the fate of Eugene MacLain, a white southerner who has both family and community ties with the other characters of the book. That his story remains marginally connected to the others does not have disturbing implications outside the consideration that he has willfully severed himself from Morgana. Rider, however, is the member of a community that has historically been oppressed. If we choose to read *Go Down, Moses* as a composite, we should therefore be careful to qualify our terminology concerning the story's role as marginal or purposefully disjunctive. Such terms may have the unintentional negative implications of separate and unequal, whereas Faulkner, I believe, was attempting to reflect the complexity of a society of inextricably linked fates by employing a form that is especially complex. By contrast, if we choose to read the book as a novel, we should be just as cautious not to perform a type of forced integration by trying to see too much cohesion where there is tension and juxtaposition.

The Confederate Stories of America

I am convinced, after reading the critical literature on the short story composite, that there are good arguments for including both *The Golden Apples* and *Go Down, Moses* as examples of this genre. However, there are also some very good reasons for calling *Go Down, Moses* a novel. I propose to resolve this genre dilemma by considering some of the culturally specific traits of the South and of southern literature that may have influenced the making of such books. I will for the space of this conclusion create a new genre, the Short Story Confederacy, the purpose of which is to illustrate how the time and place in which a work is produced wields a type of formal influence that complicates our notions of genre.

It is tempting to venture the proposition that what is most characteristic of the contemporary short story composite may have originated, in part at least, in the South. In his chapter titled "*E Pluribus Unum:* The Americanness of the Short Composite," Lundén proposes that the composite is a literary form that is more frequently employed in the United States than in other countries. He bases his analysis on what he terms "biformities in American society" such as the constitutional division of powers between the states and the federal government, ethnic diversity, and the coexistence of religious multiplicity with a type of "Civil Religion" (110–11). Such phenomena, scholars have argued, can also be seen as defining traits of the South that have spread to the nation as a whole.[9] The Short Story Confederacy, then, may be seen as a subtype of the composite, but it may also have had a formative influence on its development in America.

Culturally, the Short Story Confederacy is typical of the Bible Belt: it is the literary equivalent of the House divided that nevertheless did stand. John Gerlach's evaluation of the composite (or cycle, as he calls it, following Ingram's terminology) is relevant in this context: "The world vision of the cycle is ancient, a world close to the Biblical one, in which characters, vibrant as they may be in their individuality, are also subsumed within repeated typological patterns. Lives are told in fragments and gaps, a point Erich Auerbach long ago established about The Old Testament in *Mimesis*" (58). The story of the South is also frequently told in such a way as to repeat the thematic, rhetorical, and structural patterns of the Bible.

The Short Story Confederacy consists of stories connected by a pact against a formal foe, whether it be the unifying tyranny of the novel or the arbitrary anarchy of the loose collection. The foundation of the Short Story Confederacy is the adherence to a generic union that does not infringe on the doctrine of stories' rights: the autonomy of the individual stories ensures them the right to leave the Confederacy to join other constellations such as anthologies, and the integrity of the individual stories ensures them equal rights should they wish to stay. The literary Short Story Confederacy avoids repeating the historical phenomenon of slavery by dealing with diversity in constructive ways: stories that look or act completely different may nevertheless coexist side by side.

The Short Story Confederacy may contain a lone star story. Previously termed "fringe" story, the lone star, such as "Pantaloon in Black" or "Music from Spain," is so different from the others in the Confederacy that it claims special status and may stick out as neither completely integrated into the Confederacy nor completely independent. A lone star story is consequently likely to be the first story to secede from a Short Story Confederacy, but it may also defiantly choose to stay and contribute to the heterogeneous complexity of the genre. Rather than having kernel stories and core stories as in the composite, the Confederacy has colonel stories and deep stories. Rather than having satellites as in the composite, the Confederacy has border stories that may not resemble the deep stories because they are more hybrid in form.

To sum up, the Short Story Confederacy is a rebellious genre in between the anarchy of the collection and the despotism of the novel. This genre did not originate solely in the South and is certainly not limited to the South, but it is typical thereof. Like porch talk, a good barbecue, country music, the blues and spirituals, the Short Story Confederacy can be seen as one way of kicking back against the Americanization of Dixie, but also as an instance of the southernizing of American culture.

The coining of a new genre label may not solve the many critical problems pertaining to the discussion of *The Golden Apples* and *Go Down, Moses*, but if it adds anything fruitful to the development of our understanding of a complex genre, it may be the consideration that these two books will continue to attract our attention, wake our curiosity, and whet our appetite for categorizing and defining what we gaze at with wonder and bewilderment. Just like the South does.

Notes

1. See Lundén's chapter 6: "The Fringe Story—Or, How to Integrate the Resisting Text."

2. I will here treat authorial intention only from the very limited perspective of the genre question. Since the appearance of Beardsley and Wimsatt's seminal "The Intentional Fallacy" in *Sewanee Review* in 1946, intentionalist and anti-intentionalist theories of the role of the author have continued to evolve. For recent accounts of the current debate, see M. Bortolussi and P. Dixon's anti-intentionalist "Text Is Not Communication: A Challenge to a Common Assumption" (*Discourse Processes* 31, no. 1 [2001]: 1–25) and Raymond W. Gibbs's intentionalist "Authorial Intentions in Text Understanding" (*Discourse Processes* 32, no. 1 [2001]: 73–80). The former considers works of fiction as artifacts independent of the author, and the latter stresses the importance of reader expectations: "Authorial intentions are an essential part of our cognitive systems and function automatically in people's immediate interpretation of texts" (79).

3. Joseph Blotner documents this fact in his *Faulkner: A Biography* (New York: Random House, 1974), 437.

4. For an account of the critical reception of "Pantaloon in Black," see Sandra Lee Kleppe, "Reconstructing Faulkner's 'Pantaloon in Black'" in *William Faulkner's Short Fiction*, edited by Hans H. Skei, 212–21 (Oslo: Solum, 1997).

5. I am referring here to Roy T. Eriksen's discussion of this term in "The Building in the Text": "In an age when it has become fashionable to kill off the author and to dismiss the notion of authorial intent, I nevertheless discern . . . what may be termed the author's 'formal intention'" (2).

6. Sandra Lee Kleppe, "Rereading Faulkner: A Dialogic Interpretation of *Go Down, Moses*" (master's thesis, University of Bergen, 1993).

7. For an analysis of this song as source for the story, see H. R. Stoneback's "Faulkner's Blues: 'Pantaloon in Black,'" *Modern Fiction Studies* 21, no. 2 (1975): 241–45.

8. See Lundén's discussion of the relationship between kernel, satellite, and fringe stories in his chapter 6. Satellites and fringe stories "can be logically deleted . . . without great damage to the plot of the composite as a whole" (126).

9. The thesis that what is most characteristic about the United States as a whole originated in the South is argued cogently in both John Egerton's *The Americanization of Dixie: The Southernization of America* (New York: Harper's Magazine Press, 1974) and Peter Applebome's *Dixie Rising: How the South Is Shaping American Values, Politics, and Culture* (New York: Times Books, 1996).

Works Cited

Creighton, Joanne. *William Faulkner's Craft of Revision: The Snopes Trilogy, "The Unvanquished," and "Go Down, Moses."* Detroit: Wayne State University Press, 1977.

Eriksen, Roy Tommy. "The Building in the Text." Unpublished manuscript.

Faulkner, William. *Go Down, Moses, and Other Stories.* New York: Random House, 1942.

Gerlach, John. "Faulkner's *Unvanquished* and Welty's *Golden Apples*: The Boundaries of Story, Cycle, and Novel." *Short Story* 2, no. 2 (Winter–Spring 1992): 51–62.

Gretlund, Jan. *Eudora Welty's Aesthetics of Place.* Odense: Odense University Press, 1993.

Ingram, Forrest. *Representative Short Story Cycles of the Twentieth Century.* The Hague: Mouton, 1971.

Lundén, Rolf. *The United Stories of America: Studies in the Short Story Composite.* Amsterdam: Rodopi, 1999.

Mann, Susan Garland. *The Short Story Cycle: A Genre Companion and Reference Guide.* New York: Greenwood Press, 1989.

McHaney, Thomas. "Falling into Cycles." In *Eudora Welty: The Eye of the Storyteller*, edited by Dawn Trouard, 173–89. Kent, Ohio: Kent State University Press, 1989.

O'Connor, Flannery. *Mystery and Manners: Occasional Prose.* Selected and edited by Sally and Robert Fitzgerald. New York: Farrar, Strauss and Giroux, 1993.

Thornton, Weldon. "Structure and Theme in Faulkner's *Go Down, Moses.*" *Costerus* 3 (1975): 73–112.

Welty, Eudora. *The Golden Apples.* New York: Harcourt Brace Jovanovich, 1949.

The Queer Short Story

Axel Nissen

There is something queer about the short story. As I have been rereading many of the classic statements on the form written during the last hundred years, it strikes me how many of them have the character of a defense or an apologia and how concerned their authors are with defining the short story, with categorizing it, with dissecting it, and with comparing it to the dominant form of fictional narrative.

The novel and the short story have been locked in a lethal, loveless embrace for more than a hundred years now. As we know, binary oppositions such as woman/man, black/white, homosexual/heterosexual, and for that matter, short story/novel are not innocent. The two halves are not on equal terms, so to speak; they do not carry the same authority, nor do they have the same claim on normalcy or cultural centrality. Thus it has been with the traditional categories of gender, race, and sexuality, and thus it has been with the longstanding generic pairing of the novel and the short story. While the short story is often seen to be minor, fragmented, underdeveloped, superficial, immature, and simple, the novel is considered major, whole, fully developed, exhaustive, mature, and complex. The short story is the "other" of fictional prose narrative. As the other it must continually justify its existence, worry about the circumstances of its being and becoming, agonize about its value and identity. Not unlike homosexuality, the short story was born into the world as a generic problem, a problem that required a solution or at least a definition. It is a curious coincidence, then, that the modern homosexual and the modern short story were invented at the same time, toward the end of what is no longer the last century.

This essay is divided into two parts. In the first part, I will raise general, theoretical questions that have to do with the relationship between the short story genre and the narrative representation of gender and sexuality. In the second part, I will give one specific answer to this set of questions that relates to how one nineteenth-century American author used the genre of the short story to represent love between men in the setting of the California Gold Rush.

Maybe short story theory has something to learn from what is known as "queer theory." That something has to do, I think, with the dangers of definition, even self-definition, and with the ways in which disciplines discipline and limit us as much as they free us and allow us to create new and startling insights. It has to do with a whole new approach to the literary text and what we are accustomed to calling its context.

Queer theory is largely concerned with questions of sexual ideology, history, and identity, and with how sexuality interacts with gender, ethnicity, and class. It is especially interested in the role played by deviant sexualities and identities in contemporary, Western life, but also in other periods, climes, and cultures. The advantage of the word "queer" both for gender theory and in the context of discussing the otherness of the short story is that the word "queer" has functioned and continues to function as a more than usually slippery signifier, whose meaning cannot be given a priori nor be determined for all time. Queer allows us to discuss deviance, sexual indeterminacy, and nonreproductive, nonheterosexual sexuality and eroticism without having to use potentially anachronistic labels about phenomena that may be unnamed or indeterminate in the period or the text in question. Queer is maybe more an absence than a presence—an absence of or deviation from whatever is the normative sexual or gender behavior or identity in a given period or culture.

As with sexuality and sexual identity, we may wonder if maybe the short story cannot be defined transhistorically or outside a specific cultural context. Maybe it does not need to be so defined. Maybe its role during the last one hundred years has primarily been to act as the novel's other, as the homosexual has been the heterosexual's other. Maybe the proper response to this unequal and at least partially oppressive relationship would be not to continue to produce ever more sophisticated definitions and taxonomies of the short story, but rather to emphasize differences between the various forms of short fictional narrative in prose in their various national and historical contexts or the many structural and stylistic commonalities between shorter and longer prose narrative forms. Rather than generic essentialism, then, I propose a manner of social constructionism in relation to the nature, form, function, and identity of the short story at any given point in time and in any given culture.

An antiessensialist approach to the short story has, of course, long ago been suggested by Norman Friedman and Mary Louise Pratt. Yet in addition to an analysis of the dangers of essentialism, queer theory can provide us with new questions and new reading strategies. I am thinking now particularly of the way in which queer theorists such as Judith Roof have shown how narrative and traditional narrative patterns are implicated in heterosexual ideology or what she calls "heteroideology" (xxii). In her book from 1996, *Come as You Are: Sexuality and Narrative*, Roof suggests that "narrative and sexuality inform each other" (xiv) and in turn "our very understanding of narrative as a primary means to sense and satisfaction depends upon a metaphorically heterosexual dynamic within a reproductive aegis" (xxii). In other words, sexuality is inseparable from narrative, and the narrative of sexuality also imbues fictional narrative, including stories that appear not to be about sexuality at all.

Roof takes Freud's narrative of sexual development as a primary model of heteroideological narrative and writes suggestively about the role of what she calls "perversions" in such a narrative: "Supplanting the proper conclusion, perversions cut the story short, in a sense preventing a story at all in its preparations. But this premature abridgement only has significance in relation to the 'normal'; we only know the story is cut short because we know what length the story is supposed to be. Perversion, then, acquires its meaning as perversion precisely from its threat to truncate the story; it distorts the narrative, preventing the desirable confluence of sexual aim and object and male and female, precluding the discharge of sexual substances, and hindering reproduction. And yet the aberrations are the foreplay necessary to ever getting to the end at all. . . . An integral threat, the perversions are absolutely indispensable to the story; their possibility and presence complicate the narrative of sexuality" (xxi). Thus perversions are whatever complicate the story line on the way to its reproductive end. Roof locates an opening for perverse or queer sexuality in the middle of the story. "The narrative middle . . ." she writes, "provides the scene for doubt, risk, and uncertainty. The middle . . . is the locus of homosexual suggestions, the place where such a possibility is made visible on the way to a reproductive end" (xxxiv).

In her book Roof discusses both modern short stories and novels, but she does not ask whether the short story and the novel might be differently implicated in the perpetuation of heteroideology. This brings me to my set of interrelated theoretical questions:

- What difference might it make to the link between narrative and heteroideology that the short story is short or that, in some cases at least, it might be said to be all middle?
- Several critics, including Brander Matthews (53), Mary Louise Pratt (187), and Clare Hanson (2–6), have discussed the short story's independence from the traditional "love plot" and the way in which the genre allows for different subject matters and voices to express themselves. Is this a matter of degree or of kind? Is the short story innately better suited to treating certain subject matters, or do we need to limit our generalizations to specific times and places?
- Has the short story by virtue of its brevity allowed for different kinds of stories to be told, and what has been the role of homosexuality, deviance, or what Roof calls perversion in those narrative patterns?
- In sum, what is queer about the short story?

I will offer no answer to most of these questions here, because I do not think there is a single non-context-specific answer to any of them. To avoid the dangers of essentialism, then, I want to concentrate on one example taken from my current research project, a project in which I had not initially considered the significance of genre to the understanding of my chosen textual examples. This essay gives me an occasion to do so.

But before I do that, let us remind ourselves how many short stories we have read, written about, and taught that indeed diverge from the traditional love plot but are still vitally implicated in the gender and sexual politics of their time and place. How many of these stories do not, in fact, seem to be a perverse reminder of other possibilities, other dreams, and other desires than those promulgated by the adult, mature, responsible novel? Limiting myself to stories I have taught in recent years, I have to ask: What's the deal with Reverend Hooper and that black veil? Why does the lawyer-narrator feel he has to tell Bartleby's story? Why does Sister live at the P.O., and why is Uncle Rondo running around in a flesh-colored kimono? Why does Kate Chopin describe the lovemaking scene in "The Storm" from what appears to be the man's point of view? Why doesn't Homer Barron want to settle down with Miss Emily? Why does the ideal woman in Thomas Bailey Aldrich's story "Marjorie Daw" turn out to be the figment of one man's imagination in his letters to another? I won't even get started on Henry James. To the extent that queer theory has had an impact on short story criticism, it would appear to be largely in the subfield of James studies.[1]

The object of my book-in-progress is to write a cultural poetics of gender and sexuality in Victorian America with major emphasis on affective relations between men. My interest is in how white, middle-class American men in the years between 1850 and 1900 understood and represented their own gender, what they would have called their "manliness" or "manhood." More specifically, I am interested in those various authors such as Bayard Taylor, Bret Harte, Charles Warren Stoddard, and Henry James, whom we might want to identify as "queer," a queerness consisting in their, for various and often unclear reasons, registering an unease and a dissatisfaction with the circumstances of life in the United States and a yearning for something more or different.

As these men clearly were, I am interested in exploring the limits on and possibilities for same-sex emotional and sexual relations in nineteenth-century America. One of my claims will be that the group of writers in question used various forms of narrative to resist dominant injunctions on gender behavior and limitations on same-sex interaction and to explore ways of living with and loving members of the same sex. I call the literature they created "male-identified" and I will suggest that it was not only women writers who had, in Jane Tompkins's words, "sensational designs." In line with new historicist insights into the interactions between texts in a culture, I will choose to see these literary texts as engaging, often subtly but no less subversively, in a dialogue with other types of texts relating to gender roles and gender performance.

I have chosen to call the dominant, white, middle-class sexual and gender ideology in the mid-to-late-nineteenth-century United States "the domestic mind." Like the "straight mind," as conceptualized by Monique Wittig, the domestic mind is a specific set of attitudes, a normalization of certain ideas about right and wrong in the world, and the active exclusion of or simple ignorance about alternative possibilities. The domestic mind is clearly a precursor of the straight mind, as much as the code of normative gender relations it enforces, what I will call "compulsory domesticity," is a precursor of compulsory heterosexuality (Rich). I use these terms to highlight the fact that we are dealing with an entirely different sex/gender system than our own and one that is not based on the heterosexual/homosexual binary. I will not now discuss the characteristics of this sexual ideology in detail, but let me point out that it placed a central emphasis on the necessity of marriage and procreation to the attainment of full manhood and womanhood. The rigidity of the "doctrine of separate spheres" paradoxically allowed for greater emotional (and at times sexual) freedom both inside and outside marriage than is often the case today, including passionate romantic friendships between members of the same sex.

While romantic friendship has come to be identified almost exclusively with women through the pioneering work of Carroll Smith-Rosenberg, Lillian Faderman, and Martha Vicinus, research is beginning to show that romantic friendships were also prevalent among men. In my study I hope to demonstrate that same-sex, male romantic friendships, as represented both in fiction and other textual sources from the period, reveal some important parallels not only with female romantic friendship but also with cross-sex courtship practices, the companionate marriage ideal, and the cult of true love. These similarities can explain why romantic friendships were accepted and even admired during much of the nineteenth century. Both romantic friendship and the cult of true love placed an emphasis on:

- The uniqueness and exclusivity of the relationship
- The sense of intimacy and the need to know each other deeply and reveal oneself as to no one else
- The idealization of the partner
- The promise of faithfulness until death
- The sense of intellectual and spiritual companionship
- The aesthetic admiration of the lover's beauty of form and feature, possible because, both in same-sex and cross-sex love relationships, the erotic was de-emphasized

Yet despite the extent to which the dominant sexual ideology could accommodate romantic friendship and even borrow some of its defining terms in formulating its ideal of marriage, there is evidence that what we would call the heterosexism of domestic ideology—its overwhelming emphasis on cross-sex courtship and marriage—was more offensive to some men than to others. Quite a few nineteenth-century American men dreamed of a world in which relations between males would not be governed and structured by competitiveness and self-interest. In some cases, they also dreamed of spending their lives with a man rather than a woman.

The resistance to or revisions of domestic ideology are numerous in the years between 1850 and 1900, and it is these texts and their authors I am particularly interested in. Unlike the canonical texts of the domestic mind, which are male- and female-authored conduct books, medical manuals and reform treatises, an opposing or alternative discourse primarily comes to light in short stories, sketches, and some novels. If not usually presenting alternatives to domesticity, these works often try to create *alternative domesticities.* I am thinking here of Charles Warren Stoddard's domestic idylls set in the South Seas and Horatio Alger's stories focusing on working-class boy couples in New York City. I am thinking of Bret Harte's all-male, gold-mining communities, such as the Roaring Camp of his most famous short story, or his faithful-until-death partnerships, such as that of Tennessee and his partner. I am thinking of Bayard Taylor's autobiographical narrative of two men on a boat on the Nile, and last but not least, numerous examples of what I would call "romantic friendship fiction," starting with novels such as Theodore Winthrop's *John Brent* and *Cecil Dreeme,* and including the "high realism" of William Dean Howells and Henry James. The aim of this literature was to imagine and describe what making another man the object of one's affections might be like and what a man's life with a man might be like.

When Mary Louise Pratt discussed the way the short story was often the genre used to introduce new and stigmatized subject matters into the literary arena, Bret Harte was one of the authorities she cited (187). Nearly sixty years before Pratt published her justly famous essay, Edward O'Brien wrote truer than he knew when he called Harte "the wicked fairy at the christening of the short story" (107). This is not the time to enter into the intriguing details of Harte's own sexual makeup, a subject that I fear will remain a mystery to us despite my best efforts (see Nissen). Suffice it to say that at the time of writing the story I will focus on in the remainder of this essay, Harte had kept the Atlantic Ocean between himself and his wife for nearly twenty years, and during those years he had not seen her nor three out of their four children.

I had originally intended to discuss some of Harte's stories that focus on male romantic friendship, but since so many of them are not being read today, I could easily have gotten overinvolved in retelling the plots. I have thus chosen to focus on Harte's final depiction of the love "passing the love of women," a short story he wrote in 1897 and published in December of that year both in the notorious *New York Sun* and in the illustrious *Illustrated London News.* The story is called "Uncle Jim and Uncle Billy" and stands out among the many stories Harte wrote about love relationships between men by virtue of having a happy ending. In the first of Harte's stories about "men without women," the autobiographical "Notes by Flood and Field" (1862), the hero, George Tryan, is drowned, while the witness-narrator lives on to tell the story. In Harte's most famous short story of this kind, "Tennessee's Partner" (1869), Tennessee is hanged for highway robbery despite his partner's efforts to save him, and his partner later dies of grief. In "An Apostle of the Tules" (1885), the young preacher Gideon Deane resists the blandishments of the gambler Jack Hamlin and marries the unattractive Widow Hiler to give her a husband and a provider for her three children. In "Captain Jim's Friend" (1888), Captain Jim expends his dying breath trying to exonerate his worthless friend, Lacy Bassett, who has in fact shot him. In the year of Oscar Wilde's three trials and final imprisonment, 1895, Harte wrote and published "In the Tules," in which the gambler and killer Jack Despard and the rugged settler Martin Morse take turns saving each other's life and finally are buried in the same grave.

The plot of "Uncle Jim and Uncle Billy" is both convoluted and elliptical. In the prologue we are introduced to "Uncle Jim" (James Foster) and "Uncle Billy" (William Fall), who since 1849 have been partners both in domestic life and in the unpromising "Fall and Foster" gold mine and who are the veteran residents of Cedar Camp. Their quiet, unambitious, harmonious existence is interrupted by the hotheaded young miner Dick Bullen, who breaks in on their customary game of euchre one rainy evening and delivers a diatribe on the need for the partners to get on in life and take on adult responsibilities. As a result, Uncle Jim leaves the camp to seek his fortune in San Francisco, and Uncle Billy is left behind to fend for himself and to be cheered by the remaining camp residents, who make biweekly visits to his cabin "carrying their own whiskey and winding up with a 'stag dance' before the premises" (65). When Billy strikes it rich to the sum of $20,000, he decides to seek out his partner in San Francisco, and after a series of complications that defy summary, he is finally joyously reunited with him. It turns out Uncle Jim has been making his living as a crossing sweeper and has saved up $956, which money he wants to use to buy a little ranch with Uncle Billy. Fearing that Uncle Jim might withdraw from him if he knew how much he was worth, Uncle Billy sets aside the small amount he needs to join his partner in buying the ranch and gambles away the rest. The two partners live happily ever after on the prosperous "Fall and Foster" ranch in Napa.

A story about the trying and testing of love, "Uncle Jim and Uncle Billy" does not so much represent an alternative to the wedlock or domestic plot of the novel as an inversion of it. It is also an ironic commentary on what Joseph Allen Boone has called the "American quest romance" in that it contains "the ever-present male bond; maintained by its radical mutuality—of spirit, of gender, of democratic fraternity" (237), but the quest itself does not revolve around the men's quest for gold, but rather evolves into a quest for each other. The making of fortunes, in fact, becomes an obstacle to the men's relationship rather than the relationship becoming an obstacle to the fortune hunting.

What fascinates me about Harte's fiction is the vivid antiessentialism of his imagination in a cultural environment rife with biological theories about race, gender, and what we call sexuality. Writing in a period—the 1890s—and in a nation—England—that was pathologizing and criminalizing man-loving men to an unprecedented degree, Harte chose to make his protagonists the law-abiding, sober, modest, and avuncular citizens of Cedar Camp that their nicknames suggest. While Tennessee had been a highway robber and Jack Despard of "In the Tules" a gambler and "cop killer," Uncle Jim and Uncle Billy have subsisted peaceably for years on grub wages, and their homely cabin has become the social center of the community.

As he did most famously in "The Luck of Roaring Camp," Harte shows that men can create a home without women and without all the appurtenances of bourgeois domestic establishments. Thus, he is not transcending domestic ideology but transforming it and creating an alternative, same-sex domesticity that problematizes and subverts the essentialism of Victorian domesticity's gender roles and ideals. I am not suggesting that Harte was the only voice, the lonely voice in the period that shouted "No, in thunder!" to the cult of domesticity. Due to the increasingly commercial character of his fiction, as witnessed by its continued wide popularity, he was intimately implicated and invested in domesticity. As result he has something to tell us today about mainstream nineteenth-century attitudes concerning gender and sexuality, including that forgotten bond, romantic friendship.

In a story such as "Uncle Jim and Uncle Billy," which appears to have shocked or offended no one, we see how Harte incorporates and develops contemporary ideas about bachelors and bachelorhood to deflect some of the potentially disturbing elements of his story. These ideas have to do with the *feminization* of men involved in long-term, adult, same-sex liaisons and the *infantalization* of men who failed to marry and have children.

In a widely popular lecture titled "The Argonauts of '49" given in the early 1870s, Harte had this to say about partnerships in the pioneer days of California: "In these unions there were the same odd combination often seen in the marital relations: a tall and a short man, a delicate sickly youth and a middle aged man of powerful frame, a grave reticent nature and a spontaneous exuberant one. Yet in spite of these incongruities there was always the same blind unreasoning fidelity to each other."[2] Twenty-five years later he described Uncle Jim and Uncle Billy thus: "They even got to resemble each other, after the fashion of old married couples, or, rather, as in matrimonial partnerships, were subject to the domination of the stronger character; although in their case it is to be feared that it was the feminine Uncle Billy—enthusiastic, imaginative, and loquacious—who swayed the masculine, steady-going, and practical Uncle Jim."[3] By describing the couple in marital terms, the relationship is rendered less dangerous, as it remains in a sense a conventional attraction between opposing feminine and masculine principles. At the same time, Harte shows that a marriage and marital devotion and fidelity are not necessarily limited to cross-sex couples.

Harte also introduces the viewpoint of the domestic mind in the unlikely form of the handsome, long-haired, broad-shouldered miner Dick Bullen (46, 49), who delivers a lengthy invective on the older men's style of life: "Here you are,—two men who ought to be out in the world, playing your part as grown men,—stuck here like children 'playing house' in the woods; playing work in your wretched mud-pie ditches, and content. Two men not so old that you mightn't be taking your part in the fun of the world, going to balls or theatres, or paying attention to girls, and yet old enough to have married and have families around you, content to stay in this God-forsaken place; old bachelors, pigging together like poorhouse paupers" (47). According to the domestic mind, warm, confiding moments of friendship, such as we witness in "Uncle Jim and Uncle Billy," were worthy of a child but not of a man.[4] In the words of John W. Crowley, "romantic friendship had to be outgrown by the adult male in order to reach a position of power in the patriarchal power structure" (317). Yet men who persisted in maintaining strong bonds within their own sex, rather than marrying and fathering children, were viewed throughout much of the nineteenth century with tolerant indulgence, rather than the virulent hatred that marked the final decades of the century.[5]

Among the five closural signals discussed by John Gerlach, the one most frequently used by Harte is natural termination. As I have already noted, the natural termination of most of Harte's stories about love between men is death, but if not death, then the replacement of the primary male same-sex bond with one or two cross-sex relationships. The question is, What is a natural termination for a story about two men in love in an adamantly heterosexist society? That the end is not necessarily death or marriage is suggested by "Uncle Jim and Uncle Billy." At its close, Harte's story reaches a point of rest that is both the same as yet different from the opening. Here the perverse possibilities of the middle have become a beginning and an end. That the relationship between James Foster and William Fall is finally rendered nonnarratable—something about which nothing more need be said—rather than unspeakable—something about which nothing *should* be said—is to the credit of Harte's imagination. It is also the result of a romantic tradition of love between men that we are only beginning to recover.

Notes

1. See, for example, Sedgwick, *Epistemology of the Closet*, 182–212.
2. Quoted in Nissen, *Bret Harte*, 236.
3. "Uncle Jim and Uncle Billy," 35–36.
4. Rotundo, *American Manhood*, 87.
5. See Crowley, "Howells, Stoddard, and Male Homosocial Attachment," 313–14.

Works Cited

Boone, Joseph Allen. *Tradition Counter Tradition: Love and the Form of Fiction.* Chicago and London: University of Chicago Press, 1987.

Crowley, John W. "Howells, Stoddard, and Male Homosocial Attachment in Victorian America." In *The Making of Masculinities: The New Men's Studies,* edited by Harry Brod, 301–24. Boston: Allen Unwin, 1987.

Faderman, Lillian. "Female Same-Sex Relationships in Novels by Longfellow, Holmes, and James." *New England Quarterly* 51, no. 2 (1978): 309–32.

———. *Surpassing the Love of Men: Romantic Friendship and Love between Women from the Renaissance to the Present.* London: Women's Press, 1985.

Friedman, Norman. "What Makes a Short Story Short?" In *Short Story Theories,* edited by Charles E. May, 131–46. Athens: Ohio University Press, 1976.

———. "Recent Short Story Theories: Problems in Definition." In *Short Story Theory at a Crossroads,* edited by Susan Lohafer and Jo Ellyn Clarey, 13–31. Baton Rouge: Louisiana State University Press, 1989.

Gerlach, John. *Toward the End: Closure and Structure in the American Short Story.* Tuscaloosa: University of Alabama Press, 1985.

Hanson, Clare. Introduction to *Re-reading the Short Story,* edited by Clare Hanson, 1–9. New York: St. Martin's Press, 1989.

Harte, Bret. "Uncle Jim and Uncle Billy." In *The Works of Bret Harte,* vol. 13, pp. 35–92. Argonaut edition. New York: P. F. Collier, 1906.

Matthews, Brander. "The Philosophy of the Short-Story." In *Short Story Theories,* edited by Charles E. May, 52–59. Athens: Ohio University Press, 1976.

Nissen, Axel. *Bret Harte: Prince and Pauper.* Jackson: University Press of Mississippi, 2000.

O'Brien, Edward J. *The Advance of the American Short Story.* New York: Dodd, Mead, 1923.

Pratt, Mary Louise. "The Short Story: The Long and Short of It." *Poetics* 10, no. 2–3 (1981): 175–94.

Rich, Adrienne. "Compulsory Heterosexuality and Lesbian Experience." *Signs* 5, no. 4 (1980): 631–60.

Roof, Judith. *Come as You Are: Sexuality and Narrative.* New York: Columbia University Press, 1996.

Rotundo, E. Anthony. *American Manhood: Transformations in Masculinity from the Revolution to the Modern Era.* New York: Basic Books, 1993.

Sedgwick, Eve Kosofsky. *Epistemology of the Closet.* Berkeley: University of California Press, 1990.

Smith-Rosenberg, Carroll. "The Female World of Love and Ritual: Relations between Women in Nineteenth-Century America." *Signs* 1, no. 1 (1975): 1–29.

Tompkins, Jane. *Sensational Designs: The Cultural Work of American Fiction, 1790–1860.* New York and Oxford: Oxford University Press, 1985.

Vicinus, Martha. "Distance and Desire: English Boarding School Friendships, 1870–1920." In *Hidden from History: Exploring the Gay and Lesbian Past,* edited by Martin Duberman, Martha Vicinus, and George Chauncey, 212–29. Harmondsworth, U.K.: Penguin, 1989.

Wittig, Monique. "The Straight Mind." 1980. In *The Straight Mind and Other Essays,* 21–32. Boston: Beacon Press, 1992.

Melville's Stories as Novel Alternative

Hans B. Löfgren

The prominence of the short story and the novella among narratives of the Romantic period suggests something about the structure as well as the historicity of the short narrative form. When applied to narrative, the Romantic ideal of creative process as a dialectical unfolding of consciousness defines a new dilemma: the narrator strives to represent a process that is universal and comprehensive, yet the narrative standpoint is itself outside that process. Evidently, the short story form, in introducing more self-reflexive narrative techniques, proved more adaptable to this contradictory claim on narration than the novel. Similarly, the short story appears to have offered certain possibilities for managing the new social position of the writer. The position of the Romantic writer is characteristically experienced as alienation, whether defined as narrative dilemma, as the divided self, or in social terms, as the exposure to a commercialized reading public whose demands contradict the ideals of an artistic vocation. New forms of irony that are not just limited to representation, but that pervade narrative technique as such, are apparently more readily adopted by short fiction, which can thus effectively mediate a new and ambivalent relation to the public.

This dilemma of narration in the Romantic period and its resolutions in short stories that anticipate a new type of realism emerge conspicuously in the literary production of Herman Melville. The novels of Melville's major phase in the 1850s remain caught in the narrative contradictions of the Romantic consciousness, but his short stories from the same period invent a particular narrative doubleness that goes a long way toward resolving formal contradictions and enables a more effective treatment of thematic content. While *Moby-Dick* and *Pierre* are marked by the contradiction of a self-objectifying narrative consciousness, stories like "Bartleby, the Scrivener" and "Benito Cereno," in using ironic modes of narrative discourse, achieve a formally consistent treatment of topics whose delimitation is characteristic of short rather than long narrative. In the short narrative form, the double nature of Romantic consciousness becomes the effective vehicle, rather than the obstruction, to narration. In addition, this development of the short story seems to have had implications for the further development of the novel. When Melville returns to the novel in *The Confidence-Man*, he produces a formally more achieved and consistent work than his earlier novels, while in its episodical nature this work also, significantly enough, bears a strong resemblance to short fiction.

Melville's stories are a novel alternative in a double sense: they provide an alternative form to those novels in which Melville had wrestled with certain technical problems, and they lead him toward an alternative form of the novel that takes the short story form as its basis. As Thomas Leitch has argued in his article on the debunking form of the American short story, it is the story rather than the novel that now becomes the "unmarked mode," so that many American novels after the emergence of the story assume the form of "story-novels" (146). This observation gives some support to my view of Melville's story as a kind of laboratory in which a new technique was developed that could subsequently be adapted to the novel. There is a new period in the history of narrative technique, as it were, a transformation of narrative that is subsequently recuperated on behalf of the novel.

To put it as concisely as possible, this transformation has its origin in the shift from a world-representing novel to a type of narrative that must foreground its own operations. There is a shift from a narrative practice that does not normally problematize representation to a practice that can only effect representation indirectly, in terms of self-reflexive technique. What I am asserting here has affinities with Georg Lukács's theory of critical realism. For Lukács, the privileged form of realism was not one that reflected the surface of reality but one that could penetrate surfaces in order to lay bare the inner dynamics of social structure. Melville's short stories, however, achieve their critique of realistic surface indirectly. External reality is approached through a critique of naive consciousness as embodied in narrative point of view or focus, rather than through the representation of social relations as such.

While the traditional novel could occupy a spatiotemporal dimension of indefinite scope, the new story is increasingly affected by the spatiotemporal constraints of narration. The eighteenth-century form of the novel becomes defunct for nineteenth-century writers because the centered epistemology of traditional realism is no longer available as narrative standpoint. This constitutes a situation in which primarily poetry becomes the vehicle for an art of prophesy and revelation, while, for writers like Herman Melville, the same situation compels prose fiction to tell its truth by indirection and the disillusionment of expectations. Though European fiction influenced Melville's stories (Dickens's influence on "Bartleby" has in particular been cited), aspects of a characteristic American romance persist, even if for Melville realism consists in the ironic distancing of this romance.

Let us first review certain aspects of narrative technique in the two novels that preceded the short stories. In *Moby-Dick*, Melville's heroic attempt at truth telling is obstructed by the insufficient separation of narrative standpoint and subject matter. The narrator ends by developing not only his theme but also his own narrative standpoint and consciousness, so that the stable position from which the novel's meaning might be determined is undermined. The urge to tell the unspeakable truth leads in part to a technically flawed work and thus to an inadvertent blurring of the meaning promised by the literary conventions employed, particularly the tragic. This concerns not only the much-noted shift from first-person to third-person point of view but also the projective relation between the first person and its chief focalizer, Ahab. Ishmael's claim that the Narcissus image is the "key to it all" is brilliantly exemplified by the text but also confirmed symptomatically.

Similarly, narration is blurred in Melville's next novel, *Pierre*. The generic frame of reference gradually shifts from sentimental romance to satire as Pierre moves from a heroic—though youthfully and romantically tragic—to a satirized position. One may perceive in Pierre the caricature of Melville himself, with an ambivalent mixture of positive and negative traits. Significantly, Pierre fails as the writer who adamantly seeks both to tell the truth and to profit financially from the sale of his books.

Yet with his stories, composed in the next stage of his career, Melville has some financial success, even as he maintains his commitment to truth telling. The short stories were published in magazines, most of them in *Putnam's*, which, as Sheila Post-Lauria has shown, appealed to a relatively small readership that was "intellectual and politically liberal": "The common stance of *Putnam's* writers against sentimental rhetoric goes far in accounting for the strategies that Melville employed in 'Bartleby, the Scrivener,' one of his most stylistically challenging stories. In this tale, the author employs a sentimental style as a methodological weapon against itself and, in doing so, reinforces *Putnam's* editorial stance" (197). *Putnam's* readership must have represented views that were relatively congenial to Melville, and his choice of this magazine over *Harper's*, as Post-Lauria argues, is an indication of special narrative strategies in "Bartleby." Nevertheless, as he turns to magazine publication, Melville's ambition to make money is more clearly in evidence. The ideal that he attributed to Hawthorne, but that is even more apt as applied to himself, to say "No! in thunder," is applied in a more circumspect manner.

Telling the truth indirectly is now not only a matter of covert symbolism but also of writing in such a way as to challenge and expand the reader's ability to reflect on and revise the entire process of encoding and decoding. There is a shift from the reliance on plot and symbol to narration itself. Instead of the representation of a process of revelation or disillusionment at the story level, this process is shifted to the level of narrative discourse. Moreover, not only is the truth question raised within narrative point of view or focalization, but the unreliability of these creates ironies that purposefully shift the question onto the reader. In this way, Melville accomplishes his objective to tell the truth covertly, and in "snatches"; in fact, he implicitly redefines the conception of truth itself as something that must in part be constructed by the reader.

Several critics have discussed Melville's stories in the context of short story theory. For my purposes, two examples in particular provide useful points of departure. In an important early literary history of the short story, Robert Marler argues for the centrality of nineteenth-century American literature and the transformation of the romance and supernatural tale into the realist short story. In Marler's view, "the decay of the immensely popular tale fostered the development of the short story as a new genre" (165). "Overall, the composite fictional worlds of the three leading authors demonstrate a broad shift from Poe's overt romance and verisimilitude to Hawthorne's neutral ground of actual and imaginary and thence to Melville's mimetic portrayals and reliance on facts for the profound probing of everyday reality" (176–77). Marler states that Melville's stories, with the exception of "Benito," depend for their "illusion of actuality" on the "credibility of . . . first-person narrators" (176).

While Marler sheds light on the emergence of the modern short story against the background of the tale, I would claim that Melville's realism is tempered by the extraordinary success of stories that use unreliable narration and that therefore depart from simple mimesis. Thus I also find valuable the quite different reading of Melville, and different theory of the short story, that Charles May offers in this connection. Like Marler, May uses Melville's stories, and "Bartleby" in particular, in an argument about the short story genre: "In 'Bartleby, the Scrivener,' instead of a realistic character entering the realm of primary process, as is the case in Poe's tale ['The Fall of the House of Usher'], the movement is reversed, and an obsessed aesthetic figure invades the realm of secondary process reality, realistically represented as the practical and prudent world of the law office on Wall Street. We can no more ask what is the matter with Bartleby than we can of Usher" (70). May argues that the figures cannot be explained in secondary process terms by the narrators; they must be understood by the discourse as "rhetorical structure and metaphor" (71).

Thus, while Marler associates the emergence of the short story with realism, May rather emphasizes the persistence in the short story of a primordial tale that he analyzes in Freudian primary process terms. Moreover, he emphasizes the foregrounding of rhetorical structure and the fruitlessness of seeking interpretations at the level of story, or *fabula*. I believe that May is right that the ultimate issue in "Bartleby" does not concern its external realism. At the same time, however, the shift from the narrated to narration, from the red herring question about Bartleby's identity to the salient question of the lawyer's narrative construction of Bartleby, opens up a new kind of realism that is quite historically specific, even as it is based in the analysis of consciousness. What is the matter with Bartleby is rather his narrator and biographer—more precisely, his profession. We *can* say that what is the matter with the *lawyer* is that the practice of his profession as a smug, prudent, and profitable enterprise leads him to make use of employees in a dehumanizing manner. The Wall Street of the story is in this sense not primarily its actual literal physical appearance but a metaphor for the unsatisfactory relations and practices of the human beings who make their living within this setting. These relations and practices construct the symbolic walls between individuals, of which the lawyer's office and the jail alike are the external manifestations.

My point here, however, is not so much to argue for a certain interpretation of "Bartleby" as to suggest that the meaning of the story is inaccessible except as the critique of an unreliable narration that is itself the source of the reality it deplores. The meaning of "Bartleby" becomes accessible to the reader who perceives the ironic cues that Melville has planted within this narration, the way in which the implied author has made the narrator give himself away by confessing to his commitment to the pale values of comfort and prudence. The truth is thus told, one might say, not by an Ishmael who figures as the substitute voice of an Old Testament prophet but by the ostensibly well-intentioned character whose narrative value is that he indirectly reveals the nature of his inability to perceive and speak the truth. His final apostrophe on the tragic fate of human communication is the ultimate aestheticization of cognitive failure: "Ah, Bartleby! Ah, humanity!" The readers who take this statement at face value remain inscribed within the sentimentality whose latent insensitivity Melville critiques.

A similar type of pseudoresolution and pseudorevelation of truth also forms the conclusion to "Benito Cereno." As Henry Sussman has argued, the ironic narrative alternates sublime situations with dialectical revelation, and it is the sublime, aesthetic alternative that is given the final word in the description of the unflinching gaze of Babo's impaled head. In Sussman's reading, the climax of the Hegelian allegory lies in the deposition that purportedly reveals the facts of the slave rebellion aboard the *San Dominick*. But the deposition does nothing to explain the profounder issues involved in the practice of slavery and the nature of evil; it is rather an instance of the systematic way in which truth can be repressed. In "Benito Cereno," as in "Bartleby," Melville's chief technique of indirect truth telling lies in his use of ironic narration, this time by means of the good-natured and optimistic Captain Delano, whose faculties of perception and judgment focalize the narration of attempts to cover up the signs of a reversed racial hierarchy aboard the slave ship on which a violent mutiny has occurred.

Delano's sentimental liberality is analogous to the lawyer's in its double failure: it prevents the understanding of violent action beyond a facade of loyalty and generosity, and in so doing it becomes complicit with this violence. Once again, reality is constructed within the narrative act. In the case of the lawyer, the violence done to Bartleby is fairly direct, as it is the lawyer who treats his clerk as a shadow, reducing him to a voice behind a wall for the sake of his convenience. But Delano is also responsible for what he sees and what he fails to see, in the sense that slavery could not be possible unless the cruelties on which it depends are repressed by a sentimentally optimistic view of human nature. By contrast, there is no recovery from the revelation of truth for Don Benito, who gradually wastes away in monastic seclusion.

Just as "Bartleby" ironizes the lawyer's contradictory position as one that creates the problem it tries to solve, by placing walls between people in the interests of comfort and monetary gain, so "Benito Cereno" ironizes the position of the consciousness that feels a type of compassion that is premised on a presumed racial superiority. This type of consciousness has profound ideological implications since it enables slavery, in the sense that it makes possible the exploitation of another race behind the cover of a falsely rationalized clear conscience. As I have already suggested, these narrational ironies constitute a new way of telling the truth. Truth is no longer what can be directly stated, not even if these direct statements are symbolically recoded, but must be created as a potential reading constituted by narrative structure.

This is not to say, of course, that Melville's concept of truth telling can be assumed by the critic. If the new form of the short story provides an advantage over the traditional novel in the context of a post-Enlightenment, postrepresentational world, this form also has its own limitations. Even in Melville's short fiction, in which the critique of the ideology of slave masters and employers is so incisive, the discourse of the Other remains unheard. As some critics have pointed out (for example, Sussman), Melville never gives us the possibility of the blacks' point of view in "Benito Cereno." Similarly, the use of ironic narration in "Bartleby" is compromised by its correlation with a kind of privileging of the victim's position, a sympathy with the passive character who might be said to enact a kind of masochistic rebellion.

The critique of a self-interested point of view in "Bartleby" and "Benito Cereno" opens up a new relation to the Other, but this Other will remain silent until the more radical challenge posed to capital and to colonialism in the twentieth century. As we will see, this historicity of Melville's narrative is evident also in the way in which *The Confidence-Man* adopts the short story form.

The resumption in a novel of the doubled narrative perspective developed in the stories correlates with the emergence of a contradictory figure that represents both polarities in the lawyer-Bartleby as well as the Delano–Don Benito relation. I am referring to the confidence man and the novel of that name, in which the central figure is both antagonist and protagonist—purposefully both vehicle and object of satire. Looking back to the novels that precede the stories, one might make comparisons also to the split protagonist of *Moby-Dick* constituted by the Ishmael-Ahab relation, as well as the self-divided Pierre, and observe that these are all expressions of contradictory deep-structural actants, to use a term from A. J. Greimas. In *The Confidence-Man* this contradictory actant is now actualized at the surface level in such a way that it for the first time becomes wholly objectified by narrative point of view.

When Melville returns to the novel in *The Confidence-Man*, he adopts the double narrative standpoint developed in his stories, while at the same time freeing narration from a discrete narrator or focalizer. This move has the effect of further removing the narrative standpoint from represented story world that is a subject of critique or satire, and it shifts the responsibility to the reader even more radically than the short story had. The scope is now enlarged in a manner consistent with the often larger representational ambition of a novel, yet this type of novel also depends on short story technique. The narrative of *The Confidence-Man* is episodic: its plot is more a matter of the metonymic relation of microstories than it is of any overarching story as such. This is a feature that is quite consistent with the shift of emphasis from story to narrative discourse and narration that I have attempted to identify in the two *Piazza* tales. Melville's last novel to be published in his lifetime is a striking early instance of that novel that we must read as if in one sitting—the work that we cannot read, but only reread, in the sense that its meaning lies not primarily in syntagmatic elaboration of story but in the paradigmatic reconstruction of its narrative discourse. More precisely, the meaning of such a novel lies in the resynchronization of the diachronic experience of reading.

The augmented involvement of the reader in the discursive relation of the narrative that results from the broadening of narrative perspective in *The Confidence-Man* implies a further shift of narrative dialectics. As I argued initially, the narrators of *Moby-Dick* and *Pierre* are implicated in the dialectical process of their own narration, so that the narrative standpoint doubles on itself in a contradictory manner. By contrast, the use of ironic narration in "Bartleby" is correlated with a static structure. To borrow from Sussman's reading of "Benito," the sublimity of enchantment, which arrests perception at an enigmatic surface, dominates the story entirely. There is no dialectical reversal except insofar as the reader reverses the lawyer's meaning. In "Benito," the displacement of ironic structure from unreliable first-person point of view (intrahomodiegetic narration) to the focalized character of a third-person point of view (heterodiegetic narration) correlates with the partial reemergence of a dialectical story. It is still the reader who must perform the dialectical reversal at the level of narration, but at the same time the story also contains a reversal: the moment in which the scales are said to fall from Delano's eyes, so that Babo is revealed as the instigator of horrible crimes, a revelation of the truth that later finds its legal elaboration in the court deposition that describes in detail the slave mutiny. Clearly, however, this is an instance of a pseudodialectic, a revelation that is determined as false within the ironic narrative focalization that centers on the stupidly innocent Delano. The dialectical movement, falsely represented by the story line, is properly completed at the discursive level.

When ironic structure is shifted not only from first-person point of view to third-person focalization but also to omniscient and explicitly neutral narration, the narrative dialectic undergoes a further displacement. Aboard the Mississippi steamer *Fidèle*, several confidence men, who seem to be one man in several disguises, swindle their fellow passengers while engaging them in various discussions concerning the confidence that might be placed in humankind. Typically, each episode in *The Confidence-Man* enacts a dialectical reversal, as the victims of the eponymous protagonist come to express, in what we might call mock Socratic dialogues, the opposite of their professed beliefs in humankind. But if expressions of trust give way to mistrust, and vice versa, it is not clear that either of these is the ultimate revelation of truth. Nor is it clear whether the transformation of the confidence-man figure into the cosmopolitan is a further deception or a revelation, though this central turning point is prompted by the unprecedented refusal of one character to yield to the persuasion of the protagonist. Though one might argue, as James Kavanagh does, that Don Benito has understood the horrors of slavery in a way that the ideologically constrained Delano cannot, *The Confidence-Man* implies that both of these attitudes are inadequate. Reliable representations of the world cannot be projected either by faith and hope or by doubt and despair. In *The Confidence-Man*, irony and narrative dialectics are equally situated at the levels of story and its narration. It is still the reader who must construct meaning by decoding a double narrative technique, but this construction no longer takes the simple form of a reversal of the meaning constructed at the story level: the reversals of *The Confidence-Man* appear to be indefinitely repeatable.

It is by no means clear, however, that this achievement of narrative technique is an entire success, with respect to the issues raised in and by the novel, nor have readers by any means uniformly praised *The Confidence-Man*, even during the age that has seen the elevation of many of Melville's other works to canonical status. Though I have argued that this last novel to be published in Melville's lifetime represents something of a perfected artistic achievement, as the purposeful application to the novel of an ironic narrative technique developed in his most celebrated stories, I would not claim this narrative represents an ideal. The paradoxical value we encounter with *The Confidence-Man* in this respect might be explained by once again returning to the distinction between story and its discursive or narrational realization. While in the modern short story the narratological category of story can be characterized as an absence, something deduced from narrative discourse rather than its obvious a priori, for Melville the priority of narration over narrated is rather a symptom that story is constituted as a lack, as loss. *The Confidence-Man* might therefore be read as an attempt to return to the type of novel in which story is still the ground of meaning, even as this story is absent, even as meaning is now constituted discursively. The omniscient narrator remains but no longer claims the privilege of unequivocally representing the world or the ability to find a coherent sequence of events naturally occurring within it. Nina Baym has argued that Melville was by temperament not actually a writer of fiction, discussing his turn to poetry and abandonment of fiction after *The Confidence-Man* (with the exception of the unfinished and only posthumously published *Billy Budd*). One might also argue that Melville succeeded only too well with a new form of narration defined in negative terms as lacking in the traditional omniscient point of view and the possibility of reliable representation. As a new novel, sometimes read as anticipating the modern, even postmodern novel (see Sten), *The Confidence-Man* might nevertheless be said to fail precisely in its impossible attempt to fuse the forms of the new short story—a genre associated in its modern emergence with the primacy of narrative discourse—with a traditional form of the novel in which story (*fabula*) depends on the stability of omniscient narration. Melville's stories and novels of the 1850s are thus instructive as to the nature of modern narrative and the conditions of its emergence.

Works Cited

Baym, Nina. "Melville's Quarrel with Fiction." *PMLA* 94 (1979): 909–23.

Kavanagh, James. "'That Hive of Subtlety': 'Benito Cereno' and the Liberal Hero." In *Ideology and Classical American Literature*, edited by Sacvan Bercovitch and Myra Jehlen, 352–83. Cambridge: Cambridge University Press, 1986.

Leitch, Thomas M. "The Debunking Rhythm of the American Short Story." In *Short Story Theory at a Crossroads*, edited by Susan Lohafer and Jo Ellyn Clarey, 130–47. Baton Rouge: Louisiana State University Press, 1989.

Lukács, Georg. *Studies in European Realism*. Introduction by Alfred Kazin. New York: Universal Library-Grosset and Dunlap, 1964.

Marler, Robert F. "From Tale to Short Story: The Emergence of a New Genre in the 1850s." In *The New Short Story Theories*, edited by Charles E. May, 165–81. Athens: Ohio University Press, 1994.

May, Charles E. "Metaphoric Motivation in Short Fiction: 'In the Beginning Was the Story.'" In *Short Story Theory at a Crossroads*, edited by Lohafer and Clarey, 62–73. Baton Rouge: Louisiana State University Press, 1989.

Post-Lauria, Sheila. "Canonical Texts and Context: The Example of Herman Melville's 'Bartleby, the Scrivener: A Story of Wall Street.'" *College Literature* 20, no. 2 (1993): 196–205.

Sten, Christopher. "The Dialogue of Crisis in *The Confidence-Man*: Melville's 'New Novel.'" *Studies in the Novel* 6, no. 2 (1974): 165–85.

Sussman, Henry. "At the Crossroads of the Nineteenth Century: 'Benito Cereno' and the Sublime." In *America's Modernisms: Revaluing the Canon*, edited by Kathryne V. Lindberg and Joseph G. Kronick, 77–100. Baton Rouge: Louisiana State University Press, 1996.

Contributors

GERD BJØRHOVDE is professor of English literature and pro-rector at the University of Tromsø, Norway. She is the author of *Rebellious Structures: Women Writers and the Crisis of the Novel, 1880–1900* (1987). She has published numerous essays and has a special interest in "marginal" writers of all kinds.

LAURA CASTOR is associate professor/chair of the English Department at the University of Tromsø, Norway, where she teaches courses in American literature and culture. Her 1994 doctoral dissertation was titled "Historical Memory, Autobiography, and Art: Redefining Identity through the Writing and Theater of Isadora Duncan, Hallie Flanagan, and Lillian Hellman." Her research interests include autobiographical narrative, Native American literature, and gender and ethnicity in literature. She has published articles on the relationships between gender, discourse, and media and on contemporary Native American literature.

JOHN GERLACH is the author of *Toward the End: Closure and Structure in the American Short Story* (1985). He has published numerous articles on American literature, narrative, and short fiction in journals such as *Arizona Quarterly, Journal of Narrative Technique,* and *Modern Fiction Studies and Extrapolation* and fiction in journals such as the *North American Review, Prairie Schooner,* and the *Ohio Review.* He has been assistant dean, College of Arts and Sciences, and is currently chair of the Department of English at Cleveland State University.

JAN NORDBY GRETLUND is associate professor of American and British literature at the University of Southern Denmark. He has held ACLS and Fulbright fellowships at the universities of Vanderbilt, Southern Mississippi, and South Carolina. He is the author of *Eudora Welty's Aesthetics of Place* (1997) and *Frames of Southern Mind: Reflections on the Stoic, Bi-Racial, and Existential South* (1998). He is the editor of *The Southern State of Mind* (1999) and has coedited another four books on southern literature: *Realist of Distances: Flannery O'Connor Revisited* (1987), *Walker Percy: Novelist and Philosopher* (1991), *Southern Landscapes* (1996), and *The Late Novels of Eudora Welty* (1998). He is a member of the editorial board for the *South Carolina Encyclopedia* and is literary editor of the EAAS's *Southern Studies Forum Newsletter.*

ANDREW K. KENNEDY is emeritus professor of British literature at the University of Bergen and a life member of Clare Hall, Cambridge University. He has been a visiting fellow at the universities of Edinburgh, Cambridge, Washington, and Princeton. His publications are centered on drama and dialogue, including the well-known *Six Dramatists in Search of a Language* (1975). His current main interest is short fiction, and the essay written for the present volume is based on reflections on his story collection, *Double Vision* (1999).

SANDRA LEE KLEPPE is currently writing a book on the poetry career of Raymond Carver, financed by a grant from the Norwegian Research Council. She holds a post-doctoral position at the University of Tromsø and has published articles on American literature in *Mississippi Quarterly*, the *Flannery O'Connor Bulletin, Literature and Theology*, and most recently, in *Classical and Modern Literature* on Carver's use of the catalog poem.

HANS B. LÖFGREN, a graduate of the University of California at Santa Cruz, is associate professor of English literature at Göteborg University in Sweden. His research interests lie in American literature and literary theory. He has recently completed a monograph titled "Landlessness: Four Psychohistorical Studies in American Narrative" and is currently working on a project titled "Cultural Theory as Negative Totality: A Model of Semiotic Change."

SUSAN LOHAFER is a professor of English at the University of Iowa. She is the author of *Knave, Fool, and Genius: The Confidence-Man as He Appears in Nineteenth-Century Fiction* (1973, under the name Kuhlmann), *Coming to Terms with the Short Story* (1983), and *Reading for Storyness: Preclosure Theory, Genre Poetics, and Culture in the Short Story* (2003). She has coedited two collections of essays on short fiction theory, *Short Story Theory at a Crossroads* (1989) and *The Tales We Tell: Perspectives on the Short Story* (1998). With Charles E. May, she edited a special theory issue of *Studies in Short Fiction* (1996). Her articles and short fiction have appeared in literary and scholarly journals such as the *Southern Review* and *Style*. From 1996 to 2002, she was president of the Society for the Study of the Short Story; she is now a trustee of that organization.

JAKOB LOTHE is professor of English literature at the University of Oslo. He has also taught comparative literature at the universities of Bergen and Oslo. His books include *Conrad's Narrative Method* (1989) and *Narrative in Fiction and Film* (2000). He has edited and coedited several volumes, most recently *Franz Kafka* (2002) and *European and Nordic Modernisms* (2004). He is the author of numerous essays, including contributions to the Cambridge Companions to Joseph Conrad and Thomas Hardy.

CHARLES E. MAY is emeritus professor of English at California State University, Long Beach. He is the author of *Edgar Allan Poe: A Study of the Short Fiction* (1991) and *The Short Story: The Reality of Artifice* (1995). He is the editor of *Short Story Theories* (1976) and *The New Short Story Theories* (1994). He is also the author/editor of *Twentieth Century European Short Story* (1989), *Fiction's Many Worlds* (1993) and *Interacting with Essays* (1996). May has published more than two hundred articles and reviews on short fiction.

GITTE MOSE, a graduate of the University of Copenhagen, was associate professor of Danish literature at the University of Oslo from 1995 to 2001 and is currently senior researcher at the Danish Institute for Advanced Studies in the Humanities in Copenhagen. Her fields of research include the Todorovian and Borgesian fantastic in Scandinavian novels after 1978, and the Jena-Romantic fragments and short short fiction in 1990s' Scandinavian literature. Her main project at present is titled "Writing on the Web — Flash Fiction Strategies in Cyberspace," in which the aim is to develop strategies for reading hyperfictions as literary "texts."

W. H. NEW is University Killam Professor at the University of British Columbia. A fellow of the Royal Society of Canada, and for seventeen years the editor of the critical quarterly *Canadian Literature,* he is internationally known for his publications on postcolonial writing. Among his more than forty books are *Dreams of Speech and Violence: The Art of the Short Story in Canada and New Zealand* (1987), *A History of Canadian Literature* (1988; rev. ed. 2003), *Land Sliding: Imagining Space, Presence, and Power in Canadian Writing* (1997), *Borderlands: How We Talk about Canada* (1998), *Reading Mansfield and Metaphors of Form* (1999), and *Grandchild of Empire* (2003). He is also the author of two books for children and four collections of poetry (most recently *Riverbook and Ocean,* 2002) and the editor of various collections, including *Canadian Short Fiction* (2nd ed., 1997) and *Modern Stories in English* (4th ed., with H. J. Rosengarten, 2001). His most recent book is *Encyclopedia of Literature in Canada* (2002), and he is currently at work on a study of short fiction in Australia.

AXEL NISSEN is associate professor of American literature at the University of Oslo. His doctoral dissertation on the life and literary career of Bret Harte was awarded H. M. the King of Norway's Gold Medal in 1997 and was later published as *Bret Harte: Prince and Pauper* (2000). Nissen has published numerous essays in international journals and essay collections on the theory and practice of biography, queer theory, and gender studies, and on authors such as Ernest Hemingway, Toni Morrison, Wallace Stevens, and Eudora Welty. His most recent book is an anthology titled *The Romantic Friendship Reader: Love Stories between Men in Victorian America* (2003).

MARY ROHRBERGER is author or editor/coeditor of ten books, including *Hawthorne and the Modern Short Story* (1966), *Reading and Writing about Literature* (1971), *The Art of Katherine Mansfield* (1977), *Story to Anti-Story* (1979), *Speaking of the Short Story* (1997), *Postmodern Approaches to the Short Story* (2003); nine chapters in books; and some 350 articles. She is also the recipient of a *Festschrift* collected in her honor by Harold Kaylor, titled *Creative and Critical Approaches to the Short Story* (1997). She is founder and executive editor of *Short Story*; founder and executive director of a series of biennial International Conferences on the Short Story; executive editor and founder of a press, Textual Studies and Production; and executive director and founder of the Society for the Study of the Short Story. She received her Ph.D. from Tulane University and has taught at Oklahoma State University, the University of Northern Iowa, Tulane University, and the University of New Orleans.

STUART SILLARS is professor of English at the University of Bergen, having previously taught at the University of Cambridge, England. His writings include *Art and Survival in First World War Britain* (1987), *British Romantic Art and the Second World War* (1990), *Visualisation in Popular Fiction* (1995), *Structure and Dissolution in English Writing, 1910–1920* (1999), and articles in journals and collections. He is currently working on a book on eighteenth-century Shakespeare paintings and a volume of essays on the relation between verbal and visual texts.

HANS H. SKEI is professor of comparative literature at the University of Oslo and chair of the Department of Scandinavian Studies and Comparative Literature. He has published three books on Faulkner's short story achievement: *William Faulkner, the Short Story Career* (1981 and 1984), *William Faulkner, the Novelist as Short Story Writer* (1985), and *Reading Faulkner's Best Short Stories* (1999). He also edited *William Faulkner's Short Fiction: An International Symposium* (1997) and has published widely on southern fiction as well as on Norwegian literature and literary theory.

PER WINTHER is professor of American literature at the University of Oslo. His publications include *The Art of John Gardner: Instruction and Exploration* (1992) and articles on Emily Dickinson, Ernest Hemingway, Robert Lowell, Ralph Ellison, Alice Walker, and Canadian short fiction; he currently serves as the editor of *American Studies in Scandinavia* and as president of the American Studies Association of Norway. He initiated and is chair of the Oslo Short Fiction Project at the University of Oslo.

Index